PRE-INTERMEDIATE

Language
LEADER

TEACHER'S BOOK
and Test Master CD-ROM

PEARSON
Longman

Grant Kempton

CONTENTS

CONTENTS

List of photocopiable worksheets

1A	World weather	Pairwork	Present simple, present continuous; types of weather
1B	Dictionary crossword	Individual, pairwork, group work	Dictionary entries; unit vocabulary
2A	Murder at Chester House	Group work	Past simple, past continuous
2B	The family company	Individual, pair and group work	Personality adjectives; past continuous
3A	What's on	Individual, pair and group work	Media; relative pronouns
3B	Front page	Individual and group work	Media
4A	History quiz	Individual and pairwork	Present perfect
4B	The advice game	Group work	Giving advice and reasons
5A	The shipping line	Group work	Expressions of quantity
5B	Charities	Group work	Comparatives and superlatives; environment, animals, charities, giving opinions
6A	How will it be?	Group work	*will*, *might* and *may* for predictions, first conditional, expressing opinions
6B	Wordsearch	Individual and pairwork	Unit vocabulary
7A	Scientific duties	Individual and group work	Science; *must* and *have to*
7B	New for my town	Group work	Developing an argument
8A	Don't trust your future!	Individual and group work	Future patterns
8B	Preferences bingo	Individual, pair and group work	Expressing preferences
9A	The job for you?	Individual and group work	Job conditions
9B	How to make …	Group work, individual and pairwork	Present passive
10A	Firsts crossword	Individual and pairwork	Past passive
10B	University opening	Individual and group work	Adding emphasis, present continuous for future arrangements
11A	Phrasal verb snap	Group work	Phrasal verbs
11B	Missing persons	Pairwork	Question tags
12A	Second conditional chains	Group work, whole class, individual	Second conditional
12B	Wordsearch	Pairwork, individual, pair and group work, whole class	Unit vocabulary

INTRODUCTION

To the teacher: introduction by the authors

We are pleased to welcome you to this new course: *Language Leader*. In this introduction we outline some of our ideas about the course. We have done our very best to write a series of books that teachers (and students!) will enjoy using, and we very much hope that, although we may be physically far apart, we share with you – as teachers – a common set of beliefs and practices, and a common sense of purpose.

Approach

Language Leader is an international course with a global focus, and is aimed at citizens of the 21st century world – people who cross (and communicate across) national borders. We believe that students are curious about the modern world, and that this course engages with it. *Language Leader* enables students to be better informed and helps them understand and express their ideas and feelings about the world.

We believe it is important to offer students stimulating topics that engage their interest and increase their motivation for learning. We have made use of our diverse backgrounds, personalities and interests as authors, in the hope of providing students with a rich variety of different topics. Each unit contains an 'umbrella topic' with a different subtopic in each lesson, allowing us to explore a range of issues within a single topic and also to recycle vocabulary. We think that the approach to the topics in the course will challenge students and allow them to develop their powers of expression and analysis and their critical thinking skills. *Language Leader* reflects our belief that language learning is not merely a form of training, but should be situated in a broader educational context. We hope that students who use the series will not only learn English, but – through English – will also learn interesting things about the world and about themselves. Perhaps, sometimes, they may not even be aware that they are actually learning English!

Language Leader is not based on one particular teaching 'philosophy' or methodology, but is informed by sound pedagogical principles, plus an intuitive sense – the result of many years' experience – of what works in the classroom. Having said this, we use a broadly communicative methodology and a text and task-based approach. Pair and group work is an important part of the learning process. The Common European Framework has informed many of the speaking activities.

Language development

Throughout the units, there is careful development and logical staging of new language, as well as substantial recycling of previous language, enabling students to move forward rapidly. The Review, Language Reference and Extra Practice sections consolidate and extend students' learning.

The texts in *Language Leader* not only provide context for grammar and vocabulary but systematically develop students' reading and listening skills. The reading texts are authentic or semi-authentic, or at lower levels based on real sources, and are taken from a variety of genres (for example, newspapers, magazines, literature and publicity materials). Listening skills are also developed throughout the course. Each unit has a number of listening activities and there is a wide variety of different listening texts (for example, radio programmes, conversations, interviews, talks and lectures), as well as a varied range of activity types.

There is considerable variety in the length of these reading and listening texts: some are relatively short, but *Language Leader* also offers students an opportunity to deal – in a supported way – with some longer texts. Students who suddenly find themselves in an English-speaking environment – whether in their home country or abroad – often have difficulty with the large quantities of spoken and written English that they are exposed to. This course helps them to build up their confidence in handling extended amounts of English. In addition, many of the reading and listening exercises are based on exam-type questions.

There are constant opportunities throughout the course for students to improve their speaking skills, with speaking exercises in every unit. Students can comment on the topics and discuss the issues that arise, as well as talk about more personal experiences and knowledge, through a variety of exercises, such as information gaps, personalised question and answer activities, role plays and debates.

The Scenario lessons are, we believe, an important communicative feature of *Language Leader*. Every unit includes a Scenario lesson, devoted to extended speaking practice in a real-life situation. Information has to be processed – and decisions made – leading to a specific outcome. Students are given language support to carry out the task.

The course covers all the key grammar points. These points are all contextualised and students are generally encouraged to analyse and understand grammar through an inductive approach with reference to examples in the texts. The grammar is practised in motivating and interesting activities. The Language reference and Extra practice section at the back of the book extends students' knowledge of grammar and provides essential further practice. It can be used in the class or for independent study at home.

Lack of vocabulary is one of the main problems many students face. Consequently, students struggle to make sense of texts and express themselves. They need more words. To address this, *Language Leader* has a wide range of vocabulary, and students are able to acquire and use this vocabulary through contextualisation and recycling.

Writing skills and study skills

Writing in English has become increasingly important, but is often students' weakest skill and something that they don't really enjoy. Even with very able students, it often drags down their scores in examinations in which they would otherwise do well. We consider, however, that writing is also a skill in which – with a little help – students can make significant progress. *Language*

Leader has a page in every unit that is devoted to the development of writing skills, and there are also further writing activities throughout the course. Because of the systematic approach to the development of writing skills in the course, students should be able to make real progress in their writing, and derive great satisfaction from this. Again, there is wide variety in the length and type of tasks. We place considerable emphasis, even at the lower levels, on discourse features of written English, with frequent analysis of text models and plenty of writing practice at both paragraph and text level. In addition, we have included activities designed to encourage students to be rigorous in checking their own writing.

Each unit also includes a Study skills page, which aims to encourage students to be independent learners with a high level of self-awareness. The skills that we cover in this section are not just for students who are on educational courses in schools, colleges and universities; they are also transferable skills which will be useful to students in many different contexts, including their careers and personal lives.

Flexibility

Of course, we hope that you will use every page in the book! But the *Language Leader* format deliberately lends itself to different teaching situations and can be adapted easily depending on the length and type of course you are teaching.

To conclude, we trust that you and your students will find *Language Leader* interesting, motivating and enjoyable. We also hope that it will meet your students' needs as well as providing something new. We welcome your comments on the course and hope to have the pleasure of meeting you in the future!

Gareth Rees, Ian Lebeau (Elementary and Pre-intermediate)
David Cotton, David Falvey, Simon Kent (Intermediate and Upper Intermediate)

Language Leader: course description

Language Leader is a general English series for adults and young adults. The course has a topic-based multi-strand syllabus which includes comprehensive work on grammar, vocabulary, pronunciation and integrated skills, where strong emphasis is placed on reading, writing and study skills as well as speaking and listening. With its purposeful approach *Language Leader* is particularly suitable for general English students working towards exams, and those learners who may go on to, or are already in, further education.

Language Leader has four levels and takes learners from Elementary to Upper Intermediate; each level offers 90 – 120 hours of work.

Coursebook

The twelve Coursebook units are divided into double-page lessons, each with a clear aim, which are designed to make the course flexible and easy-to-use.

- **Input lessons:** in *Language Leader Pre-intermediate* there are two input lessons in each unit. Here, new language is presented through informative texts with a balanced mix of grammar, vocabulary, pronunciation and skills work.
- **Scenario:** in the third lesson, learners integrate and practise the language presented in the previous lessons through a communicative task. This major speaking activity is carefully staged; the Key language section gives extra support by developing functional exponents and the Other useful phrases boxes provide helpful fixed phrases.
- **Study and Writing Skills:** the fourth lesson consists of a Study skills section, followed by Writing skills, which helps students to write a particular text type.

Language Leader Coursebook also features the following:

- **Review:** the Review spreads occur after every three units; these provide mixed practice for ongoing revision. The Language check section is a quick self-edit exercise and Look back encourages reflection on the previous units.
- **Language reference/ Extra practice:** this section consists of one cross-referenced spread for each unit. The left-hand page includes a grammar summary for the unit, plus reference lists for Key language and Vocabulary. The right-hand page provides extra practice for consolidation.

CD-ROM

- This component is attached to the back of the Coursebook.
- It provides extra practice and self-assessment for the learners with a variety of exercises, including listening. With the help of the Language Reference and the Dictionary, the CD-ROM helps learners develop their learning skills. The unique Writing section includes models for different writing tasks from everyday notes to academic essays.

Class CDs

- These provide all the recorded material from the Coursebook.

Workbook

- This contains further practice of areas covered in the corresponding units of the Coursebook and introduces Extra vocabulary to build lexis in the topic area.
- To help the development of language skills, useful strategies are introduced through Read better and Listen better boxes.
- In each unit there is a Translation exercise for students to compare English with their L1, and Dictation exercises provide more listening and writing.

Workbook CD

- Attached to the back of the Workbook, the CD contains all the recorded material for extra practice.

INTRODUCTION

Teacher's Book

- This provides all the support teachers need from detailed teaching notes to extra photocopiable activities.
- There are **warning points** to alert teachers about possible problem areas as well as **teaching tips** to help them. Taking into account teachers' busy schedules, the Teacher's Book notes are designed as lesson plans, with ideas for **extension** and **adjustment,** which are especially useful for mixed ability groups. There are **extra practice** suggestions as well as **project** ideas.

⚠ **warning points**   Ⓢ **extension**   Ⓔ **extra practice**
💡 **teaching tips**   🔧 **adjustment**   Ⓟ **project**

Test Master CD-ROM

- Attached to the back of the Teacher's Book, the Test Master CD-ROM is an invaluable resource to accompany *Language Leader*. The tests are based strictly on the content of the Coursebooks, providing a fair measure of students' progress.
- The audio files for the listening tests are conveniently located on the same CD-ROM.
- The tests can be printed out and used as they are, or can be adapted using Microsoft® Word to edit them to suit different teaching situations.
- The Test Master CD-ROM contains the following:
  - Placement Test (to identify levels)
  - Unit Tests (one 'A' and one 'B' test for each unit)
  - Progress Tests (one 'A' and one 'B' test for every three units plus additional optional speaking and writing tests)
  - Final Test (one 'A' and one 'B' version)

Syllabus areas

- **Topics:** to motivate learners the units are based on up-to-date topics of international interest or new angles on familiar subjects. Themes have been carefully chosen to engage the learners and to provide a springboard for their own ideas and communicative needs.
- **Grammar:** *Language Leader* follows an established syllabus progression and learners are actively involved in developing their knowledge of grammar. The Grammar sections in the input lessons focus on the main language points presented through the texts and learners are encouraged to work out the rules for themselves. They are supported by the Grammar tip boxes and cross-referred to the corresponding Language reference and Extra practice pages at the back of the book for reinforcement.
- **Vocabulary:** vocabulary input is derived from the unit topics and texts, allowing the teacher to build on words and phrases the students already know to create lexical sets. Additional attention is paid to word building and lexical patterns. The vocabulary is recycled through the speaking activities in each unit, revised in the Review lesson and Extra practice and practised further in the Workbook.

- **Pronunciation**: regular pronunciation sections are integrated with the presentation of new language or included on the Scenario spread as part of the communicative task. The pronunciation syllabus covers word and sentence stress, difficult sounds, contractions and intonation.
- **Reading**: there is a wide range of reading material in *Language Leader* and a variety of exercise types developing the reading skills. The informative texts have been chosen for their interest and to provide a context for the grammar and vocabulary items being studied. The texts are based on real-life sources (magazines, websites, etc) and related activities include comprehension, vocabulary and reading sub-skills work.
- **Listening**: students are given many opportunities to develop a wide range of listening skills in *Language Leader,* both in terms of text types and activity types (e.g. checking predictions, table and note-completion). There is more listening practice in the Workbooks and CD-ROMs to further build the learners' confidence.
- **Speaking**: opportunities for oral practice of language and freer discussion appear regularly in every lesson. There is at least one explicit speaking activity per lesson and a major communicative task in the Scenario lesson.
- **Writing**: the writing syllabus introduces students to different genres and develops students' writing through analysis of models and practice in producing different text styles.
- **Study skills**: a systematic approach to developing study skills fosters independent dictionary use, encourages students to take notes effectively and gives them help in approaching exams and learning outside the classroom.

External organisations and link to examinations

- **Common European Framework of Reference:** the ethos of the CEFR is reflected throughout *Language Leader* in a variety of ways. For example, the outcomes of the Scenario lessons reflect the 'Can do' descriptors and help students use the language they have learnt effectively. Also, great emphasis is placed on the development of independent learning across the course including the extensive work on study skills, good study habits and self-assessment. For more information on *Language Leader* and the CEFR see the website www.pearsonlongman.com/languageleader.
- **Bologna Process:** as part of this initiative to harmonise tertiary education, many institutions now offer credit-bearing English language programmes. *Language Leader* reflects the values of the Bologna Process with its emphasis on individual responsibility for learning.
- **Link to examinations:** ELT examination exercise-types occur regularly throughout *Language Leader* to help prepare students for a range of common exams (IELTS in particular). The website provides grids correlating *Language Leader* to international ELT exams.

INTRODUCTION

How a unit works (Pre-intermediate)

Input lesson (1)

The contents of each unit are clearly labelled at the top of the opening page.

Stimulating topic-related quotation to engage learners.

Listening exercises guide students through audio texts and encourage different styles of listening.

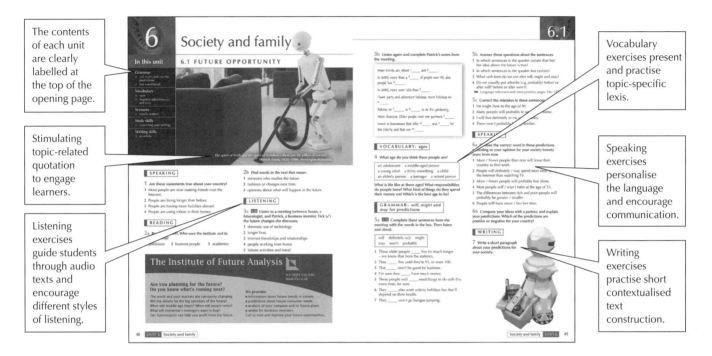

Vocabulary exercises present and practise topic-specific lexis.

Speaking exercises personalise the language and encourage communication.

Writing exercises practise short contextualised text construction.

Input lesson (2)

Reading exercises aid comprehension of the text and develop skills.

The informative reading text provides a context for the language and vocabulary being studied.

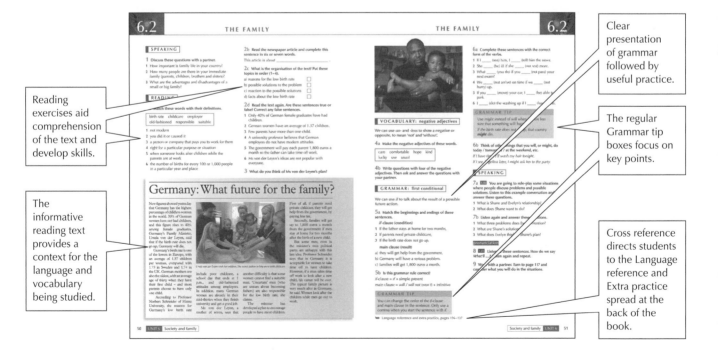

Clear presentation of grammar followed by useful practice.

The regular Grammar tip boxes focus on key points.

Cross reference directs students to the Language reference and Extra practice spread at the back of the book.

INTRODUCTION

Scenario

Scenario lessons practise Key language from the unit through a meaningful final task.

Students are given preparation for the task through different activities.

The Key language of the lesson is presented and practised.

Students are given practice in correct pronunciation of the Key language.

The clear, well-structured communicative Task enables students to practise language in a meaningful context.

The regular Other useful phrases boxes provide extra help for students to carry out the task.

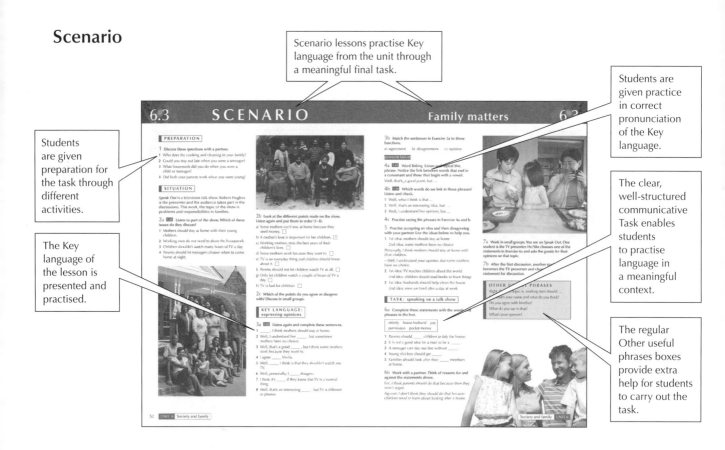

Study and writing skills

The Study skills section develops students' ability to work on their own and in the classroom environment.

Students are given real life tasks.

Writing Skills focus on a different genre of writing in each unit.

Students are given model texts to follow and analyse.

Students are given a guided writing task

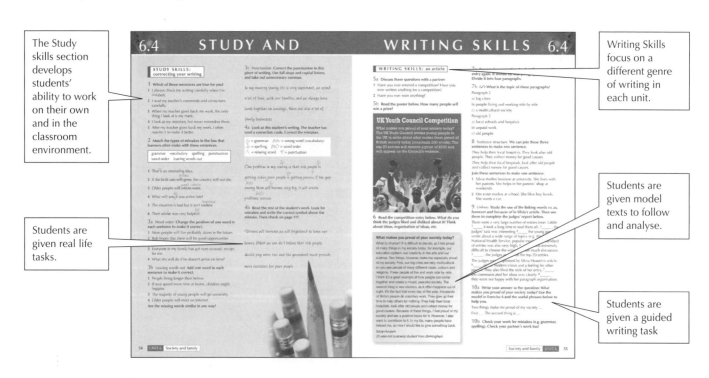

INTRODUCTION

Other sections

Review

Review lessons occur after every three units; they revise and consolidate the Grammar, Vocabulary and Key language from the previous units.

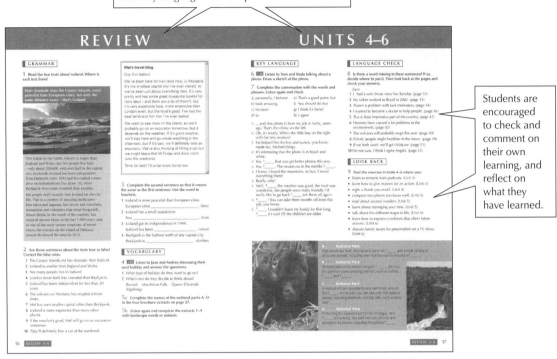

Students are encouraged to check and comment on their own learning, and reflect on what they have learned.

Language reference / Extra practice

There is one Language reference and Extra practice spread for each unit at the back of the book.

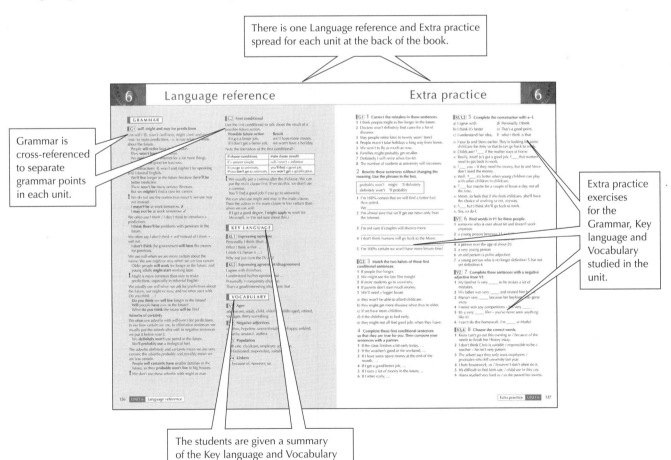

Grammar is cross-referenced to separate grammar points in each unit.

Extra practice exercises for the Grammar, Key language and Vocabulary studied in the unit.

The students are given a summary of the Key language and Vocabulary they have studied in the unit.

Weather

1.1 EXTREMES

Lesson topic and staging

This lesson looks at the topic of weather, particularly extreme weather such as hurricanes and blizzards. The first section provides students with the basic vocabulary needed. Students then practise listening, gaining a deeper insight into the topic. The listening also provides the basis for the grammar focus, which is present simple and present continuous. Students will have already met these forms, but the introduction of state and action verbs is new and will need some attention. The final speaking activity personalises the topic and gives opportunity for the free practice of the present simple and the present continuous.

Objectives

By the end of the lesson, students should have:

- learned about different types of extreme weather
- learned and practised vocabulary of extreme weather
- practised listening skills, listening for gist as well as specific information
- revised the present simple and present continuous
- learned the difference between state and action verbs
- talked about extreme weather in their country, using the practised forms

Timings

If there is not enough time, leave out exercises 4c or 5 and give them for homework (although students would need some pre-teaching).

Possible lesson break: before exercise 4a or after 4c.

VOCABULARY: the weather

This is not just a warm-up activity for the listening. It also provides important vocabulary which will be needed later.

1a Students look at the pictures and describe what they see. This can be done by the whole class or in pairs. To complete exercise 1a, students will either have to know the words or have to guess. Let them guess or elicit the meanings.

blizzard (n) – a storm with a lot of wind and snow

drought (n) – a long period of dry weather when there is not enough water

hurricane (n) – a bad storm with very strong winds

storm (n) – very bad weather with a lot of wind, rain or snow, and sometimes thunder.

(!) Some students may have trouble with the pronunciation of some words. You may like to show the differing stress for the following.

  •   •
hurricane   *blizzard*

- Ask the students if these extreme weathers would happen in their country. Ask them if they know any other words to describe the four situations.

> **A** hurricane; **B** storm; **C** drought; **D** blizzard

1b Students do activity as per Coursebook. Have a class discussion about which situation the students think is the most serious. There is no correct answer.

2 Students do activity as per Coursebook, preferably on their own to begin with, although they could check their answers in pairs.

> **1** wind; **2** rain; **3** dry; **4** hot; **5** dry; **6** snow;
> **7** windy; **8** ice

- You might like to check if students know that *wind* is a noun and *windy* is an adjective. Elicit that with types of weather we can put *-y* on the end of some nouns to make them adjectives (e.g. *snowy, rainy*).

LISTENING

`1.2`

Students are going to listen to a news report about hurricanes. Make sure they remember what hurricanes are.

3a Students do activity as per Coursebook. They shouldn't need more than one listening.

> 1b; 2a; 3d; 4c

3b Students do activity as per Coursebook.

> **1** false; **2** true; **3** false; **4** false; **5** true

---

Track 1.2

Reporter, Man, Woman, Chief of police

R: Only two things are happening in Florida right now, waiting or leaving. The people of Florida are either waiting for Hurricane Helen, or they're leaving in their cars.

continued...

M: I'm staying here. I have a lot of food in my house and, at the moment, I'm covering the windows with wood. I know about the danger, especially after Hurricane Katrina, but, well, I'm not leaving.

W: I'm getting out of here. They're saying that this is a really dangerous hurricane and I don't want to meet it. Of course, the roads are really busy because many people are leaving.

R: The hurricane's moving north across the Caribbean Sea and it's coming towards Florida. Strong winds and heavy rain are hitting the coast, and the hurricane is getting bigger and faster. It's now a Category four hurricane, which means the wind speed is 100 kilometres per hour ... I'm now in the police station with the chief of police.

C: Our emergency plan's going well. As you know, we often get hurricanes in Florida so we know what to do. We do this kind of thing every year, and this summer is no different. On the streets, my men are doing their jobs and they're checking that people are safe. Each year some people leave the area, and others stay. Either way, we always help everyone.

R: Hurricane Helen is a very strong hurricane. And the question is – why are there more strong hurricanes every year? Research shows that the number of strong hurricanes is increasing and that they're getting stronger. Some scientists say this is because of global warming: the sea's getting hotter, and warm seas cause hurricanes. The American government doesn't agree with this connection between global warming and hurricanes. Right now though, the people of Florida are just trying to save their houses and their lives. This is Joanne Webb, live from Florida. Back to Nick in the studio.

GRAMMAR: present simple and present continuous

4a Ask students to look at the four sentences. Remind them that they are taken from the recording. Then students do activity as per Coursebook. This should not be difficult as they should already know these forms. When they have finished the task, you can elicit the structure of each form on the board, including in the negative.

> **Present simple:** 2, 4; subject + *do/does* + *not* + main verb
> **Present continuous:** 1, 3; subject + *am/are/is* + *not* + *-ing* of main verb

4b Students do activity as per Coursebook. If students are having problem with this, refer them to the Language reference section at the back of the Coursebook.

> 1b; 2a; 3d; 4c

- Once students have finished the activity, you might want to elicit more examples for each grammar note in the feedback session, just to make sure they fully understand the point.

4c Students do activity as per Coursebook.

> **1** 'm listening; **2** falls; **3** hits; **4** is falling;
> **5** doesn't snow; **6** 's not raining

5 This will be the first time that students will have met state and action verbs in English, but they should pick this up quickly as the concept exists in most languages. Go through the explanation with the class as a whole. Elicit more state and action verbs as examples. Then students do activity as per Coursebook. Once students have finished, they should be able to answer the last question easily but make sure they understand that state verbs are not normally used in the present continuous.

> **1** *is* – state; **2** *'s coming* – action; **3** *have* – state;
> **4** *are getting* – action; **5** *know* – state
> Present simple

6 Students do activity as per Coursebook, individually or in pairs. In the class feedback session, ask students why they chose the present continuous or the present simple.

> **1** are hitting; **2** are; **3** get; **4** is causing; **5** are not
> working; **6** are moving; **7** are giving; **8** is looking;
> **9** don't usually fly; **10** isn't

E Students can do exercise 2 from the Extra practice activities on page 127 either in class or for homework.

SPEAKING

7 The activity works better if you have a multinational class. If not, you may need to go through this quite quickly. In one-country classes, it may be possible to talk about extreme weather in different parts of the country. For questions 3 and 4, get students to tell each other their opinion and encourage them to use the list of words.

HOMEWORK OPTIONS

Ask students to go on the Internet and discover examples of extreme weather around the world, and be prepared to tell the class about them in the next lesson.

Students can do exercise 6 from the Extra practice activities on page 127.

Students do the exercises on pages 4–5 of the Workbook.

1.2 WINTER

IN THIS LESSON

Lesson topic and staging

This lesson focuses on seasons and in particular winter. Students start by discussing seasons and winter before doing an extended reading activity. The reading is the basis for a quick revision of modifiers and then a more detailed revision of present simple and present continuous questions, as well as question words. Students get to practise these in a free communication activity and then finish with a short free writing activity.

Objectives

By the end of the lesson, students should have:

- learned about extreme winter conditions in Siberia
- discussed winter in their own country
- completed skimming and scanning reading activities
- revised or learned and practised present simple and present continuous questions
- revised and practised question words
- done a general knowledge quiz about winter
- written a composition

Timings

Exercises 5c or 6 can be dropped if there is not enough time. Exercise 7 can be done for homework.

Possible lesson break: before exercise 3a or after 3b .

READING AND SPEAKING

1   This exercise sets the scene for the reading text. Before students answer the questions, first elicit the meaning of *seasons*. Make sure they know *spring, summer, autumn* and *winter*.

- Ask students as a class about seasons in their country. Ask them how many seasons they have (some countries don't have four seasons). They can ask the other questions in pairs but also do class feedback and share the ideas.

(!) Some students (especially from Arab countries) may not have much of a concept of 'winter' or 'snow'. You may have to teach these concepts.

- At some stage (depending on your class) you may like to check they understand the following words:

familiar (adj) – well-known to you and easy to recognise

last (v) – to continue for a particular length of time

melt (v) – to change from solid to liquid or to make something do this by heating it

scary (adj) – frightening

burst (v) – to break open suddenly and violently

community (n) – a group of people who live in the same town or area

2a   Students do activity as per Coursebook. Ask students why they chose the answer.

> 3 (a magazine about TV programmes)

2b   Students do activity as per Coursebook, first individually and then checking in pairs.

> A5; B4; C10; D7; E3; F2; G9; H6; I1; J8

2c   Students do activity as per Coursebook, first individually and then checking in pairs.

> 1 nine months; 2 normal; 3 the sun;
> 4 dangerous gases; 5 freeze; 6 fur

💡 Ask students to go back to the text and find words that mean the following:
very cold (*freezing*)
pieces of clothing that you wear on your hands (*gloves*)
to break open suddenly (*to burst*)
something expensive that you want but do not need (*luxury*)
under or below something (*sub*)

VOCABULARY: modifiers

Students should have already been introduced to modifiers and should know these quite well. However, it may be a good idea to ask them to look at the four sentences in exercise 3a and to identify first the adjectives and then the modifiers. Make sure they know the modifier comes before the adjective. Then ask students what the modifier's role is (to give extra information about the adjective).

3a   Students do activity as per Coursebook.

> 1C; 2A; 3B

3b   Before starting this activity you may want to revise different types of weather. You could use photocopiable activity 1A to do this.

Students should do this activity in pairs and then share with the rest of the class.

> students' own answers

GRAMMAR: present simple and present continuous questions

Students will already have met present simple and present continuous questions, as well as question words.

4a Students do activity as per Coursebook.

> **Present simple:** 1, 2, 4, 5, 6, 7, 8, 9, 10
> **Present continuous:** 3

4b Students do activity as per Coursebook.

⚠ Students may be unsure of what an auxiliary verb is. Make sure they see the examples of *do/does* and *am/is/are*. You may like to elicit some examples of auxiliary verbs as a concept check.

> 1c; 2a; 3b

5a Students do activity as per Coursebook. You can then elicit all the other question words they know and examples of how they are used. Students who find this difficult can refer to the Language reference.

> **1** Why; **2** How; **6** What; **7** What, How much;
> **8** What, What; **9** what; **10** Why
> Other question words: where, how many,
> how often, who, whose, when, which

⚠ Students may not associate auxiliary verbs with question words. Show your students how auxiliary verbs can work with question words (e.g. *How do you know … ?*) and without question words (e.g. *Is it getting warmer?*)

5b Students do activity as per Coursebook. You may like to check their sentences are correct before they ask each other questions.

> **1** Do you feel sad on cloudy days?
> **2** What's your teacher wearing today?
> **3** Are you learning English for fun?
> **4** How do you spend your free time?
> **5** What are your friends doing now?

5c Students do activity as per Coursebook. Make sure they look at the reading text before writing the questions.

> **Possible questions:**
> **2** Where is the temperature sometimes minus 60 or 70 degrees?
> **3** Why does the sun produce very little heat?
> **4** What is stopping the surface from freezing?
> **5** Is the temperature increasing in Siberia?
> **6** Do your fingers freeze in the cold weather?

Ⓔ Students can do exercises 1, 3 and 4 from the Extra practice activities on page 127 either in class or for homework.

SPEAKING

6

Put your students into groups of three and tell them to turn to page 110 for the quiz. Ask students to read the questions and predict what the answers are. Then put two groups together and ask students to agree on the answers. You can then read the answers out to the students or ask them to check them on page 112. Ask them if they are surprised by the answers.

- OPTION A: In the feedback session, you can write one answer on the board and students have to match the answer to the questions or you can put each of the answers on slips of paper and give them to the students to sort out.

- OPTION B: Cut up the quiz into two parts. Give the first four questions to one group with the answers for 5–8 on a separate sheet. Give answers 1–4 and questions 5–8 to the other group. After they have guessed the answers to their questions, they have to ask the other group questions to find out the answers.

> Students check their answers on page 112.

WRITING

7 Students can do this either in class or at home.

Ⓟ If you have a class of students from one country, brainstorm different issues related to winter in your country (e.g. weather, what people wear, what people eat, etc.) and give them to students. These sentences could then form the basis of a class presentation on winter in their country.

- If students have trouble coming up with ideas you could use the following prompts:
  What's the weather like? What do people do? Do they have any problems? Are winters changing?

HOMEWORK OPTIONS

Students do the exercises on pages 6–7 of the Workbook.

1.3 SCENARIO: LATIN AMERICAN ADVENTURE

IN THIS LESSON

Lesson topic and staging

The lesson looks at the topic of adventure holidays. Students are introduced to the vocabulary of adventure activities through pictures and reading. The scene is set through a variety of short readings (an advert, an email, notes). Students then listen and respond to a discussion on choosing adventure holidays. The listening text introduces the language of agreeing and disagreeing with short answers, while the pronunciation section focuses on the intonation of these forms. Finally students are given a task to complete which involves speaking and taking notes, using the 'Other Useful Phrases' box, plus the vocabulary learned and the language of agreeing and disagreeing.

Objectives

By the end of the lesson, students should have:

- learned about different types of adventure holidays
- taken information from a variety of different written texts
- listened for general and specific information
- learned and practised short answers to show agreement or disagreement
- completed a task using the language of agreement and disagreement

Common European Framework

Students can use language effectively to exchange opinions.

Timings

Possible lesson break: after exercise 3b.

WARM-UP

Adventure holidays are becoming more and more popular, especially with young people. The activities described in Lesson 1. 3 are examples of common adventure holidays. Many of these holidays have an age limit and whoever wants to go on these holidays may have to have a medical examination before they can take part.

- Ask students to look at the pictures on pages 10 and 11. Ask students what subject the pictures are about (elicit *adventure holidays*). Ask students what they know about adventure holidays. Find out it any of the students have been on an adventure holiday.
- You can also ask if students know any of the activities being shown in the pictures.

1a Students do activity as per Coursebook. Students answer the second question in pairs. You can get classroom feedback but make sure students tell you why they would like to go on one of their trips.

> Double here means 'consisting of two parts' – the holiday offers two locations and a different activity in each location.

1b Students do activity as per Coursebook. You may want to teach the sport phrases (*white-water rafting*, *diving*, etc.) at the end of the exercise, but try and get your students to tell you their meaning from the pictures.

> **A** mountain biking; **B** white-water rafting;
> **C** trekking; **D** sea kayaking; **E** diving;
> **F** snowboarding; **G** wildlife watching;
> **H** island cruises; **I** snorkelling; **J** horse riding
> **Note:** Skiing isn't illustrated.

2a Students do activity as per Coursebook.

> to suggest two countries for new holiday destinations in Latin America

2b Students do activity as per Coursebook individually and then compare answers in pairs. Finally do class feedback. Do not give a clear answer here as your students will hear a discussion about this later.

> students' own answers

1.3

3a Students do activity as per Coursebook. Students should only need to listen once.

> Belize – longer holiday season and more interesting activities

3b Students do activity as per Coursebook.

> 2B; 3B; 4D; 5B; 6B; 7S

> **Tracks 1.3 and 1.4**
> *Simon, Diana*
> S: So, Diana, any thoughts?
> D: Well, I like the sound of Argentina. I think the Antarctic wildlife cruise is a great idea.
> S: Mmm, so do I. It's unusual, and everyone loves penguins. Er, any problems with this trip?
> D: Well, I suppose the season for the Antarctic trips is short; November to February – that's only about four months long.
> S: Yeah, I agree, and I don't like the weather in the mountains.
> D: No, neither do I. It's windy and changeable in the summer. But, is that a problem for our customers? They like adventure after all!
> S: True, but it's not nice walking in the wind all the time. In fact I don't like the activities – they're very ordinary.
> *continued…*

D: Don't you? I do. Horse riding is always popular, and everyone can go trekking. I think those activities are fine, especially if we want to attract first timers.

S: Well, I'm not sure. I think our customers want new activities, or unusual ones. Anyway, what about Belize?

D: Well, I think this is excellent because the activities look interesting.

S: And exciting.

D: Exactly. Diving in clear blue water, white-water rafting. In fact, I don't think there are any problems with the activities.

S: Neither do I. But what about the weather? When's the best time to go?

D: Well, I think the trips should be in the dry season.

S: Yes, so do I, especially because of the hurricanes in the rainy season.

D: Yes, and also it's a little cooler from November to May.

S: So, how long is the holiday season? Let's see, er, November, December, January, February, March, April, May … How many's that?

D: Seven months. I think that's good.

S: Do you? I'm not sure. In the USA, the holiday seasons are longer. And also, I don't want to offer trips anywhere near the hurricane season. You know that hurricanes are getting stronger and stronger and, well, we don't know what's happening really.

D: Sure, so, let's say the holiday season is six months long.

S: OK. Fine. So, which do you prefer?

D: Personally, I prefer Belize to Argentina.

S: Mmm, so do I, but the Antarctic cruise is a great idea. Let's look at the other two, and then decide.

KEY LANGUAGE: agreeing and disagreeing

`1.4`

4a

Students do activity as per Coursebook. Write the target structures on the board.

> **1** So; **2** neither; **3** Don't; **4** Do

> **Track 1.4**
> *Underlined in audioscript for Track 1.3.*

4b Ask and answer the questions as a whole class. Make sure that students understand that 4 is a more polite way of disagreeing.

> **1** agree; **2** agree; **3** disagree; **4** disagree

pronunciation

`1.5`

5a Students do activity as per Coursebook. Make sure that they notice the question mark is a signal for the changing intonation.

> **1**a; **2**b; **3**a; **4**b

> **Track 1.5**
> **1** So do I.
> **2** Don't you?
> **3** Neither do I.
> **4** Do you?

5b Students practise as a class, then individually.

To give more practice, you could call out other sentences and get students to respond with personal opinions, using the right intonation, e.g.:

TEACHER: I love chocolate. Mehmet?

STUDENT: So do I.

Then let students make sentences that other students respond to.

E Students can do exercise 5 from the Extra practice activities on page 127 either in class or for homework.

6a Students should respond with their own opinions in this activity. This should be done individually.

Note: Exercise 5 from the Extra practice activities could be done here.

6b Put students into pairs. Students use their responses from 6a to tell partners. Their partners should respond with their own opinions.

Note: Exercise 5 from the Extra practice activities could be done here.

TASK: designing a holiday

7 Tell students they are now going to find out about two other Double Action Adventures holidays. Put students into pairs and label them A and B. Tell Student As to turn to page 113 and read the task. Tell Student Bs to turn to page 111 and do the same. When they have finished reading, tell the students that they will now ask and answer questions to find out about each other's holiday. Before they do this, however, make sure they take note of the OTHER USEFUL PHRASES box. Go through it with them, checking they know how to use it.

If you have a weaker class, you may practise the questions and answers from the OTHER USEFUL PHRASES box before starting the activity.

8a Ask students to read the email in exercise 2a again. Make sure that students know they now have four countries to consider (Argentina, Belize, Peru, Chile), not two. Students should work alone for a few minutes answering the questions in 8a, making notes and preparing to tell their partner about it.

8b With their partner, students should now discuss the four countries and decide on the best countries for 'first timers' and 'older adults'. Remind them to use the language of agreeing and disagreeing as they discuss. When they have finished, have a class feedback.

☼ Students, in groups, plan an adventure holiday in their country. Each group presents suggestions and the class decides on their best choice.

HOMEWORK OPTIONS

Students can do exercises 7 and 8 from the Extra practice activities on page 127.

Students do the exercises on page 8 of the Workbook.

1.4 STUDY AND WRITING SKILLS

IN THIS LESSON

Lesson topic and staging

This lesson looks at the study skill of using a dictionary and the skill of writing a guidebook entry. Students start by recognising that words in a dictionary have more than one definition. They learn to use example sentences and make the most of dictionary definitions. They then investigate how opposites are presented in dictionaries. The writing skills section focuses on guidebook entries. Students first discuss what should be in a guidebook, study a guidebook entry and then finally write one themselves. As they do this they also revise the linkers *and, but, also* and *when*.

Objectives

By the end of the lesson, students should have:

- learned how to make use of dictionary entries, especially definitions, example sentences and opposites
- studied guidebook entries and considered what they should include
- read for specific information
- revised linkers
- written their own guidebook entry

Timings

Exercise 4b can be omitted if there is not enough time. Exercise 8 can be given for homework.

Possible lesson break: after exercise 4b.

STUDY SKILLS: dictionary skills (understanding meaning)

Some students may not have used a monolingual dictionary before. You need to be careful when introducing this section so as not to put your students off using one. Ideally, for this lesson, students should have access to a monolingual dictionary, but if not, everything they need is in the Coursebook.

1 Focus students on the dictionary entry for *cold*.

- Tell them that this has come from a monolingual dictionary. Ask them to read the whole entry. Ask them if they understand it.

- Students do activity as per Coursebook. When they have finished, check their answers. Explain to them that monolingual dictionaries are written for students so that even though the definitions are in English, they are usually easy enough to understand. You may have to teach the word *definition*, and then check by asking students how many definitions there were for *cold* (three). Make sure they understand that when there is more than one definition, the first one may not always be right (a common mistake made by students with bilingual dictionaries).

> 1c; 2a; 3b

💡 Write the words *definition*, *word type*, *example sentence*, *pronunciation*. Ask the students to identify each part of the entry. This should be easy but just reminds students of what a dictionary entry looks like.

2 Students do this activity as per Coursebook. They should do this individually and then check in pairs.

> a 3; b 2; c 4; d 3; e 4; f 1; g 2; h 3; i 2

3 Students work in pairs and do this activity as per Coursebook. Then make pairs into groups of four. If students have a dictionary, encourage them to use it rather than turning to page 111.

> 1 white or grey; 2 near the ground; 3 leaves fall off the trees; 4 violent, with strong winds; 5 storm, lot of wind, snow; 6 light and heat

4a Encourage students to look at the entry and point out where the opposite is given. Then they can quickly do the activity.

> 1 short; 2 weak; 3 light; 4 minor

4b Students do activity as per Coursebook.

> 1 minor; 2 short; 3 weak; 4 light

💡 As a final activity, students use their dictionaries to find a word that they think the other students know but is not too easy, preferably an adjective as it must have an opposite. They should take note of the opposite, the definition and the example sentence.

Divide students into groups. In each group each student first reads out the definition, then the example sentence (without saying the actual word) and, finally, the opposite. If someone guesses the word from the definition, the group gets three marks, from the example sentence two marks, and from the opposite one mark. The group that gets the most marks win.

WRITING SKILLS:
a guidebook entry

5 This activity is a discussion activity. Begin by writing the word *guidebook* on the board. Elicit from the students what a guidebook is and what you use it for. Then ask students to do the activity as per Coursebook individually. When they have finished doing it individually, get them into groups of three or

four. Finally, have a short class discussion on what the whole class feels.

> students' own answers

6 Students do activity as per Coursebook.

You could check they understand the following words:

damp (adj) – wet, usually in a cold and unpleasant way

mild (adj) – quite warm

period (n) – a length of time

> 1 The sun isn't too strong, prices are still quite low and the weather is warm. 2 It becomes very dry. 3 late October; 4 It can snow in the high mountains and it's extremely cold in some towns. It's also the rainy season. 5 prices, how crowded it gets at the coast, when hotels and restaurants close; 6 beach, mountains, inland, countryside, coast, towns

7a Students do activity as per Coursebook.

> and x7; but x2; also x2; when x2

7b Students do activity as per Coursebook. You can ask students to give example sentences to show they understand the different usage as well as meaning. Make sure they can see that *also* usually comes after the verb and does not join two words or parts of a sentence.

> 1 words; 2 time; 3 different; 4 fact

7c Students do activity as per Coursebook.

> 1 and; 2 also; 3 but; 4 when; 5 but; 6 and, also

8 Students should do this activity as per Coursebook. Make sure students are aware that they have a template in the Mallorca reading.

🅟 You may like to develop the Guidebook project further. If students are from one country, one city or one institution, then they could prepare a guidebook entry covering areas such as those listed in exercise 5.

🅔 You can do photocopiable activity 1B to revise vocabulary taught in this unit.

HOMEWORK OPTIONS

Exercise 8 can be given for homework.

Students do the exercises on page 9 of the Workbook.

2 People

2.1 INSPIRATION

Lesson topic and staging

This lesson focuses on people who inspire others. The topic is an easy way to introduce personality adjectives. The lesson starts with a short text which students read for gist and for specific information. Students then listen to an interview, identifying gist and then specific information. The reading and the listening are a platform both for the teaching of personality adjectives and the recycling of the past simple, which students then practise. They also learn about the use of prepositions in time expressions (e.g. years, months, days, clock time). Finally, students learn and speak about Mother Teresa and another person who inspires them, using the language they have studied in the lesson.

Objectives

By the end of the lesson students should have:

- read for gist and specific information
- listened for gist and specific information
- learned and practised personality adjectives
- revised and practised the past simple
- learned and practised time expressions
- completed a speaking activity which required the use of all of the above language

Timings

Exercise 8c could be left out if there is not enough time.

Possible lesson break: after exercise 4b.

READING

1a Choose five or six famous people your students will know (e.g. Nelson Mandela, Albert Einstein, Ronaldinho, Bill Gates). Elicit from students why they are famous. Write the names on the board, together with the word *inspiration*. Ask students if they know what it means (someone who achieves something difficult or important can be an inspiration to others). Elicit related words from students, as they will need them:

inspiration (n), *inspire* (v), *inspirational* (adj)

- Elicit from students which of the famous people on the board they think are inspirational. They can also tell you why.
- Students look at the picture and headline. Ask them what information about the person in the picture they expect to find out. Students then read the text and check their answers.

> students' own answers

1b Before students do the activity as per Coursebook, you may like to check they understand the following words:

housewife (n) – a woman who stays at home doing the cooking, cleaning, etc.

poverty (n) – when people are extremely poor

marathon (n) – a race in which people run about 26 miles or 42 km

in her honour – in order to show respect to someone

2 Students do activity as per Coursebook.

> **1** housewife and mother; **2** professional athlete; **3** to pay for her children's education; **4** She's a hero and an inspirational person.

LISTENING

1.6

3a Tell the students that they are now going to find out more about Chimokel by listening to an interview. Students do activity as per Coursebook.

> Topics talked about: 1, 3, 5 and 6

3b Students do activity as per Coursebook.

> 1g; 2a; 3c; 4d; 5e; 6b; 7h; 8f

> **Track 1.6**
> *Journalist, Interpreter*
> J: Chimokel, did you want to become an athlete when you left school?
> I: Oh, no, I didn't. I come from a very poor place, and my mother died when I was sixteen, so I left school and then I married Benjamin a year later, in 1995. I didn't think about running or sport at that time. I had a lovely husband, a home, and then I became a mother. I have four beautiful boys.
> J: So, why did you start running?
> I: We are a poor family: we have just a few animals – three sheep and seven chickens in fact – and a little land for potatoes. We're a hard-working family, but in our local area most people earn under a dollar a day. So, we didn't have any money, but we wanted to send our boys to school. Then, last year, my neighbour told me about the running races and the prize money. So, I decided to start running, and here I am now!
> J: How did you train and look after the children at the same time?
> *continued…*

I: My husband Benjamin was very helpful. I trained every morning; I ran in the hills and Benjamin made breakfast for the boys. They're very young – the oldest is only nine – so it wasn't easy for my husband. But he didn't get angry; he always smiled! He's a patient, friendly man. And last week he sold one of his sheep and a chicken to pay for my ticket to come to Nairobi. He helped me very much – he's very kind.

J: Did you win much money yesterday?

I: Oh, yes, I did. Oh, a lot, a lot. A lot for me and my family. I won $12,000. It's incredible. I still can't believe that I won the race. Now we can send our children to a good school. When we were young, we didn't have the chance to finish our education, but perhaps our children can go to university.

J: Was this marathon your last race?

I: Oh, I don't think so! They want me to race in Europe next year! Can you imagine? I live in a tiny village in the Kenyan countryside, and they want me to run in Paris and London. I hope I can take my family, and that we don't need to sell any more sheep and chickens.

VOCABULARY: personality adjectives

4a Elicit again from students the meaning of *inspiration*, and then *inspirational*. Tell students that this is an example of a personality adjective. Tell them the words in the box are all personality adjectives. Then students do the activity as per Coursebook.

> **Chimokel:** dedicated, determined, inspirational, talented
> **Benjamin:** lovely, helpful, patient, friendly, kind
> **the family:** hard-working

4b Students do activity as per Coursebook. If they do not have access to a dictionary, first try to elicit the meanings and then teach them. Alternatively, you can read out the meanings below and students have to guess which you are describing:

dedicated (adj) – working very hard at something because you think it's important

determined (adj) – wanting to do something very much and not letting anyone or anything stop you

kind (adj) – caring about other people and wanting to help them

talented (adj) – having a natural ability to do something well

patient (adj) – able to stay calm and not become angry when waiting for something or doing something difficult

> **1** dedicated; **2** helpful; **3** determined;
> **4** inspirational

To further practise personality objectives, ask students to nominate someone they know for each adjective. Tell them they should be prepared to tell the class why.

GRAMMAR

5a Students should have already studied the past simple so this should be revision for them. They do activity as per Coursebook.

> **1** Her mother died when she was sixteen.
> **2** She left school in the same year. **3** She married Benjamin one year later. **4** She started training one year ago.

5b Students do activity as per Coursebook. Once the students have completed the exercise, encourage them to give more examples for each of the four notes. You can write these on the board, especially for types 2, 3 and 4.

> **1** started; **2** died; **3** married; **4** left

5c Put *She married Benjamin* up on the board. Elicit the negative form, i.e. *She didn't marry Benjamin*. From this, elicit the rule (subject + *didn't* + infinitive). Then elicit the yes/no question form, i.e. *Did she marry Benjamin?* and elicit the rule (*Did* + subject + infinitive). Finally elicit the answer to the questions, i.e. *Yes, she did*, and the rule (*Yes/No* + subject + *did/didn't*).

- Make sure students know that it's wrong to include the infinitive in a short answer. Make sure they understand that the question form also works when using a *wh-* question (*wh-* + *did* + subject + infinitive).

- Write *She was a housewife* on the board and go through the process again.

(!) Make sure that students notice that *did* has only one form but when using *to be*, they need to decide between *was* and *were*.

- If students are still having trouble, let them look at the Language reference. As a final practice students can do exercise 1 from the Extra activities on page 129.

> **Negatives:** *did + not +* infinitive of main verb
> **Questions:** *Did +* subject *+* infinitive of main verb … ?
> **Short answers:** *Yes, +* subject *+ did*.
>   *No, +* subject *+ didn't*.
> **When the verb is** *be*:
> **Negatives:** *was/were + not*
> **Questions:** *Was/Were +* subject … ?
> **Short answers:** *Yes, I/he/she was.*
>   *Yes, you/we/they were.*
>   *No, I/he/she wasn't.*
>   *No, you/we/they weren't.*

6 Students do activity as per Coursebook.

> **2** trained; **3** ran; **4** was; **5** got up; **6** Did … eat;
> **7** ate; **8** Did … watch; **9** didn't come; **10** didn't have; **11** stayed; **12** spoke

[i] Since winning the Nairobi Marathon in 2004, Chimokel Chilapong has not run much, finishing second in the Belgrade Marathon in 2005 and eleventh in the 2005 Nairobi Marathon after falling over.

7a Show students the grammar tip. Do some quick concept check questions with the words in the box. Students then prepare sentences individually before working in pairs.

7b This activity is done in pairs. When completed ask students to tell the whole class about their partner.

> students' own answers

SPEAKING

The woman in the picture is Mother Teresa. Information about her is contained in the communication activity that the students do.

8a Students do activity as per Coursebook in pairs. Then have classroom feedback; however do not confirm or deny information as students will find out for themselves in the following activities.

> students' own answers

8b Students should be in pairs, one being student A and the other student B. Student As turn to page 112 and Student Bs turn to page 114. Students should do the activity together as per the instructions, without looking at each other's book.

[☼] If you have an odd number of students, make groups of three where one student records all the answers needed.

> **1** geography; **2** 1946; **3** a room; **4** the Nobel Peace Prize; **5** the poor people of Kolkata
> **a** the principal of the school; **b** an open-air school for homeless children; **c** her first centre in another country; **d** $6,000; **e** 1997

8c Students should prepare this before they share it with their partners. This can then be presented to the class.

HOMEWORK OPTIONS

Exercise 8c can be extended into a composition for homework.

Students do the exercises on pages 10–11 of the Workbook.

2.2 CREATIVE LIVES

IN THIS LESSON

Lesson topic and staging

The focus in this lesson is on creative lives, especially the life of the painter Frida Kahlo. The lesson begins with some warm-up speaking questions about creative people. This is followed by a reading activity on the life of Frida Kahlo. This involves reading for gist, reading for specific information and working out meaning from context.

The reading text is the context for the presentation of past continuous. This should simply be revision for most students. The past continuous and the past simple are compared and practised. There is also some practice of the pronunciation of *was* and *were*, as well as further practice (following on from Lesson 2.1) of time expressions, but with past continuous. Finally students do a speaking task supported by a listening for specific information task.

Objectives

By the end of the lesson, students should have:

- read for gist, specific information and to work out meaning from context
- recycled and practised the past continuous alone and then in comparison with the past simple
- practised pronunciation of *was* and *were*
- completed a speaking activity, using the past simple and the past continuous, about famous creative people

Timings

Exercise 3a (or 3b) and/or 4b can be left out if there is not enough time.

Possible lesson break: after exercises 3b, 5 or 7.

1 Students do activities as per Coursebook in pairs. Make sure students understand the meaning of *creative* (adj) – someone who is good at thinking and making new ideas or things. Do feedback on question 1 alone (as you will re-visit 2 at the end of the lesson).

> students' own answers

2a This is a quick reading for gist activity. To make this really effective give your students a time limit that is challenging, e.g. two minutes. Otherwise it will be less about reading for gist and more about reading for specific information.

> students' own answers

2b Students do activity as per Coursebook.

> **1** true; **2** true; **3** false; **4** false; **5** text doesn't say; **6** false

2c Students do activity as per Coursebook.

> **1** damaged; **2** recovering; **3** proud; **4** philosophy; **5** admired

- You can also check they understand the following words:

  recent (adj) – having happened a short time before

  stormy (adj) – when people argue a lot and have strong feelings

  portrait (n) – a painting, drawing or photograph of a person

(!) Students are not always very good at finding meaning from context and you may have to identify an area where the word can be found.

3a Students do the activity as per Coursebook as a class discussion.

3b Students need to have time to think about this activity. Students share their thoughts in pairs and then in groups.

GRAMMAR: past continuous

This is a revision section, so you may want to start by eliciting the rule instead of giving students the description at the top of page 17. To do this, write sentences a) and b) on the board and elicit the rule from the students.

4a Students do activity as per Coursebook.

> 1a; 2b

4b Students do activity as per Coursebook

> While she was staying in Paris, she appeared on the front cover of *Vogue* magazine.
> When she wasn't working, she liked singing and telling jokes at parties.

(!) Students may identify *He was doing a painting* as an answer. Explain that this is an example of a different use of the past continuous which they will look at next.

4c Take example a) from exercise 4a and put it on the board. Elicit from students how to make it negative (*She wasn't travelling on a bus …*) then elicit the form (subject + *wasn't/weren't* + *-ing* form). Do the same for the question form. Elicit from students the form (*Was/Were* + subject + *-ing* form) then focus on the presentation of the second usage of the past continuous (action in progress in the past). Again, you may prefer to write up the example sentences on the board and elicit the usage before reading the description.

- Students with difficulties with this tense may check the Language reference on page 128. Students may then do exercises 2, 3 and 4 from the Extra practice activities or for homework.

(!) Students may not remember that state verbs don't use the past continuous. Remind them of this, e.g. *I knew him*, not *I was knowing him*.

> **Affirmative:** subject + *was/were* + *-ing* form of the verb
> **Negative:** subject + *was/were* + *not* + *-ing* form of the verb
> **Questions:** *Was/Were* + subject + *-ing* form of the verb

---

[1.7]

5 Students should first read the texts and predict the answers for the blanks.

(☼) To make things quicker, divide the class into groups of three. One student in each group reads text A, one reads B and one reads C. Each student predicts the answers and shares them with the rest of the group.

- Students listen to the recording to check the answers and find out the names of the people.

> **A** (3) John Lennon **1** was returning; **2** shot; **3** killed
> **B** (1) Hassan Fathy **4** designed; **5** was teaching; **6** built
> **C** (2) Junichiro Tanizaki **7** wrote; **8** was living; **9** destroyed; **10** moved

> **Track 1.7**
> **A**
> John Lennon was an inspirational British musician from Liverpool and in the most famous pop group of all time – the Beatles. In 1980, he was returning to his home in New York when someone shot and killed him.
> **B**
> Hassan Fathy was an important Egyptian architect. He designed his first building in the 1930s, when he was teaching at the Faculty of Fine Arts in Cairo. He built modern houses in the traditional Egyptian style.
> **C**
> Junichiro Tanizaki was a Japanese writer. He wrote about Japanese culture, and the influence of western countries on Japan. In 1923, when he was living in Tokyo, a great earthquake destroyed his home, and he moved to Osaka.

---

pronunciation

[1.8]

6a Students do activity as per Coursebook.

> **1** weak form: /wəz/; **2** weak form: /wəz/, strong form: /wɒz/; **3** weak form: /wə/; **4** weak form: /wə/, strong form: /wɜː/

[1.9]

6b Students do activity as per Coursebook.

> **Tracks 1.8 and 1.9**
> **1** I was singing.
> **2** – Was she eating?
> – Yes, she was.
> **3** We were studying.
> **4** – Were they running?
> – Yes, they were.
> **5** He was painting.
> **6** – Was she working?
> – Yes, she was.
> **7** Where was he living?
> **8** – Were they telling jokes?
> – Yes, they were.
> **9** Why were they helping him?
> **10** What were you reading?

7 Students do activity as per Coursebook.

SPEAKING

`1.10`

8a Read through the instructions with the students. Students listen and fill in the answers. The objective of the listening is to provide a template for exercise 8b.

> **1** musician; **2** energy and abilities; **3** sing, play instruments and dance; **4** the history of jazz, blues and pop; **5** generous; a lot of money to poor children; **6** you were singing in the streets

Track 1.10
I'd like to invite Louis Armstrong because I think he was the greatest musician ever. I know that his early life was very hard – he came from a very poor family in New Orleans. But he had amazing energy and abilities. He could sing, play instruments and dance. He made many records and he changed jazz – he made it into an art. So, he had a big influence on the history of jazz, blues and pop. Erm … he was also a generous man. For example, later in his life, when he was rich, he gave a lot of money to poor children – so they could learn music. Er … so, I'd like to invite Louis Armstrong because he brought happiness and pleasure to millions of people. What would I like to ask him? Well, perhaps this: How did you feel when you were eight years old, and you were singing in the streets of New Orleans for money?

8b Students work in pairs to prepare the questions for the creative person they are going to invite. They should prepare at least one question in the past continuous, e.g. *What were you doing when you were my age?*

8c Do activity as per Coursebook. Make sure that each member of the pair joins a different group. There should be at least four people in each group.

💡 You could make this a balloon debate with students taking the part of the creative people they have talked about.

💡 Alternatively, students could write about their choice using the title *A creative person I admire.*

E You can now do photocopiable activity 2A to revise the past simple and past continuous.

HOMEWORK OPTIONS

Students do the exercises on pages 12–13 of the Workbook.

2.3 SCENARIO: SHARING A FLAT

IN THIS LESSON

Lesson topic and staging

This lesson is about sharing a flat, in particular giving and sharing opinions about other people. The lesson starts by talking about people sharing a flat and students are encouraged to think about what qualities they would expect from a flatmate. This is an introduction to learning more personality adjectives, including the word stress in adjectives with different numbers of syllables. Students are then introduced to the situation through a listening activity which involves listening for gist and for specific information. Next, students discover and practise the key language of describing people before tackling the speaking task.

Objectives

By the end of the lesson, students should have:

- talked about important characteristics of a flatmate
- learned and practised new personality adjectives and recognised the different stress patterns of these adjectives
- listened for gist and for specific information
- learned and practised the language for describing people
- completed a speaking task using personality adjectives, the language of personal description and language for agreeing/disagreeing

Common European Framework

Students can use language to describe other people.

Timings

If there is not enough time, exercises 5b and/or 5c could be given for homework as could the first part of 5d. Exercise 5b could be omitted.

Possible lesson break: after exercise 4b or 5c.

PREPARATION

1a Students do activity as pairs and then feed back to the class.

⚠ In some cultures people don't share flats with friends. If you know this is the case you may want to jump this activity.

1b Students do the activity first individually and then in pairs. You may need to check they understand the following vocabulary:

honest (adj) – someone is honest if they do not lie, cheat or steal

tidy (adj) – someone is tidy if they keep their things neat (in the right place) and clean

students' own answers

1.11

2   Students first work individually to match the pairs of adjectives, then listen and check. You may need to teach the following vocabulary if students cannot finish the task, or in the feedback session:

shy (adj) – nervous or embarrassed about meeting or talking to other people

rude (adj) – speaking or behaving in a way that is not polite

chatty (adj) – someone is chatty if they talk a lot

1c; 2e; 3a; 4b; 5d; 6h; 7f; 8g

Track 1.11
1   The opposite of polite is rude.
2   The opposite of friendly is unfriendly.
3   The opposite of confident is shy.
4   The opposite of nice is horrible.
5   The opposite of cheerful is miserable.
6   The opposite of hard-working is lazy.
7   The opposite of clever is stupid.
8   The opposite of chatty is quiet.

pronunciation

3a Students do activity as per Coursebook. Students may have difficulty understanding the meaning of the word *syllable* and you may need more examples than just *confident*.

One syllable: nice, shy, rude
Two syllables: polite, friendly, cheerful, clever, chatty, stupid, quiet, lazy
Three syllables: confident, hard-working, horrible, unfriendly
Four syllables: miserable

1.12

3b Students do activity as per Coursebook. Ask them to practise saying *confident* to confirm they understand.

1

Track 1.12
confident   confident

1.13

3c Students do activity as per Coursebook. As you check get students to pronounce the adjective rather than just say 'it's the second syllable'.

Track 1.13
1   po<u>lite</u>
2   <u>friend</u>ly
3   <u>con</u>fident
4   nice
5   <u>cheer</u>ful
6   hard-<u>work</u>ing
7   <u>clev</u>er
8   <u>chat</u>ty
a) shy
b) <u>horr</u>ible
c) rude
d) <u>mis</u>erable
e) un<u>friend</u>ly
f) <u>stup</u>id
g) <u>quiet</u>
h) <u>laz</u>y

3d Students work in pairs to complete this activity. You should go round the class checking the pronunciation.

SITUATION

Read through the introduction with the students. You can ask the following concept questions.

Who share a flat? (Stephanie and Xu Ming)

How many bedrooms does it have? (three)

Where is Stephanie now? (Germany)

Who saw the people coming to the flat? (Xu Ming)

Who is giving the information about the people? (Xu Ming)

1.14

4a Students do activity as per Coursebook. Ask students why they chose the answer.

not really

4b Students do activity as per Coursebook.

1 doctor; 2 friendly; 3 chatty; 4 tidy; 5 sport;
6 smoking; 7 professional; 8 nice; 9 brown;
10 quiet

Track 1.14
Stephanie, Xu Ming
s: Hello.
x: Hi Stephanie, it's Xu Ming.
s: Oh, hi. How are you? How did the interviews go?
x: Oh, I'm fine. The interviews were fine too. Have you got ten minutes or are you busy?
s: I'm fine for time. Tell me about the people. Who did you see first?
x: Well, the first person was a guy called Martin. He's a young doctor and he's Canadian.
s: Oh, that sounds good. What's he like?

continued…

x: Well, I'm not sure. At first he wasn't very friendly, and he certainly isn't chatty. He works long hours, so … he's hard-working, I guess. He seems honest and tidy.

s: I see, so erm, what does he like? What are his interests?

x: Well, he likes watching sport on TV, but he doesn't play any. Er, what else? He doesn't smoke, in fact he hates smoking. Oh, he said he likes cooking, when he's got time.

s: OK, so perhaps he's a bit quiet. What does he look like? Does he look tidy and smart?

x: Well, he's a doctor, so he looks professional. He wears nice clothes. He's got short brown hair. In fact, he looks like that Hollywood actor, you know, Tom Cruise.

s: Really? I'm not sure that's a good thing! So, what do you think? Would you like to live with him?

x: Mmm, yes, I think so. I'm happy to live with a quiet person.

s: What, like me?!

x: Yeah, exactly! And I'd like to live with a Canadian, you know, my sister lives in Toronto. Also, doctors are usually honest and responsible. What about you?

s: Well … erm … he sounds quite quiet … tell me about the others first …

KEY LANGUAGE: describing people

1.15

5a Students do activity as per Coursebook. Make sure students predict the answers first before listening. Do not investigate the differences between the four uses of *like* until exercise 5b.

> **1** like; **2** look; **3** does; **4** Would

> **Track 1.15**
> 1 What's he like?
> 2 What does he look like?
> 3 What does he like?
> 4 Would you like to live with him?

5b Students do activity as per Coursebook. Now is the time to draw their attention to different uses of *like*.

> **1** Personality; **2** Appearance; **3** Likes/Dislikes; **4** Xu Ming's opinion

5c Students do activity as per Coursebook. Let students first fill in the blanks and then decide which question goes with each answer.

> **1** got (answers question 2); **2** looks (answers question 2); **3** seems (answers question 1); **4** isn't (answers question 1); **5** so (answers question 1); **6** likes (answers question 3); **7** wears (answers question 2)

5d Exercises 5a, 5b and 5c have made a connection between the things we want to know, the questions we ask to find them out and the way we answer. Exercise 5d gives students the opportunity to practise this before they do the task. Students prepare individually first, then work in pairs.

☼ Alternatively, students could prepare at home before this exercise (see 'Timings' above).

E Students can do exercise 5 from the Extra practice activities on page 129 either in class or for homework.

TASK: choosing a new flatmate

6a This task requires the students to use all the key language for describing people and personality adjectives. It is an information gap so divide students into pairs. Students should follow the instructions in the Coursebook, with Student A turning to page 113 and Student B to page 114. Make sure they know not to show the information they have to their partner.

6b Read through the instructions with students and check understanding. Then go through the language in the OTHER USEFUL PHRASES box. Model the OTHER USEFUL PHRASES to the students before starting the activity. Students first work in pairs. Then join two pairs together. Finally do a class feedback session.

E You can now do photocopiable activity 2B to revise the past simple, the past continuous and the functional language of this lesson.

HOMEWORK OPTIONS

Students can do exercises 6 and 7 from the Extra practice activities on page 129.

Students do the exercises on page 14 of the Workbook.

2.4 STUDY AND WRITING SKILLS

IN THIS LESSON

Lesson topic and staging

This lesson focuses on the learning styles of students and how to keep a learning diary. Students are encouraged to discuss their learning styles. Firstly, they listen to people talking about learning experiences. Students use the skills of listening for gist and listening for specific information. Students then share learning experiences. Next, they do the learning styles questionnaire and analyse the results. As part of discovering their learning styles, students can keep a learning diary of their experiences and this is what they are encouraged to do in the second half of the lesson. Students look for specific information in an extract from a student's learning diary. They then do some revision on linkers. Finally they are asked to start a learning diary.

Objectives

By the end of the lesson, students should have:

- listened for gist and specific information
- discussed learning styles and identified their own style
- found out about the use of learning diaries
- read for specific information
- revised linkers

Timings

Exercise 7 shouldn't be done in class, but as homework. Possible lesson break: before the Writing Skills section.

KEY LANGUAGE: learning styles and strategies

`1.16`

1a Tell students that they are going to investigate how people learn things. Tell them that first of all they are going to listen to two learning experiences. Students do activity as per Coursebook.

> **Person 1: 1** to drive a car; **2** not especially
> **Person 2: 1** Russian; **2** yes, very much

1b Tell students that they are now going to find out why the two people found the learning enjoyable or not. Students do activity as per Coursebook.

> **Person 1: 1** initially his father, then a driving instructor; **2** neither difficult nor easy; **3** neither proud nor excited
> **Person 2: 1** her Latin teacher; **2** easy; **3** really proud

You can go a little deeper into this subject by asking the students the following questions:

Why did the first person not enjoy the learning experience?
(father was impatient and started shouting, instructor wanted him to go faster, learned in the city where everyone drove fast)

Why did the second person enjoy the learning experience?
(excellent coursebook, Russian was quite easy, the teacher was good, the lessons were enjoyable, loved the sound of words)

> **Track 1.16**
> **1**
> I started learning to drive when I was eighteen. I had my first lessons with my father, but he was very impatient with me. He always shouted at me when I made a mistake. So I went to a driving school instead. I wasn't a confident driver and I can still hear the words of the instructor: 'More gas. More gas!' He always wanted me to go faster. Learning to drive wasn't especially easy or difficult, but I didn't enjoy it very much. I was living in a big city and there was a lot of traffic – everyone was driving fast, too. It wasn't much fun then. I failed my test the first time, but I passed the second time. I didn't feel proud or excited – I was just happy it was finished.
> **2**
> I learned Russian at school. There was a teacher who taught Latin, but he also knew Russian. It was funny because I was the only student in the class – it was really a private lesson. I had an excellent coursebook. I can't remember much about it … erm … the front cover was red and it was very modern. Learning Russian was quite easy. I was surprised. The teacher was good so that helped a lot. Also, I'm quite good at learning languages. It was really enjoyable, too. I loved the sound of the words. I felt really proud when I could read a short story in Russian and when I passed my exam.

2a Students should do the activity in groups of three to five. You can give them some time to think about what they will say before doing the activity.

2b Give students an example of what is meant by 'things that you learned', e.g. *I learned that I like learning through reading* or *I like to have lots of practice*, otherwise students might not understand. Get class feedback to make sure all students have understood.

- Read through the paragraph together. You can also, after reading this, brainstorm different ways of learning before students do the questionnaires (e.g. people like to read or see, listen and speak, or do).

3   Students do the questionnaires individually or in
    pairs. If in pairs, Student A reads out the sentence and
    Student B gives his/her answer and a mark out of 5.

    When students have finished this, ask them to read
    the descriptions and the tips on page 112. Check they
    understand the following words:

    tip (n) – a helpful piece of advice

    regularly (adv) – often

    highlight (v) – to mark words on paper or computer
    screen using colours so that they are noticed more
    easily

    sound file (n) – a computer file that holds sounds

    aloud (adj) – in a voice that people can hear

• Find out which students have which learning styles
    and elicit from students the types of activities you can
    do in class to accommodate these styles.

WRITING SKILLS

Write the word 'learning diary' on the board. Ask
students what they understand by this. Then ask them
what things they think should be in a 'learning diary'
(make sure students' books are closed at this time). Ask
students to open their books and read the introductory
paragraph. You might like to do a concept check by
asking students the uses of the learning diary (thoughts
and feelings clearer, thinking time, helps organise
our ideas, helps make plans, helps see progress and
development, helps us become better learners).

4   Students do activity as per Coursebook.

> **1** phrases like *So do I* and *Neither do I*; **2** yes; **3** the
> teachers and students are great; **4** in a group; **5** he
> understood a film in English

5   Read through the list so that students take note of the
    things they can put in a learning diary. Then students
    should find examples in Michal's diary.

> **1** the teachers and students are great, at the
> moment I'm very happy here; **2** I had a lot
> of trouble with [listening] until I came here.
> **3** I wrote down some of the expressions they used
> in my vocabulary book. **4** I now realise that I enjoy
> working with other people like this.

6   This should be revision for the students. First get them
    to identify uses of the linkers in the text. Make sure
    they realise the following about linkers: *at first* and *at
    the moment* usually come at the beginning or end of
    a clause or sentence; *then* and *until* usually connect
    clauses. Students should also notice that *at first* and
    then usually appear together. Make sure they also
    understand the differences in meaning for each linker.
    Students can then do the activity as per Coursebook.

> **1** At first, then; **2** At first, Then; **3** at the moment;
> **4** at first, then; **5** until; **6** afterwards

E Students can also do exercise 8 from the Extra
practice activities on page 129.

7   This activity can be started in class but should
    continue for up to a month. It is up to you how you
    want to do this and whether you make it compulsory
    or voluntary. If compulsory, you may want to collect
    learner diaries on a regular basis. If voluntary, give
    students the option of showing you their diaries.

HOMEWORK OPTIONS

Exercise 7 on an ongoing basis.

Students can do exercise 8 from the Extra practice
activities on page 129 either in class or for homework.

Students do the exercises on page 15 of the Workbook.

The media

3.1 MY MEDIA

Lesson topic and staging

This lesson looks at the different types of media, particularly newspaper and magazines, television and radio and computers and the Internet. Students begin by studying media-related vocabulary and talking about media in their own country. They do a quick reading for gist activity, followed by listening for specific information. The reading and listening texts provide the examples for the grammar focus, a revision of articles. After the grammar practice, students discuss their personal use of media.

Objectives

By the end of the lesson, students should have:

- learned more about the media
- learned and practised vocabulary connected with the media
- read for gist
- listened for specific information
- revised and practised articles
- discussed personal use of media

Timings

Exercise 5b can be done for homework if there is not enough time.

Possible lesson break: after exercise 3b.

VOCABULARY AND SPEAKING: the media

1a Before students open their books, write up the word *media* on the board and elicit its meaning. Ask what different types of media there are. Students then do activity as per Coursebook. Once they have completed it individually, get them to check in pairs. Finally do a class feedback, checking they understand the words. You can pre-teach the following:

celebrity (n) – a famous living person

documentary (n) – a film or television programme that gives information about a subject

search engine (n) – a computer programme that helps you find information on the Internet

soap opera (n) – a programme about the same group of characters that is shown on TV regularly

webcast (n) – a programme shown or heard on the Internet

journalist (n) – someone who writes reports for newspapers, magazines, television or radio

E Get students to add more words to the list, e.g. *blog*, *headline*, *front page*, etc.

> **A Newspapers and magazines:** advert, article, celebrity, journalist
> **B Television and radio:** advert, celebrity, comedy, documentary, drama, journalist, presenter, producer, programme, reality TV show, series, soap opera, station
> **C Computers and the Internet:** advert, article, computer game, email, search engine, webcast

1b Get students to discuss in groups and then do class feedback. You could add the following topics:

Children watch a lot of TV.

Most presenters are young, attractive women.

Everyone uses email.

These statements could be titles for a composition for homework.

> students' own answers

READING

2a Students do activity as in Coursebook. Make sure they justify their answers so you are sure they have read the text. Give students no more than two minutes to read otherwise it will become reading for specific information.

> students' own answers

2b Students do activity as in Coursebook.

> 1b; 2d; 3a; 4c

If you want to do more with this text, you could ask the following questions:

When he was an English teacher, how many countries did Callum work in? (four)

When did he present his first radio series? (1998)

Does he produce TV programmes? (No, he produces webcasts and features for radio and online.)

What are his favourite sports? (racket sports, scuba diving, hill walking)

Why is it hard for Callum to suggest something to learners? (because every learner is different)

LISTENING

Students read the introduction. You can pre-teach the following words before either exercise 3a or 3b:

trade magazine (n) – a magazine for people in a certain type of industry or business

medium (n) – a way of communicating information or ideas

indispensable (adj) – so important or useful that you cannot manage without

`1.17`

3a Students do activity as per Coursebook.

> TV, radio and the Internet

3b Students do activity as per Coursebook.

> **1** true; **2** false; **3** true; **4** true; **5** true; **6** false; **7** true

Ask what Callum's opinions are on the following:

- American TV programmes
- talk radio
- the Internet.

- Ask students whether they agree with Callum or not. Do this as a class discussion.

Track 1.17

Callum, Helen

C: Hi, Callum Robertson.

H: Hello Callum. Helen Francis, from *The Nation*.

C: Hi. How are you? Thanks for the email.

H: I'm fine. Thanks for agreeing to do the interview. As I mentioned in the email, it's pretty simple really. Just a few questions about the media. You can say as much or as little as you like.

C: Fine, go ahead.

H: OK … first question: which newspapers do you read?

C: I don't buy a newspaper every day because I don't really have time to read one. I cycle to work every day and it's a bit difficult to read a newspaper while you're cycling. If I travel by train, I get one of the free newspapers, like the *Metro* that we have here in London. But when I get to work we have the daily papers here, so at lunchtime, I read *The Guardian* or I have a look at one of the tabloids.

H: What about magazines?

C: I subscribe to a computer magazine, *Mac World*, because I have a Mac at home and I like to keep up with what's going on with Macs. And at work I look at some of the trade magazines and some other computer and Internet magazines but apart from that I don't spend a lot of time with magazines.

H: Uh-huh. What do you watch on TV?

C: I watch a great deal of television. I probably watch too much television. I like documentaries and comedies. I like American drama series like *The Sopranos* and *ER* and things like that. But I do have square eyes I think.

continued…

H: Do you ever listen to the radio, apart from the programmes you make?

C: I listen to the radio a lot. I think it's a great medium. When I'm cooking in the kitchen, I always have the radio on. When I'm in the bath, I have the radio on and when I go to sleep at night I have the radio on. And it's actually on throughout the night, and when I wake up in the morning I have the radio on. It's mainly talk radio; news station BBC Five Live is the station I tend to listen to, that or Radio 4, another BBC station. I don't listen to very much music on the radio, but I love the radio – it's great.

H: Can I ask you how you use the Internet?

C: I use the Internet a great deal. At work it's part of my job, and at home I use it a lot, obviously for email. And these days I use it for all of my banking and a lot of my shopping and so it's an indispensable tool for me now, the Internet, for business use and for personal use.

H: OK, finally, do you think the Internet is changing the way we use media? For example, do you think newspapers have a future?

C: I think the Internet allows people to get their news from different places and do research. Er, but I don't think the Internet will destroy newspapers, because having something physical in your hand, for reading and turning, is important. You can write on it, you can do the crossword on it. So, the Internet can give us a lot but I don't think it can ever replace newspapers.

H: Great! That's it. Thanks very much.

C: My pleasure. I'm looking forward to the article!

H: Well, we can send you a copy when it's ready.

C: Thanks, Helen. Goodbye.

H: Goodbye.

GRAMMAR: articles

4 This is revision of articles. Direct students to the first sentence of the reading text. Tell them there are four examples of the use of articles in that line. Check they understand the meaning of 'article', then elicit the answers (*a* BBC website, learners, English, *the* world). Then ask them to find more examples in the web page. (Students often forget that some nouns do not have an article at all. Remind them that 'no article' is an option.)

> **1** no article (material, live webcasts and features for radio, racket sports, badminton, squash, scuba diving, hill walking, learners)
> **2** a/an (an English teacher, a radio series, a single tip)
> **3** the (the site, the BBC, the irregular verbs tables, the phonemic symbols)

- Read with students the explanation for using *a* and *the* together. Read the example sentence together with students and elicit why *a* and *the* are being used.

5a Students do activity as per Coursebook. There are only two examples. If students have trouble, let them look at the Language reference.

E Students can also do exercises 1 and 2 from the Extra practice activities on page 131, either in class or for homework.

> I work on a BBC website / I write materials for the site
> presented a radio series / the series lasted for 40 episodes

5b Students do activity as per Coursebook.

> **1** a; **2** the; **3** An; **4** a; **5** The; **6** an; **7** The; **8** the; **9** the; **10** a; **11** the; **12** the; **13** the; **14** the

E Students can do exercises 1 and 2 from the Extra practice activities on page 131 either in class or for homework.

5c Students do activity as per Coursebook.

SPEAKING

6 Read through the instructions with the students and then make sure they identify the questions from the audioscript, e.g.:

Which newspapers do you read?

What about magazines?

What do you watch on TV?

Do you ever listen to the radio?

Can I ask you how you use the Internet?

- Put students into pairs. Then students take it in turns to ask each other the questions and note the answers. Have a feedback session afterwards comparing the use of media between the partners.

HOMEWORK OPTIONS

Students can do exercise 5c.

Students do the exercises on pages 16–17 of the Workbook.

3.2 WORLD NEWS

IN THIS LESSON

Lesson topic and staging

In this lesson, students find out about different news programmes both on TV and Internet and what they can offer the user. They begin by discussing what news they watch and where. Next, they read a text for gist and for specific information. They also work out references in the text and discuss other issues connected with the news. Students then look at nouns and how the noun form changes according to whether we are talking about people or the job/subject. Students are then introduced, for the first time, to relative pronouns. They use and then practise joining sentences together with relative pronouns and finish the lesson by making questions for a crossword using relative pronouns.

Objectives

By the end of the lesson, students should have:

- discussed news programmes
- read for gist and for specific information
- worked out references in the text
- studied and recognised the differences between nouns for people and nouns for subject or job
- learned and practised relative pronouns

Timings

Exercise 1 can be omitted if there is not enough time.

Possible lesson break: after exercise 5b.

READING AND SPEAKING

1 This introduces the topic of world news. Students discuss each topic one by one, first in pairs and then as a class.

2a This activity is better done with books closed to stop students glancing across at the text. Its aim is to check what students know, so don't give them any information about these channels at this time. Do this as a whole-class activity.

2b This activity practises reading for gist. Students do activity as per Coursebook. If you have a good class, you may elicit from them why the other options are not appropriate.

> **2** (Choose the news)

3a Students do activity as per Coursebook. This activity practises reading for specific information.

> 1 BBC World, CNN; 2 OneWorld, AllAfrica.com, WNN.com; 3 Al Jazeera International, OneWorld; 4 BBC World, CNN, Al Jazeera International; 5 OneWorld; 6 OneWorld; 7 AllAfrica.com, WNN.com

3b This will be the first time that students have done reference questions on this course so you may want to model it first. If so, write the following on the board:

Peter is on holiday in Spain. He's coming back next week.

Elicit from students how many people are mentioned in the two sentences (one). Elicit who that person is (Peter). Elicit from students how Peter is mentioned in the second sentence (he).

Tell students that *he* is a reference word as *he* refers to Peter. Get students to look at exercise 3b and do the same thing with the five items.

> 1 BBC World and CNN; 2 Al Jazeera International; 3 OneWorld; 4 non-professional journalism; 5 Internet news sites

4 Students do activity as per Coursebook in pairs and then together as a class.

VOCABULARY: nouns

5a Students do activity as per Coursebook. Check the answers and then ask them how they can know. Make sure they see that for people we can use the suffix *-ist* and for jobs we can use the suffix *-ism*. Elicit from the students other ways of showing the difference (suffixes *-er* and *-ian* for a person, no suffix or suffix *-y* or *-ics* for a job or subject). If they don't know at this stage, don't tell them but elicit again after exercise 5b.

> 1 journalist; 2 Journalism

5b Students do activity as per Coursebook. If they didn't do so in 5a, elicit other suffixes after they have completed the task.

> A (person): photographer, scientist, politician, artist, psychologist
> B (job or subject): art, photography, science, psychology, politics

You can write the following sentences on the board and ask students to fill in the gaps.

1 A _____ is someone who does experiments to understand the world.

2 _____ is the study of mind and human behaviour.

3 A _____ is someone who works in government and makes new laws.

4 _____ takes pictures with a camera.

5 An _____ is someone that paints pictures and makes sculptures.

- Check students' answers (1 scientist; 2 psychology; 3 politician; 4 photographer; 5 artist).

GRAMMAR: relative pronouns

6a Students look at the example sentence. Before looking at the explanation try to elicit from the students the two pieces of information. Then students do the same with sentences 1–3. Students do it individually and then in pairs.

> 1 BBC World and CNN are popular channels. BBC World and CNN make good quality news programmes.
> 2 OneWorld is an Internet site. OneWorld has stories about the developing world and human rights.
> 3 The writers for this company are often local people.
> The writers for this company write the stories for free.

6b Students now look back at the answers for 6a and fill in the gaps to construct the rules. If students are not clear on this let them use the Language reference on page 130.

> 1 who, that; 2 which, that

E Students can do exercises 3 and 4 from the Extra practice activities on page 131 either in class or for homework.

7 Students do activity as per Coursebook.

! Students may include the relative pronoun but not delete the subject from the second sentence. To avoid this, you might like to model this activity using the two sentences from 6a.

> 1 Politicians are very important people who/that make the laws in a country.
> 2 The United Nations is a global organisation which/that tries to solve world problems.
> 3 Nelson Mandela was a great leader who/that made his country a fairer place.

8 Students do activity as per Coursebook.

> 1b – who/that; 2c – which/that; 3a – which/that

3.3 SCENARIO: THAT'S ENTERTAINMENT!

SPEAKING

9 Put students into pairs, one student being A and the other B. Make sure students know what a crossword is and pre-teach the meaning of *across* and *down* in crosswords. Once they have learned this, direct Student As to page 114 and Student Bs to page 117. Make sure students can see that their crosswords are incomplete. Tell them that they must use the language in the 'Useful Phrases' box to identify and define the missing words. It can be helpful to model the definition sentences for students, e.g. *This is someone who … works in a classroom* (*teacher*). Don't use words that are in the crossword.

[N] Students can make their own crosswords and bring them to the next class.

[E] You can now do photocopiable activity 3A to practise relative pronouns and the vocabulary of this lesson.

HOMEWORK OPTIONS

Students do the exercises on pages 18–19 of the Workbook.

3.3 SCENARIO: THAT'S ENTERTAINMENT!

IN THIS LESSON

Lesson topic and staging

This lesson looks at the topic of TV programmes and prepares students to complete the task of planning a TV programme. The lesson begins by checking students' knowledge of different types of factual TV programmes. Students then listen for gist as well as specific information to find out more about the kind of scenario they are going to work with. They are then introduced to sentence stress and practise how to stress important information in speech. There is further listening practice. Before students begin the task, they learn the language of making suggestions. Finally, students use everything they have practised in this lesson to complete the task.

Objectives

By the end of the lesson, students should have:
- found out more about factual TV programmes
- listened for gist and specific information
- learned and practised sentence stress
- learned and practised the language of making suggestions

Common European Framework

Students can use language effectively to make suggestions.

Timings

If sentence stress is not an issue for your students and if there is not enough time, you can omit exercises 3a–3d. If students are already familiar with the language for making suggestions, you may like to omit 5c.

Possible lesson break: after exercise 4b or 5d.

SITUATION

1 Students do activity as a whole class. This will work better with classes where students are all from the same nationality and all know the same programmes. If not, it could be better to emphasise the second question rather than the first. Try and get through this activity quite quickly, as its objective is simply to set the scene.

`1.18`

2a Students do activity as per Coursebook. You can check students' understanding of the following after this activity or after 2b:

fame (n) – the state of being known by a lot of people because of your achievements

fortune (n) – a very large amount of money

deputy (n) – someone in an organisation who is directly below, for example, the president or the manager, and who replaces them when they are not there

current (adj) – happening, existing or being used now

hot (adj) – a subject is 'hot' when a lot of people are talking about it

chart (n) – an official list of the most popular songs, usually published every week

headlines (n) – important new stories on radio or television

> politics, pop music, films, business, celebrities and fame

2b Students do activity as per Coursebook.

ⓘ 'The Hoodies': a hood is that part of a coat or jacket that you use to cover your head. 'Hoodies' are usually teenagers who wears these hoods. It has become very fashionable to be a 'hoodie' but the wearing of hoods has been banned in many shopping centres as 'hoodies' have stolen things and the security cameras could not see who the criminal was because of their hoods.

> **1** her sporting past and her current family life; **2** Ireland; **3** a chart-topping band; **4** the Google offices in the States; **5** She presents the celebrity gossip stories. **6** b

---

Tracks 1.18 and 1.19

Hello and welcome to *Fame and Fortune*, the programme that brings you the freshest news and views from the worlds of politics, business and entertainment. In today's programme, we interview the Deputy Prime Minister about her sporting past and her current family life, we meet the hottest young film directors in Ireland and there's music from the chart-topping band 'The Hoodies'. Our business specialist, Tony Cotton, visits the Google offices in the States and Lynne Miller brings you the latest celebrity gossip. First of all, over to the news studio for the headlines of the week …

---

pronunciation

1.19

3a Read the instructions with the students. Ask students to listen to the first sentence of the introduction and elicit why they think certain words are stressed (answer: these words are the most important for the listener to understand the meaning of the utterance).

⚠ This is an awareness-raising activity, not an attempt to give rules for sentence stress. Ask students if we usually stress words such as *and, to, that, from*. Ask why / why not.

3b Do this first as choral drill and then pick individual students.

1.18

3c Students do activity as per Coursebook and compare their answers. Play the recording and do a class check.

> Answers: see audioscript.

3d Do this first as choral drill and then individually. Alternatively you could ask students to practise this in their own time.

1.20

4a This and exercise 4b are more listening for specific information exercises. Check students understand *brainstorm* (v – to get together and think about new ideas). Students then do activity as per Coursebook.

> interviews with politicians, live band, high profile businesses, e.g. Google, Sony, Apple
> They reject interviews with rich people and animals with unusual talents.

4b Students do activity as per Coursebook.

> interviews with politicians but about their lives (interests, family, life before politics) rather than politics; live band that plays three or four songs rather than the more usual one; include something on high profile businesses, e.g. Google, Sony, Apple, rather than just interviewing rich people (who are often really boring)

Track 1.20 and 1.21
Jeff, Kylie, Bill

J: OK then, Bill, Kylie, you've read the brief for the new programme. To summarise, it's a magazine-style programme, with a young adult audience and it's for the early Friday evening slot. The working title is *Fame and Fortune*. Now's the time to sort out some details. Any ideas? Kylie?

K: Well Jeff, I think we should include some politics in the programme.

J: Politics? Really?

K: Yeah, I know politics is usually a turn-off for this audience, but I think we can do it in a new way.

J: Oh yes, and how do we do that?

K: Well, why don't we get some politicians on the programme? However, let's not interview them about politics. Instead, let's ask them about their lives – you know, interests, family, perhaps their life before politics.

J: OK, so er, politicians without politics.

K: Exactly.

B: I like it.

J: So do I. Anything else? Bill?

B: What about music? We should have a live band on the programme.

J: I agree, but, then again, so many programmes do that.

B: That's true, but why don't we get the band to perform three or four songs, rather than just one?

J: Nice idea, that way we get a much better idea about the band.

continued…

K: Fine, but, what about the fortune part of the programme? <u>What about interviewing rich people?</u>

J: No, I ... I don't think that's a good idea. We don't need more interviews, and rich people are often really boring. I think we should do something about high profile businesses, you know, er, like Google, Sony, Apple. You know, the big businesses that have all the exciting new ideas and products.

K: Great idea. So, we've got some politics, music and business, all with a fresh angle. I think these things are good for the target audience, but the programme is an hour long. <u>What else shall we put in the programme?</u>

B: <u>What about something with animals?</u>

K/J: Animals!?

J: And, just how are animals connected to fame and fortune exactly?

B: Well, I thought that perhaps we could find pets that have unusual talents, you know, cats that can sing. And then we could have a competition, and, you know, make them famous.

K: And you really think that young adults, after a hard week at work, are interested in that?

B: Well, I don't know, erm, well, perhaps not, erm, perhaps that's not a good idea. Why don't we ...

KEY LANGUAGE: making suggestions

1.21

5a Students listen to extracts from the same conversation again. Let them check in pairs before doing classroom feedback.

> **1** Any; **2** don't; **3** not; **4** Let's; **5** Anything; **6** should; **7** about; **8** shall; **9** What

Track 1.21
See audioscript for Track 1.20.

5b Students do activity as per Coursebook.

> **a** 2, 3, 4, 6, 7, 9; **b** 1, 5, 8

5c It is probably better if you start with the grammar before going to the audioscript. Write the following phrases on the board (<u>don't</u> write the words in brackets):

Why don't we ... (+ infinitive)

Let's not ... (+ infinitive)

Let's ... (+ infinitive + object)

(*I think*) *We should ...* (+ infinitive)

What about ... (+ -*ing* form)

What else shall ... (+ subject + infinitive)

What about ... (+ noun)

Ask students to look back at the completed sentences in exercise 5a and elicit what goes in the blanks. (Answers are in the brackets.) Students then find other examples and compare the grammar.

> I think we should include some politics in the programme. / How do we do that? / What about music? / Why don't we get the band to perform three or four songs, rather than just one? / What about the fortune part of the programme? / I think we should do something about high profile businesses.

5d Students work in pairs. You can model this with another student to give the task more focus.

As a group, students make suggestions for some of the following situations:
- somewhere to have lunch
- a place to visit
- a present to buy for your mother
- a place to go on a holiday
- something to do tonight
- You have £1000 to improve your school / university / place of work.

TASK: planning a TV programme

6a If you have classes of more than ten students, then do this activity in groups rather than pairs. Students do activity as per Coursebook. When each group finishes this task make sure they show you and you check or give advice before going on to 6b. Also make sure students use the language of giving ideas and suggestions while doing this activity.

6b Students do activity as per Coursebook. Make sure your students use the introduction from Track 1.18 as a template.

6c / 6d The idea of this activity is to guess the target audience and the broadcast times of each group's programme, based on the introduction they gave. For this reason you should check each group's introduction before they give it so as to make sure they have included the relevant information.

E You can now do photocopiable activity 3B to practise the language of media and the functional language of this lesson.

HOMEWORK OPTIONS

Students can do exercises 5, 6 and 7 from the Extra practice activities on page 131.

Students do the exercises on page 20 of the Workbook.

3.4 STUDY AND WRITING SKILLS

Lesson topic and staging

The lesson focuses first on pair and group work, in the context of discussing newspapers and TV. Students begin by discussing how they feel about pairwork and group work. They then listen to a talk on the advantages and disadvantages of working in groups, identifying the gist as well as specific information. Students then listen to group work in practice. The recording introduces certain phrases which students then have an opportunity to practise in discussion.

In the second half of the lesson students look at TV programme reviews. They study the vocabulary of programmes, read a review and identify the different sections in it. They particularly look at the size of each section and the importance of a good ending. Finally they get the opportunity to write a review for themselves.

Objectives

By the end of the lesson, students should have:

- discussed the importance of pair and group work
- listened for gist and specific information
- identified and practised the type of language used in pairwork and group work (responding to what other people say)
- learned or revised different types of TV programmes
- studied a programme review and its different sections
- written a review for themselves

Timings

Exercises 2c and/or 8c can be omitted if there is not enough time.

Possible lesson break: after exercise 4.

STUDY SKILLS: working with others

1   Ask students how often they work in pairs and groups. Elicit whether they like group work / pairwork. Divide students into groups to make a list of what they like / don't like.

1.22

2a Students do activity as per Coursebook. There are no correct answers for this activity. Let the students just discuss what they heard and maybe put some ideas on the board to compare with the answers for 2b.

2b Students do activity as per Coursebook.

1 increases; 2 confident; 3 independent; 4 variety; 5 interesting; 6 communicating

Track 1.22
One of the ways we like to work is by asking you to do things in pairs or small groups. Some students think this is a waste of time. They don't want to listen and talk to other students; they want to communicate with the teacher.
However, here at the York Language Centre, we believe there are many advantages to working in pairs or small groups. First, it increases the amount of time each student can talk; you can't all have long conversations with the teacher, but it is possible to have quite long conversations with your partner, and that speaking practice is important. Number two: it helps students become more confident, especially if they're a little shy about speaking in front of the whole class. Reason number three: it encourages students to become more independent learners – they're not always waiting for the teacher to tell them what to do. Number four: it provides variety in the lesson – sometimes the teacher is talking, sometimes you work in pairs or in groups, and sometimes you have a big class discussion – this makes the class more interesting. The fifth reason is that you can learn interesting things from other students, not only from the teacher! Last but not least, it gives the teacher the chance to see how everybody is working and communicating. The teacher can go round the class and listen carefully to students and make helpful comments. And there are probably many more reasons I haven't mentioned. So we hope that you will appreciate and enjoy working in pairs and small groups, even if you haven't learned in this way before.

2c It is possible that students have thought of more things after the listening, especially disadvantages. Ask the students if they have changed their opinion. Do they now think that pairwork / group work is important?

1.23

3a This, again, requires your students to make a personal response so there is no 'right' answer.

3b Tell students they are now going to look at the language we use in pairwork and groupwork, particularly how to respond to what your partner says. Brainstorm with your students what different phrases they know to respond to what someone says. Make a list on the board and keep them on the board until the end of exercise 3. Students then listen and do activity as per Coursebook.

1 B; 2 B; 3 R; 4 I

Track 1.23

Roberta, Ilwoo

R: OK, so the question is: *Do you always believe the news?* Right … do you want to start?

I: Yes, alright. Er, well … it depends. I believe most of the news on TV, especially the BBC or CNN news. They're big, international organisations and a lot of people trust them, including me! I believe their websites, too.

R: What do you think about newspapers? Do you believe them?

I: No, I don't believe newspapers so much. I think some of them write anything – just to sell. You know, stories about celebrities …

R: Yes, but that can be interesting sometimes when you don't want really serious news.

I: Mmm, you're right actually. It *is* sometimes interesting to read those kinds of news stories. Anyway, another thing is … the newspapers are often very political. Some are for the government, and others are against the government.

R: Absolutely. And they try to influence you.

I: I think TV news is fairer. It's more balanced. Anyway, what do you think? Do you believe the news?

R: Well, I think I agree with you, basically. I trust TV news more. But there's a special problem here in Britain, even on the TV news … you know … it's the way they talk about Europe … they seem to tell British people what they want to hear …

I: Sorry, I don't really understand. What do you mean exactly?

R: Well … when they talk about Europe in the media … it's … like it's a bad thing, you know, like it's us and them … Britain's good and Europe's bad. I'm Italian so that makes me angry.

I: So, are you saying that the British feel that they aren't really part of Europe?

R: Yes, exactly.

I: Mmm, that's an interesting point. I'm not sure I agree with you, though. Anyway, at least the British media say *something* about Europe. I never see any news about South Korea at all. My country doesn't really exist for them.

3c Students compare phrases a–j in exercise 3c with the phrases they brainstormed on the board. Are they the same or different? Students do the activity as per Coursebook to check meaning.

When they have finished the activity and you have checked it, you can ask students to look at the audioscript and practise saying the phrases. You may also like them to make their own example sentences with different endings.

1a, d; 2g; 3e; 4b, h, i; 5f, j; 6c

4 Students should do this activity in pairs. Give each pair a topic to discuss. Then change the pairs so they are talking to different people on a different topic. This will give students better practice of the phrases. Do make sure the students know they must use the phrases in 3c and do so. You can always appoint monitors to check this.

WRITING SKILLS: a TV programme review

5a Check if students understand the words in the box. If the students are all from the same country you can ask them to give examples of programmes for each category. In case students don't have a dictionary at hand, explain the following words:

chat show (n) – a programme in which people answer questions about themselves

current affairs (n pl) – important political or social events that are happening now

game show (n) – a programme in which people play games to try and win prizes

variety show (n) – a programme that has different types of entertainment, e.g. singers, comedy, etc.

5b Put students into groups but model Part one of the activity first before letting students do it.

If you have quite a weak class, you may want to model the task and then brainstorm on the board some of the language that the students will need. By modelling and brainstorming, you are making sure students understand the task and include all the points.

• Do the second activity as a whole-class discussion.

6a Ask students to read the text very quickly (give them about a minute maximum) and ask the question about the review. You can also check to see if anyone has seen this series. If so, you may also like to ask them what they think about it.

positive

6b Students do activity as per Coursebook.

1 Large collars on shirts were the fashion of the 1970s. **2** The personal computer wasn't available until the 1980s. **3** Because life in the 1970s is so alien to Sam Tyler.

7 Students do activity as per Coursebook. You can also ask your students why they gave their answers.

description: paragraph 2; writer's opinion: paragraph 3

8a Students do activity as per Coursebook. The objective of this task is to identify the key elements in a review before they do their own review.

1 paragraph 2; 2 paragraph 2 (Detective Chief Inspector Sam Tyler); 3 Manchester, 2006, then 1973; 4 paragraph 3; 5 paragraph 3 (Simm gives a convincing performance as a man who is in shock, and writer Matthew Graham makes sure that there is also plenty of enjoyable comedy.); 6 paragraph 1

8b Students discuss this in pairs and you can discuss it as a class.

students' own answers, but probably the same order as given in the text

8c Students read the point and think about it. Ask students about which they think is more important, the story or the opinions. Make sure students understand that opinions are more important.

four – the four main sentences in paragraph 2

9 This is a discussion question and there are no right answers. Students do this activity on their own and then get class feedback.

As preparation for exercise 10 (which you may give for homework) ask students to prepare their conclusions for a programme or series they saw recently, in class. These can be passed around for comment by the students.

10 This can be done either in class or as homework. You can get students to tell you their programmes in class to confirm they are on the right track. You can also get students to make their plan in class before doing the writing at home.

HOMEWORK OPTIONS

Students can do exercise 10 (see above).

Students do the exercises on page 21 of the Workbook.

Review

GRAMMAR

1

> 1 always enjoy; 2 a; 3 preferred; 4 which; 5 left;
> 6 the; 7 was working; 8 include; 9 continued;
> 10 the; 11 who; 12 watch

2

> 2 He made thrillers; 3 My local cinema is showing;
> 4 which/that shock audiences; 5 are going to the
> cinema; 6 Hitchcock designed; 7 while we were
> watching; 8 who/that makes horror films; 9 at the
> cinema; 10 I don't often watch

3 Put students into pairs to discuss the questions and then in groups. Finally do class feedback.

VOCABULARY

4a

> 1 kind; 2 helpful; 3 hard-working; 4 patient;
> 5 chatty; 6 creative; 7 talented; 8 honest; 9 rude

4b

> dedicated

5

> 1 snow ; 2 blizzards; 3 wet; 4 fog; 5 cloudy;
> 6 windy; 7 storms; 8 celebrities; 9 programme;
> 10 documentary; 11 series; 12 presenter

KEY LANGUAGE

6a Students do this activity in pairs.

`1.24`

6b Students listen and then as pairs check their answers. Pairs should be ready to give feedback to the whole class.

7

> 1b; 2a

Track 1.24
Sally, Geoff

s: Hi, Geoff. Can I talk to you for a minute?

G: Sure, what is it?

s: Well, yesterday I met that guy Steve Giles – you know, the one I thought was a possible presenter for our new reality TV show.

continued…

G: Oh, yes. What's he like?

s: Nice ... he's very polite, and cheerful ...

G: Hold on, Sally, can he present a reality TV show? I don't think we want a nice, polite person for that!

s: Don't you? Well, I'm not sure. I think the presenter has to be friendly so that people want to watch him. He's really confident too.

G: OK. What does he look like?

s: He's good-looking. He's got short dark hair, lovely eyes. He's not very smart, though, his clothes, I mean.

G: What, is he scruffy?

s: No, no, not scruffy, casual. You know, he was wearing jeans and a T-shirt. But we don't need a really smart person for this show. I think we need someone young and relaxed.

G: Yes, so do I. A lot of young people will watch it.

s: Exactly. Why don't we invite him to meet the celebrities in the show? You know, see how they all get on. I think we should arrange a meeting.

G: I don't agree, Sally. It's too soon. We don't know enough about Steve yet. What about getting him to the studio for a camera test – see how he looks on screen?

s: Oh, good idea. Let's do that. I'll ...

8

> 1c; 2e; 3a; 4b; 5d

9 Students do activity as per Coursebook. Give students a minute or two beforehand to prepare what they are going to say.

LANGUAGE CHECK

10

> The following words should be deleted: 1 now;
> 2 quite; 3 are; 4 and; 5 did; 6 are; 7 like (in *She's like ...*); 8 the; 9 it; 10 anything

LOOK BACK

11 Students do the exercise in small pairs or groups.

> learn about state and action verbs: 1.1, exercise 5;
> read a text about winter in Siberia: 1.2, exercise
> 2; write a guidebook entry for your country: 1.4,
> exercise 8; listen to an interview with a marathon
> runner: 2.1, exercise 3; talk about who to invite
> for dinner: 2.2, exercise 8; learn how to describe
> a person: 2.3, exercise 5; read an article about
> different news companies: 3.2, exercises 2/3; plan a
> new weekly TV programme: 3.3, exercise 6; write a
> review of a TV programme: 3.4, exercise 10

4 Health

4.1 DOCTORS WITHOUT BORDERS

Lesson topic and staging

This lesson focuses on health services, particularly those that provide health to poorer countries. The lesson begins by checking what medical words students know (if students have used *Language Leader Elementary*, this will be revision). Next, students practise reading for gist with a short text and then listen for gist and specific information with a recording about an international healthcare charity. The reading and listening texts provide the examples for the presentation of the present perfect which again should be simply revision. Students study and practise the present perfect in affirmative, negative and question forms. Finally, they do a speaking activity which involves using the present perfect in a freer activity.

Objectives

By the end of the lesson, students should have:

* learned more about healthcare charities
* practised vocabulary related to medicine
* read for gist
* listened for gist and specific information
* revised and practised the present perfect in affirmative, negative and question forms

Timings

Exercise 5 could be given for homework if there is not enough time.

Possible lesson break: after exercise 3b.

SPEAKING AND VOCABULARY: medical words (1)

1a Direct students to the picture and the title. Elicit from the students what they think the lesson will be about. Then elicit words they know which will be especially relevant for this lesson. You may find that some of the words they identify are already on your list to teach. If a student knows a word that others do not know, get him/her to explain it to the rest of the class.

* Students do activity as per Coursebook. When doing feedback for the activity, you can check they understand the following words:

surgeon (n) – a doctor who does operations in a hospital

clinic (n) – a place where people get medical treatment

surgery (n) – a medical treatment in which a doctor cuts open your body to repair or remove something

disease (n) – an illness which affects a person, animal or plant

malnutrition (n) – a serious medical condition caused by not eating enough good food

Note: If students have studied *Language Leader Elementary*, they should already know most of these words.

> **1** clinic – the others are people, this is a building; **2** injury – this is the health problem, the others are part of the cure; **3** operation – the others are health problems

1b Make sure students know the meaning of all the words in the box. You can use the following text as a model:

In the UK there are both private and state hospitals. The UK has a national health system which is paid by people's taxes. This means people can be treated for free by a local doctor and in hospitals, and can visit the dentist and pay little money. Of course the private hospitals offer better care and services but to use them you need to have private medical insurance.

> students' own answers

READING

Before students do exercise 2, ask them if they have heard of *Red Cross, Red Crescent* or *Médecins sans Frontières* (Doctors without borders).

i The Red Cross and Red Crescent are part of the same organisation, founded in 1876. Originally formed to nurse soldiers in war, it has now become an international humanitarian movement whose mission is to protect all human life and health without discriminating on grounds of nationality, race, religious belief, class or political opinion.

Médecins sans Frontières was formed in 1971 by a small group of French doctors. It is based in Geneva. MSF is a humanitarian non-governmental organisation found in war regions and developing countries suffering from diseases and epidemics.

Students read the pre-text to this task. You can pre-teach the following words:

charity (n) – an organisation that gives money, goods or help to people who are poor, sick, etc.

disaster (n) – an event such as an accident, flood or storm that causes a lot of harm or suffering

audio (adj) – related to recording and sound broadcasting

You can ask the following questions:

Where does IMA work? (in poor and disaster-hit areas of the world)

Where can you listen about IMA? (on its website)

2 Students do activity as per Coursebook. You can teach the following:

podcast (n) – an audio programme on the Internet

facilities (n pl) – rooms, equipment or services that are provided for a particular purpose

> **1** podcasts 1, 3 and 5; **2** podcasts 2 and 4;
> **3** podcast 6

LISTENING

`1.25`

3a Students do activity as per Coursebook. They can check their answers with each other by doing class feedback.

> **1** podcast 6; **2** podcast 3; **3** podcast 5; **4** podcast 1

3b Students first listen and answer the questions. You can then check they understand the following words:

continent (n) – one of the seven main areas of land on the earth

jungle (n) – a large tropical forest with trees and large plants growing very close together

diet (n) – the kind of food that you eat each day

reduce (v) – to make something become less in size, amount, price, etc.

raise money (v + n) – to get people to give money to help people or do a particular job

massive (adj) – very big

destruction (n) – when something is destroyed

Students then check their answers in pairs with the audiocript. Then do class feedback.

> **1** ten; **2** eight; **3** bored ; **4** the villagers can't get to government hospitals; **5** 1 January 2004; **6** January this year; **7** next week; **8** an earthquake; **9** two

---

Track 1.25
Extract 1
Sad news from head office concerning our work in Africa. Unfortunately, we've closed our mobile clinics in Ethiopia because of severe financial problems. Last year, we ran ten health centres in Africa but, this year, we've received very little money and we can't continue to offer medical services across the continent. We've decided to close the two Ethiopian centres and we hope to raise more money …

continued…

Extract 2
Working here is the best thing I've ever done. When I worked in the UK I got bored with the daily routine, but out here I find every day interesting and demanding. I'm working in a small clinic in the middle of the jungle and I've never done such important work before. The villagers in this region can't get to government hospitals, so this clinic is the only hope they have. I usually do about two operations a day and, so far, in my time here, I've probably saved about a hundred lives. When your work is very important, you …

Extract 3
The lack of food and poor diet in this region cause many of the health problems for the local people. We wanted to reduce their need for doctors like us so on 1st January 2004, we decided to educate the local people about the effects of malnutrition. Finally, after many years of planning and raising money, in January of this year, we started a training programme. So far, we've trained 500 people. By the end of the year, that number will be 1,000. Vera is doing the course at the moment. 'This course has given me many new skills. Before, I didn't know how to help people in my village. Now, I'm sure I can make a difference.' Vera finishes the course next week and then she'll return to her village …

Extract 4
I often work for IMA and I've worked in Kenya, Nepal and Peru. However, my current position, here in Sri Lanka, is perhaps the most difficult job I've had so far. Last year, an earthquake hit this area and this caused a massive amount of damage. I've never seen so much destruction before. I help the doctors in a couple of clinics – one here and another in a smaller village about ten kilometres away. I see people with diseases and serious injuries. Today I've seen forty patients, and I don't finish work for another four hours. These are busy days indeed. I started work at seven …

GRAMMAR: present perfect (1)

4a Students do activity as per Coursebook. Don't do anything more as the whole structure is presented over the following two exercises.

> **1** worked; **2** decided; **3** saved; **4** ran

4b Students do activity as per Coursebook. Do not discuss form as this will be worked on in exercise 4d. Make sure students clearly understand what each of the timelines mean.

> **1** past simple: sentences 2 and 4; present perfect:
> sentences 1 and 3;
> **2** a) sentence 4; b) sentence 2;
> **3** a) unfinished; in her life; b) no;
> **4** a) 3, b) 4, c) 1, d) 2

4c Students read the explanation at the top of the column and then do the activity as per Coursebook. During the feedback section, elicit example sentences from the students to show that they have understood.

five months ago, last year, yesterday, at five o'clock, on 20 December 2007

4d Write an example of each form on the board. Start with a sentence from the text such as *We have closed our healthcare programme*. Elicit the affirmative form (*have/has* + past participle). Elicit similar example sentences.

- Then change the sentence to negative, e.g. *We haven't closed our healthcare programme*, and elicit the form. Do the same with the question form.

- If students have difficulty understanding, direct them to the Language reference.

E To confirm comprehension, students can do exercises 1 and 2 in the Extra practice activities on page 133, either in class or for homework.

> **Affirmative:** subject + *has/have* + past participle
> **Negative:** subject + *has/have* + *not* + past participle
> **Questions:** *Have/Has* + subject + past participle … ?
> **Short answers:** *Yes, I/you/we/they have.*
> *No, I/you/we/they haven't.*
> *Yes, he/she/it has.*
> *No, he/she/it hasn't.*

5 Students do activity as per Coursebook.

> **1** went; **2** have completed; **3** organised;
> **4** have built; **5** haven't received; **6** helped

SPEAKING

6 Students should start by working in pairs. Ask your students to turn to page 115 and look at the questionnaire starting *In your life*. Tell students to read through the questions and then fill in their own questions in the blanks about things they would like to know about their classmates. Then each student in each pair goes round half the class asking other students and answering their questions. When they have finished, they should tell their partner what they have found out. Make sure that students use the present perfect throughout the activity.

The pairs prepare a graph and give a presentation based on the graph. The graph should focus on the questions they made themselves.

HOMEWORK OPTIONS

Students do the exercises on pages 22–23 of the Workbook.

4.2 BRAIN FOOD

IN THIS LESSON

Lesson topic and staging

This lesson continues the topic of health but specifically focuses on how some types of food and drink help your mental condition. Students begin by studying words and phrases connected with diet and health. Students then practise reading for specific information and using context to guess meaning with a text entitled *Feed your mind*. The text provides the examples for the grammar presentation of the present perfect with *for* and *since*. Students learn and practise this grammar point in affirmative, negative and question forms. They finish the lesson by doing freer practice of these forms, both in speaking and writing.

Objectives

By the end of this lesson students should have:

- learned more about how food and drink help your mental condition

- learned new words and phrases connected with diets and health

- read for specific information and used context to guess meaning

- learned and practised the present perfect with *for* and *since*

- completed both speaking and writing activities with the target structure

Timings

Exercises 4 and 6a could be given for homework.
Exercise 2c may be omitted if there is not enough time.
Possible lesson break: after exercise 2c or 4.

SPEAKING AND VOCABULARY: medical words (2)

1 Focus students on the title of the lesson. Elicit from the students what they think the lesson is about.

- Question 1: Make sure they understand the meaning of *diet* (what you normally eat or drink, not something you do to lose weight). Ask students to ask and answer the questions in pairs. Then do a class feedback.

- Question 2: Do this activity as a whole class. You can extend this and ask students what food they like which is healthy/unhealthy and why.

- Question 3: Students do activity as per Coursebook.

> A heart disease, high blood pressure; B depression, insomnia, lack of motivation, poor concentration, poor memory; C carbohydrates, junk food, nuts and seeds, salmon, vitamins

READING

2a Direct the students to the title and the picture. What do they think the text will be about? Ask them what is special about the picture. What types of food can they recognise?

- Question 1: Students do activity as per Coursebook. Give them no more than five minutes as they don't need to read every word.

- Question 2: This is a meaning from context exercise. Make sure students know the words in the box come from the text, so they can check what they mean.

> 1 a) ten (fruit, vegetables, chocolate, junk food, fish, olive oil, red wine, salmon, nuts, brown rice); b) none; c) six (mental illness, depression, insomnia, Alzheimer's disease, memory, concentration); d) three (schools banning junk food, UK Mental Health Foundation, research into the Mediterranean diet)
> 2 1 research; 2 healthy; 3 mental; 4 everyday; 5 illnesses

2b Students do activity as per Coursebook. Note questions 5) and 8) require students' opinions and can be discussed as a whole class.

> 1 healthy food = healthy body; 2 the effect of eating chocolate on your mood; 3 since 2006; 4 calmer and better concentration; 5 students' own answers (e.g. more processed food resulting in diets with higher salt, fat, sugar content); 6 an increase in mental illness; 7 helps you live longer and prevents Alzheimer's disease; 8 students' own answers

2c Students do activity as per Coursebook. Encourage students to find the word in the text and work out the meaning of the word from the text around it. After they have finished the activity, get students to come up with their own example sentence.

> 3 did **not** allow; 7 **old** people

GRAMMAR: present perfect (2): *for* and *since*

3a Students do activity as per Coursebook.

> 1 30 years ago; 2 yes; 3 in 1950; 4 yes

3b Before starting, ask students to identify the present perfect structure in the two example sentences in exercise 3a. Elicit the rule (given here, but which students should already know from Lesson 4.1).

> We have known this for a long time. / For a few years, there has been a campaign to improve school meals in the UK. / Since 2006, the children's behaviour in class has been a lot better. / Since 2006, they have known that it also prevents Alzheimer's disease.

Note: *The UK Mental Health Foundation has started a campaign* and *This research shows our diets have changed a lot, and the level of mental illness has increased* are not states.

3c Again, go back to the example sentences in 3a and get students to identify the time phrases (*for thirty years*, *since 1950*). Elicit from students what the difference in meaning is (*since* is used with the time when something started, *for* is used with the period of time that something has taken). Then students do activity as per Coursebook.

- If students still have problems understanding this, direct them to the Language reference section.

E Students can also do exercise 3 from the Extra practice activities on page 133 either in class or for homework.

> for: ten years, a year, an hour, a long time
> since: 2004, yesterday, two o'clock, three days ago

4 Students do activity as per Coursebook.

> 1 has been, for; 2 have known, since; 3 have had, since; 4 has been, for; 5 hasn't been, for; 6 Have … known, for

! Your students may not be expecting there to be negative and question forms in this exercise.

SPEAKING

5a Students read the instructions and the questions through individually. Make sure that for questions 1–6, they choose only one of the options (e.g. computer or video camera). Under 7–9, they should make three questions of their own. Encourage the students to be creative with their own questions.

5b Put the students into pairs and let students ask and answer each other's questions. Make sure that students find out how long their partners have had / been / known these things.

! Students may have problems understanding exactly what to do, so get one of the students to model the activity with you.

6a Students do activity as per Coursebook

6b Students then put all their summaries together and mix them up. Then they pick a summary at random, read them out in turn and guess who they think it is describing.

☼ Students think of something they do or are or have known that other students don't know about. Choose a student who will tell the rest of the class only how long they have been doing it, e.g. *I have been doing it for three years* or *since 2006* (go-karting). The class have 20 questions (the student being interrogated can only answer *yes* or *no*) to guess what it is.

Ⓔ You can now do photocopiable activity 4A to practise the use of the present perfect.

HOMEWORK OPTIONS

Students do the exercises on pages 24–25 of the Workbook.

4.3 SCENARIO: HEALTH AT WORK

IN THIS LESSON

Lesson topic and staging

This lesson looks at the type of health problems that occur at work and explores relationships between health officers and staff. Students begin by thinking about work-related health issues. They then listen to a conversation between an occupational health officer and a member of staff, looking for specific information. This leads to pronunciation practice, focusing on the intonation in *yes/no* questions. In the next recording, students listen again for specific information and are introduced to ways of giving advice with *should*. Students go on to learn and practise the language of giving advice and reasons. Finally, students use what they have learned about giving health advice, including the 'Other Useful Phrases' in the box, to complete the spoken task.

Objectives

By the end of the lesson, students should have:

* learned more about health issues in the workplace
* listened for specific information and language
* practised intonation in *yes/no* questions
* learned and practised the language of giving advice and reasons, including *should, because, to, so that* and *in order to*
* completed a spoken task putting all the language of the lesson into practice

Common European Framework

Students can use language effectively to give advice and reasons for that advice.

Timings

If there is not enough time, you could omit either exercise 3b or 3c. You may also omit 6 as it is similar to the task in 7 and 8.

Possible lesson break: after exercise 5b.

SITUATION

1 Discuss the two questions as a whole class. You may like to add the following questions:

Where are these pictures taken?

What health conditions are being shown?

What could be the cause of these conditions?

The photos show backache, stress in the workplace/overwork and a headache/migraine.

1.26

2a Students do activity as per Coursebook. Check they understand the meaning of the following words after feedback:

suffer (v) – to experience emotional or physical pain

neck (n) – the part of the body that joins your head and your shoulders

stressed (adj) – so worried and tired that you cannot relax

> **1** doctor; **2** sick; **3** back; **4** neck; **5** good; **6** headaches; **7** colds; **8** get

2b Students do activity as per Coursebook. After feedback, ask students what they think is wrong with Lucy and what they could suggest she does.

> **1** no; **2** about five days – for minor things, e.g. colds and 'flu; **3** yes – it's not very serious; result of a minor car accident three years ago; **4** no; **5** no – but wears contact lenses so not a problem; last went to optician's six months ago; **6** no; **7** not very often – about twice a year; **8** yes – she was stressed all the time in her last job

i Occupational health officers are now very common in most companies, as are medical health programmes. It is the job of the occupational health officer to check whether someone is sick enough to justify taking time off work or taking advantage of the medical health programme. They are also usually able to provide a quick and easy health service to people working in the company.

> **Tracks 1.26, 1.27, 1.28**
> *Mary, Lucy*
> M: Right, now Lucy, I need to ask you a few questions. **Have you seen a doctor recently?**
> L: No, I haven't.
> M: OK. <u>Have you had any days off sick in the last two years?</u>
> L: Erm, yes, I have … about five, I think.
> M: Right, could you tell me why?
> L: Oh, just for minor things – colds and 'flu, you know the kind of thing.
> M: Sure, that's fine for now, but I want to give you some advice later. OK? <u>Do you have a back problem?</u>
> L: Er, yes, I do, actually. It's not very serious though.
> M: OK, well, that's your opinion. How long have you had this problem?
> L: Well, for about three years. I had a minor car accident, and since then, well, I've had this problem with my lower back.
> M: I see. Well, let me know if it gets worse at work here. <u>Do you suffer from neck pain?</u>
> L: No, I don't. The problem is just with my lower back.
> M: Right. <u>Do you have good eyesight?</u>
> L: No, I don't actually, but I wear contact lenses so there aren't any problems.
> M: Fine. When did you last go to the optician's?
> L: Oh, six months ago, more or less.
>
> *continued…*

> M: OK, the last few questions now. <u>Do you often get headaches?</u>
> L: No, I don't.
> M: <u>Do you often get colds or 'flu?</u>
> L: No, not very often. Perhaps a couple of times a year.
> M: But that means you sometimes take time off work, doesn't it?
> L: Erm, yes, but not very often.
> M: I know, but we can still improve things, can't we? I can give you some advice about preventing these minor illnesses.
> L: OK, well, any more questions?
> M: Yes, the last one. <u>Do you sometimes get stressed by work?</u>
> L: Yes, I do! I was stressed all the time in my last job, that's why I've changed jobs, in order to reduce my stress. I hope things are better here …

pronunciation

1.27

3a Make sure students understand what intonation the arrows stand for. You can model the intonation each arrow represents, but don't do it with a question because it makes it too easy.

> 2

> **Track 1.27**
> See audioscript for Track 1.26.

1.28

3b Students do activity as per Coursebook. Make sure students drill both as a class and individually.

> **Track 1.28**
> See audioscript for Track 1.26.

3c Students do activity as per Coursebook. Go round the class and monitor their intonation. To make the questions more meaningful, you could get the students to give answers.

(!) It is possible that students will overuse the intonation pattern by applying it to the answers as well. By allowing students to answer the questions and identifying when they do not switch to a falling intonation, you can pick up this problem easily. Make sure your students know the difference.

1.29

4a Tell the students they are going to listen to another conversation between Mary, the occupational health officer, and a member of staff. Students do activity as per Coursebook.

> His main problem is neck pain at the end of the working day, but Mary is also concerned by the number of days off he has in a year through colds, etc.

Tracks 1.29 and 1.30

Mary, David

M: So then, David, what's the matter?

D: Well, er, the thing is that, at the end of a day at work, my neck really hurts.

M: I see. Do you do a lot of computer work?

D: Well, yes, I do. I spend all day at the computer, but I take regular breaks.

M: OK, that's good, but, do you stretch your arms?

D: Sorry?

M: Well, every half hour, you should stretch your arms **to** reduce the tension in your neck.

D: I see, well, I can do that I guess. Every 30 minutes?

M: Yes, and make sure you do that. Now, I see from your records that you're often off sick.

D: Well, not very often, but, yes, I seem to get a lot of colds and things.

M: I see. Can I ask about your general lifestyle? Do you eat well? Do you smoke?

D: Well, er, I don't smoke and I eat quite well.

M: That's good that you don't smoke. Do you eat a lot of fruit and vegetables?

D: Not really, especially not fruit.

M: Right, well, **because** you don't eat a lot of fruit, I think you should take some vitamins. You know vitamins help fight colds, don't you?

D: Sure, OK.

M: Well, if you know, why don't you take them already?

D: Well, you know, I'm very busy and …

M: No excuses, please, David. Now, you should also eat garlic **because** it helps fight colds too. And it should be raw when you have it, don't cook it.

D: Really? Erm, I don't really like garlic but well, er, perhaps …

M: There's no perhaps about it. The company doesn't welcome days off for colds. Now, finally, **in order to** improve your general health, you should do some exercise.

D: Oh, I do already. Er, I go swimming once a week.

M: Well, that's good, but you should go swimming three times a week **so that** it really helps your health.

D: I know, but, well, I don't really have a lot of free time, you know, we work long hours here.

M: I know, but the healthier you are, the more time you will have.

D: Er, I guess so. Er, anyway, time to get back to the computer – don't worry, I'll … I'll do some stretches!

M: And eat some fruit, and don't forget the garlic …

4b Students do activity as per Coursebook.

> 1 arms; 2 vitamins; 3 garlic; 4 exercise; 5 three

When you have finished doing the feedback, ask students to look back at the sentences 1–5. Elicit from students what Mary is doing when she uses these sentences. Then ask them what is the same about each sentence (*you should* + infinitive). Tell students you are going away for the weekend. Ask them to give advice about where to go or what to do using this structure.

4c Ask the class to think of more advice for David, using the *you should* structure.

KEY LANGUAGE: giving advice and reasons

`1.30`

5a Students do activity as per Coursebook. When you have finished, elicit from the students how the different structures work:

to, in order to + infinitive

because, so that + subject + verb

Audioscript and answers
See audioscript for Track 1.29.

5b Students do activity as per Coursebook. Remind students to look at the completed sentences in exercise 5a to work out which option to choose.

> 1f – in order to; 2b – to; 3e – because; 4a – so that; 5d – because; 6c – in order to

6 To do this activity, students need to use *should* with *so that, in order to, to* or *because*. Start by modelling an example with the whole class, e.g. *I am always standing in class and my feet hurt*.

• Students do each problem in pairs. One person makes the complaint and the other gives the advice with the reason. Then divide students into different pairs and repeat.

TASK: giving health advice

7a Divide the class into groups of four and label students A, B, C and D. Then turn to the OTHER USEFUL PHRASES box. Ask students to read the questions in their groups and come up with possible example answers. Check these in classroom feedback quickly. Identify the questions as the language that Student As and Bs will use. Elicit from the students what else from this lesson Student As and Bs will need (*you should, so that, in order to, to, because*). Student Cs and Ds study the role cards on page 115. Give students a few minutes to prepare what they are going to say before starting the activity.

For this activity you can provide a monitor for each group to give feedback on what they saw and the use of key language.

7b Students do a quick feedback session together, with Student Cs and Ds giving feedback to Student As and Bs. Then do this as whole class.

8 Repeat the activity with Student As and Bs now looking at the role cards on page 123.

If your students are university students or people at work, you might want them to answer the following question for homework:

The company which you work for is planning to have a health centre and an occupational health office. They have asked your opinion. Write a short report showing your advice.

E You can now do photocopiable activity 4B to practise the language of giving advice and reasons.

HOMEWORK OPTIONS

Students can do exercises 4 and 5 from the Extra practice activities on page 133.

Students do the exercises on page 26 of the Workbook.

4.4 STUDY AND WRITING SKILLS

IN THIS LESSON

Lesson topic and staging

Both parts of this lesson are based around one person's health problems. We read about his visit to the doctor in the first part and in the second half, we read an email he wrote some time later.

The first half of the lesson focuses on the study skill of guessing the meaning of unknown words. Students begin by discussing what they do when they don't know the meaning of a word in a text. Students then read a text for general comprehension and specific information and identify all the unknown words. They then find out about and practise three different strategies for finding the meanings of unknown words (using the context, dividing up the word and using their own language), and then return to the text to apply those strategies.

The second half of the lesson focuses on writing skills, particularly writing a thank you email. Students first discuss their use of emails. Next, they read an email for general meaning and specific information and then check the distinction between formality and informality in written communication. They study and practise the use of *thanks* and analyse the use of *'s*. Finally, students write their own thank you email, applying what they have studied in this lesson.

Objectives

By the end of this lesson students should have:

- discussed how to work out the meaning of unknown words
- read for general understanding and specific information
- studied and practised three different techniques to help guess the meaning of unknown words
- evaluated the techniques
- discussed personal use of email
- distinguished between formal and informal uses of greetings, opening phrases and endings
- analysed the uses of *thanks* and *'s*
- written an email to a friend, using what they have learned in the Writing Skills section

Timings

Exercise 12 could be done for homework if there is not enough time.

Possible lesson break: after exercise 6.

STUDY SKILLS: the meaning of unknown words

1 Students answer the questions as per Coursebook, firstly in pairs then as a whole class.

2 Students turn to page 116 and do activity as per Coursebook. Consider question 3 as a class.

> 1 earache, stomach ache and a pain in his chest;
> 2 His chest is clear but because he has earache, she's given him some antibiotics. The stomach problem is probably just a bug.
> 3 students' own answers

3 Students should start by doing this activity individually. They then compare in pairs, explaining words that their partner doesn't know. Make sure students do not use a dictionary at any time. You might also put them into groups of four, but only if it doesn't result in all the words being known.

- Present the idea of strategies to your students. Tell them to read the text in the first blue box (*Using the context …*).

4a First ask students to read the three sentences and identify what type of word each nonsense word is (they are all nouns).

- Check this and then encourage students to guess what the meaning is from the context.

> Suggested answers: 1 injuries; 2 hospital; 3 records

- Point students to the second strategy in the blue box (*Dividing the word …*). Elicit from the students other examples of words they may know which are compound nouns.

4b Students do activity as per Coursebook.

- Ask students if they can find other words like these in this lesson or in earlier lessons.

> 1a; 2b; 3b

- Again, read the students through the third strategy in the blue box (*Using your own language*).

4c Students do activity as per Coursebook. Do class feedback at the end of the minute.

(!) Some languages have very few words which are similar. You may want to check this before you do the activity and decide to either omit the task or extend the time period.

(N) If students find this activity simple, see if they can identify any false friends.

4d Students do activity as per Coursebook, individually and then checking in pairs. After feedback ask students if they think there are more common words than 'false friends' between English and their language (if the answer is 'yes', this is a reliable strategy).

> Suggested answers: 1 fast; 2 cold; 3 become; 4 library; 5 journey; 6 communication; 7 pain; 8 rumour

5 In pairs, students go back to the words they underlined but still don't know and try and work out their meaning using the strategies they have studied. If there are still words they do not know, put the pairs together to make groups of four and check again. Finally, do a class feedback.

(!) Some students rely heavily on you or the dictionary and find it hard to seriously try out strategies for doing it themselves. If you find that when you do the class feedback, there are still quite a few words which students do not understand, resist the temptation to turn to a dictionary or give the meanings yourself. If you do so, you will devalue the strategies in their eyes. Rather, go through the strategies with the whole class for every word they are still struggling with.

6 Have a short class discussion on this.

(!) Now you have introduced these strategies for guessing the meaning of unknown words to your students, make sure you use them in every lesson because, unless this becomes a habit, they will quickly revert to their dictionaries and asking you for the meaning.

WRITING SKILLS: a thank you email

7 Do this activity as a short classroom discussion. You could take a straw poll with question 1.

8 Students first answer the three questions individually. Tell students to then underline the words they don't know and with a partner, use the strategies to work out the meaning of unknown words. Make sure you check the unknown words and go through the strategies as well as checking the answers to the questions.

> 1 friends; 2 Abi came to stay with him last week. This was to look after him while he was ill. 3 She's Abigail from the story, and he's the man who went to see the doctor.

9 Students do the exercise as per Coursebook. When doing feedback, elicit why they thought the phrase was more formal.

> **Greetings:** Dear Sir
> **Opening phrases:** Thank you for your message of 28 February.
> **Endings:** Yours faithfully

10a Elicit from students why we use *thanks* and not *thank you* (*thanks* is more informal), before letting them do the activity as per Coursebook. Ask students to make their own examples. Get them to thank each other for things during the lesson.

> Thanks very much, thanks again for looking after me; both statements are true

10b Students do activity as per Coursebook.

> 1d; 2a; 3b; 4c

11 Students do activity as per Coursebook. Make sure students realise that *'s* has the three different meanings stated here.

> **1** has; **2** is, the possessive; **3** is; **4** has;
> **5** the possessive; **6** has

If you have time, ask students to come up with more sentences for others in the class to guess the use of *'s*.

12 This can either be done in class or for homework.

HOMEWORK OPTIONS

Students can do exercise 6 from the Extra practice activities on page 133.

Students do the exercises on page 27 of the Workbook.

Natural world

5.1 ISLANDS

Lesson topic and staging

This lesson looks at the topic of islands, particularly comparing islands in different parts of the world. As part of the introduction to islands, students learn and practise vocabulary for describing landscapes. Students read and listen both for gist and for specific information. The grammar focus of the lesson is a revision of comparatives and superlatives, including the use of *more* and *most*, *less* and *least*. The final speaking activity encourages students to talk about two places they know well, using both the landscape vocabulary and the comparatives and superlatives they have revised.

Objectives

By the end of the lesson, students should have:

* learned more about the world, particularly islands
* learned and practised vocabulary to describe landscapes
* revised comparatives and superlatives, and extended with *less* and *least*
* thought about how colours are used to enrich descriptions
* compared two places they know well in a speaking activity

Timings

Exercise 5b can be given for homework if there is not enough time, but should be done.

Possible lesson break: after exercise 3c.

SPEAKING AND VOCABULARY: landscapes

Although this section is a warm-up for the reading, it is important as it introduces the vocabulary of landscapes which will be essential for the students later. (Photo A shows Bora Bora, Photo B a fjord in Greenland and Photo C a loch in the Scottish Highlands.)

(!) Students may have a problem with the word stress in some of the words, particularly:

     •   •   •
   lagoon   mountain   tropical

1a Students do activity as per Coursebook, preferably in pairs and small groups first, and then as whole class. There will be some words in the list that the students don't know but it is advisable to let them try to guess to begin with and then teach the meanings of the words that they were not able to match with the pictures. Words which may need teaching are:

cliff (n) – a large area of rock with steep sides, usually near the sea

coast (n) – land next to the sea

lagoon (n) – an area of seawater that is separated from the sea by sand or rocks

wave (n) – a line of raised water that moves across the surface of the sea

> **Photo A:** beach, coast, hill, lagoon, mountain, sand, wave, sea
> **Photo B:** cliff, hill, rock, sea
> **Photo C:** forest, lake, mountain
> *River* is not shown in the photos.

1b Students do this activity as per Coursebook (i.e. in pairs). Go round and listen and then pick out one or two to share with the whole class.

(!) Some students may think they have never visited an island. If so, they should focus on questions 1 and 3 whilst those students who have visited an island focus on question 2.

(!) Make sure students remember that the s in *island* is silent.

READING

2a Students do activity as per Coursebook individually. To answer questions 2 and 3 of the exercise you can pre-teach the following words:

shallow (adj) – not deep

shades (n pl) – different types of one colour

transparent (adj) – clear and easy to see through

> 1 false; 2 true; 3 false; 4 true

2b Students do activity as per Coursebook individually. They can then compare their maps in pairs. You may remind students that Bora Bora is a small island. Elicit the names of big islands they know. (Australia and Antarctica are so big they are considered continents.)

(N) Ask students to go and find out more about Bora Bora and to bring information to present to the class.

LISTENING

1.31

3a Students do activity as per Coursebook.

> Greenland, Madagascar and Great Britain
> In Madagascar, lemurs and other wildlife are in
> danger because their habitats have been destroyed.

3b Students do activity as per Coursebook.

> **1** Great Britain; **2** Greenland; **3** Madagascar;
> **4** Great Britain; **5** Madagascar; **6** Greenland

3c Students do this question in pairs and then share with the class.

Track 1.31

Islands have their own kind of magic, and Greenland is one of the most magical of them all. During the summer months, it's daylight a lot of the time – and it's hard to sleep! But that gives you more time to see this strange, wild and enormous place. <u>Greenland is the biggest island in the world</u>. It lies between the North Atlantic and Arctic Oceans, off the coast of North America. It's almost two-thirds the size of Australia; 2,655 kilometres from north to south, and 1,290 kilometres from east to west. So there's a lot of land, but it's not very green. In fact, Greenland is the least green of all the islands in today's programme. And that's because an icecap – a thick layer of ice – covers 85 percent of Greenland. Snow falls on Greenland in every month of the year. The snow gets deeper and deeper and turns to ice. As a result, Greenland has the second largest icecap in the world, after Antarctica. On average, the ice is one and a half kilometres thick, but in some places it's thicker than that – more than three kilometres thick, in fact. And it's always moving. In large parts of the island, there are no people at all. About 55,000 people live around the coast, where the climate is less cold than in the centre. Their main work is fishing.

Madagascar is a world apart. <u>It's the fourth largest island in the world</u>, and lies in the Indian Ocean, off the coast of Africa. It split away from the rest of Africa about 100 million years ago. It's a land of contrasts and surprises. There's rainforest on the east coast of Madagascar. <u>In the south it's hot and dry, but the climate is cooler in the mountains that run down the middle of the island</u>. So some parts are less tropical than others. Most of the people are farmers, and rice is the main food. The population is about 18 million. But what makes Madagascar special is that there are unusual types of animals and plants that you can't find anywhere else in the world. <u>The island's most famous animals are the lemurs</u> – they look a little like monkeys and they've got long tails. But they're in danger now because people have destroyed the forests where they live. In all, about 50 kinds of wildlife are at risk on Madagascar.

continued...

Yes, it probably looks familiar ... and of course it is. I'm in Trafalgar Square, in the heart of London. Sometimes it's easy to forget that Great Britain is an island, too. In fact, Great Britain is the eighth largest island in the world, and the largest in Europe. It's interesting, too, because it's actually three countries: England, Scotland and Wales. It's rich in history, and people come from all over the world to visit famous churches, museums and castles. <u>Great Britain is more crowded than many of its European neighbours</u>, and has a population of 60 million. But in parts it's also very beautiful. Mountains cover a lot of Scotland, where there are many long, deep lakes, called lochs. <u>Wales and the north of England are hilly, while the south and east of England are flatter</u>. The area around London is probably the least impressive part of Great Britain. In 1994, the Channel Tunnel opened. This rail tunnel is almost 50 kilometres long, and links England with France. It's the second longest tunnel in the world, after the Seikan tunnel in Japan. Because of the Channel Tunnel, some people think that Great Britain is no longer an island!

GRAMMAR: comparatives and superlatives

This section should be revision but some students might be meeting the structure for the first time.

4 Start by asking a concept question:

In which part of Britain are there more hills, in Wales or the south and east of England?

- Elicit the answer from the students (Wales). Write the sentence:

  Wales is hillier / more hilly than the south and east of England.

- Underline *hillier / more hilly* and ask students what the underlined words are an example of (comparatives). Elicit the rule and how the form is constructed. Ask students what they think the superlative of the underlined words would be (*the hilliest*). Then elicit the rule and how the form is constructed.

☀ If you feel students need more revision, write the following adjectives on the board:

  tall   old   good   bad   green   terrible   frightening

  Ask students to make comparatives and superlatives in example sentences. They may then also start making comparatives and superlatives about students in the class.

- Students then do activity as per Coursebook. Make sure that students only read the audioscript to check their answers.

> **1** cooler; **2** most famous; **3** more crowded than;
> **4** flatter; **5** the biggest; **6** the ... largest

5a Students do activity as per Coursebook. *Less* and *least* are being presented for the first time. Make sure students understand the meaning of the two words. They can refer to the Language reference if they are having problems.

E Students can do exercises 1 and 2 from the Extra practice activities on page 135 either in class or for homework.

> the least green – the greenest; less tropical – more tropical; the least impressive – the most impressive

5b Students do activity as per Coursebook.

> **2b** less green than; **3b** the least hilly;
> **4b** less important than

6 Give students some time to prepare, then monitor them while they do this activity in pairs. You can pre-teach the following words:

calm (adj) – a calm sea or lake does not have many waves; calm weather is not windy or stormy

impressive (adj) – very good, very important, big, etc.

mysterious (adj) – strange or difficult to explain or understand

pleasant (adj) – enjoyable, nice or friendly

wild (adj) – wild animals and plants grow in natural conditions, without being changed or controlled by people

⚒ For weaker classes, you could, as a whole class, decide which adjectives will go with each island (and why) before doing the activity in pairs.

SPEAKING

7 Students should do this individually to begin with. Explain the stages clearly. For the note-taking part, you may like to use the following example on the board.

Lake District	Camber Sands	Conclusion
• in north of England	• south of England	Camber Sands:
• beautiful lakes	• very long sandy beaches	• better weather
• not very touristy	• touristy	• more friendly
• cold and rainy	• warm	• more enjoyable
• many old houses	• lots of things to do	• more modern
• famous for trekking	• famous because many films are made there	

• Divide the students into groups. Each student will give their presentation to the rest of the group. At the end the group may vote which is best. This presentation could then be given to the whole class.

> **Sample answer:**
> I'd like to tell you about two different places in England. One is the famous Lake District, in the north of England. The other is Camber Sands in the south of England. The Lake District is famous for its lakes. Camber Sands is less famous but has beautiful beaches. The Lake District has many beautiful lakes but it is cold and rainy. Camber Sands is by the sea and is warm, so it has better weather. The Lake District is famous for trekking but is not very touristy. Camber Sands is very touristy and there are lots of things to do. Camber Sands is therefore more enjoyable and more friendly. The Lake District is also famous for its many old houses. Camber Sands is famous because many films are made there and it is more modern.

✍ Students could write a paragraph on the same theme, either in class or for homework. Encourage them to use vocabulary from the the lesson and comparatives and superlatives, but remind them that the text should work as a meaningful whole, not just a list of five comparative and superlative sentences.

HOMEWORK OPTIONS

Students do the exercises on pages 28–29 of the Workbook.

5.2 INVASION

IN THIS LESSON

Lesson topic and staging

This lesson looks at the topic of animal invasion, i.e. animals and insects invading a new habitat and upsetting the ecosystem. Students start by revising the names of animals. They then study a reading passage, which also introduces new vocabulary. The reading is a springboard for observing how words can work as both noun and verb without their form changing. The grammar focus of the lesson is a revision of quantifiers for countable and uncountable nouns, with the introduction of the negative forms *few* and *little*. The final speaking activity encourages students to compare their lives with other students, using quantifiers.

Objectives

By the end of the lesson, students should have:

- read about how the introduction of foreign animals can upset and destroy an ecosystem
- learned and practised how words can be both nouns and verbs but retain the same form
- revised and practised quantifiers, including two new words, *few* and *little*
- talked about their lives, using quantifiers

Timings

Exercise 8 can be given for homework if there is not enough time, but should be done.

Possible lesson break: after exercise 5b, before starting on the Grammar section.

WARM-UP

The word *invasion* needs to be taught. Ask students to look at the pictures and then at the title of the lesson. Ask them what they think the word *invasion* means in relation to these pictures. You could also pre-teach *environment* (n – the land, water and air that people, animals and plants live in).

- Once you have taught *invasion*, ask students what they think the verb form is (*to invade*) and finally, what people who invade are called (n – *invader*).

VOCABULARY

1a Students do activity as per Coursebook.

> A red deer; B hedgehog; C human; D crab; E snail;
> F rabbit; G squirrel

1b Students answer the questions as a class. Pre-teach the following words:

cute (adj) – pretty or attractive (usually associated with animals or children)

extinct (adj) – a plant or animal that is extinct no longer exists

READING

2a Students do activity as per Coursebook. You can pre-teach *neighbourhood* (n – an area of a town, and the people who live there).

> 2

2b Students do activity as per Coursebook.

(i) This article gives examples of a very common phenomenon across the world today. Environmental invasion is a product of the world getting smaller and things becoming easier to transport. It is also a product of man's attempt to manipulate the world.

> **1** grey squirrels: North America; England; red squirrels
> **2** red deer: Europe; South America; plants such as young trees
> **3** rabbits: Europe; worldwide; farmers' crops
> **4** apple snails: South America; south-east Asia; rice plants
> **5** mitten crabs: China; Britain; local environments and fish in fish farms

3 Students do activity as per Coursebook.

> **1** It goes out of business.
> **2** small shop
> **3** They came as pets.
> **4** no (red deer and rabbits don't)
> **5** more small animals than large animals
> **6** There aren't many rice plants in Europe.
> **7** no
> **8** to the Chinese; as food

4 Do activity as class discussion.

VOCABULARY: nouns and verbs

5a Students do activity as per Coursebook.

> **1** verb; **2** noun

5b Students do activity as per Coursebook. Make sure your students understand the difference in meaning and function between the verb and the noun.

E Students can do exercises 7 and 8 from the Extra practice activities on page 135 either in class or for homework.

> **1** noun; **2** verb; **3** verb; **4** noun; **5** noun; **6** noun

GRAMMAR

6 Students do activity as per Coursebook.

! Students are revising *much*, *many* and *a lot of*. However, *few* and *little* are new.

> **few:** countable nouns – small number (few invaders are large land animals; there are very few positive sides)
> **little:** uncountable nouns – small quantity (grey squirrels, which cause little damage to plants)
> **many:** countable nouns – large number (many people brought grey squirrels; there aren't many native squirrels; there are many invaders that don't cause extinctions)
> **much:** uncountable nouns – large quantity (the apple snail from South America doesn't cause much damage)

7 Students do activity as per Coursebook. Make sure they refer to the Language reference if they are having problems.

> **1** false (title: *How much danger ... ?*);
> **2** true (lines 5–6: *many people*);
> **3** true (line 22: *a lot of money*; line 23: *a lot of damage*);
> **4** false (lines 22–23: *doesn't cause much damage*);
> **5** true (title: *How many invaders ... ?* line 9: *there aren't many native squirrels*)

8 Students do activity as per Coursebook. You can pre-teach the following words:

species (n) – a group of plants or animals of the same kind

pollution (n) – damage caused to air, water, soil, etc. by harmful chemicals and waste

• If students are using *a lot of* in many of the *much* and *many* spaces, tell them that in spoken English, *many* and *a lot of* are practically interchangeable, but highlight the fact that we hardly ever use *much* in affirmative sentences. In this exercise, *much* is preferred to *a lot of* in negatives and questions. As explained in the grammar tip, this is for reasons of register, as the text is semi-formal.

> **1** many / a lot of; **2** few; **3** few; **4** much / a lot of; **5** many; **6** much; **7** many / a lot of; **8** little; **9** a lot of; **10** a lot of; **11** many / a lot of

SPEAKING

9a/b Divide students into pairs and give them some time to think of sentences they can say. Model the activity in this way as an example (you may want to write this on the board or build a similar example on the board with your students):

> **A:** In my city there are many bicycles on the streets. Are there many in your city?
>
> **B:** No there aren't but there are many cars. In my city there is always a lot of rain. Is there much rain in your city?

• After they have finished the activity, students can report back to the class what they found out from each other.

P Students can choose a topic of interest to others, e.g. unemployment in their home country, animals in danger of extinction, places to visit in their home town, etc., and prepare a presentation using the language learned in this lesson. To make more use of this lesson you may like to limit the topic to animals or environmentalism.

E You can do photocopiable activity 5A to revise expressions of quantity.

HOMEWORK OPTIONS

Students can do exercises 4 and 6 from the Extra practice activities on page 135.

Students do the exercises on pages 30–31 of the Workbook.

5.3 SCENARIO: ANIMALS ONLINE

Lesson topic and staging

This lesson looks at the topic of animals, particularly charities that help to protect animals, and builds up to a task in which students role-play a meeting to choose pictures for a website. To start with, students are introduced to the different ways that animals need our support and to new vocabulary in this subject. The main skills practice, early in the lesson, is an extended listening activity in which students learn the language of describing photographs and work on the difference between strong and weak forms and the use of schwa. The task at the end of the lesson is an extended speaking activity in which students use the vocabulary and the language for describing photographs that they have learned. It also provides further revision of comparatives and superlatives, as well as allowing students to show their ability to express their opinions.

Objectives

By the end of the lesson, students should have:

- learned about animals and how charities try and protect them
- learned and practised vocabulary connected with the topic
- learned and practised how to describe photographs
- learned and practised discrimination between strong and weak forms and use of schwa
- completed a speaking activity requiring the language of describing a photograph, comparatives and superlatives and expressing opinions

Common European Framework

Students can use language effectively to describe pictures and photographs and to express opinions about them.

Timings

Possible lesson break: either after exercise 3b or before exercise 7.

WARM-UP

Ask students what they know about animals around the world: are there more of some than others? Why is that? What is being done to help animals that are few in number? You could revise here vocabulary presented in Lesson 5.2, such as *extinct*, *extinction* and *in danger*.

SITUATION

ⓘ There are quite a few animal/environmental charities around the world. The largest and most famous is the World Wildlife Fund for Nature (WWF), which works to protects the world's environment and create a future where nature and people can live in harmony. Other charities include Birdwatch, the NSPCA (The National Society for the Prevention of Cruelty to Animals) and Friends of the Earth.

1a Students do activity as per Coursebook. You can pre-teach the word *charity* (n – an organisation that gives money or things or help to people or animals that are poor, sick or need protection).

> **2** charity

- Once students have completed this activity, pre-teach the following vocabulary:

  donate (v) – to give something, especially money, to people or an organisation

  volunteer (v – can also be a noun) – to offer to do something without being told to do it

  rescue (n) – when someone is saved from harm or danger

  vet (n) – shortened form of *veterinary surgeon,* someone who is trained to give medical care and treatment to sick or injured animals

  sanctuary (n) – a peaceful place that is safe and provides protection

  captivity (n) – when a person or animal is in a prison, cage, etc. and not allowed to leave

  awful (adj) – very bad or unpleasant

💡 You may ask students why they chose answer 2. Possible answers could be:

- *because you can donate*
- *because you can volunteer*
- *because it helps animals who are sick or need protection*

1b Before students do this activity as per Coursebook, you can pre-teach *accommodation* (n – a place to live, stay or work).

> **1** C; **2** D; **3** B; **4** E; **5** A

Ⓟ Ask students if there are any local charities in their country. Get them to do a research project and to bring in everything they can find about local charities to the next lesson and perhaps give a presentation.

> 1.32– 1.33

2 Students do this activity as per Coursebook.

> **1** A, C, D, B; **2** A

1.32

3a Students do this activity as per Coursebook.

> **1** four; **2** pulling; **3** people; **4** head; **5** water;
> **6** unusual; **7** team; **8** professional

1.33

3b Students do this activity as per Coursebook.

> **1** water; **2** bird; **3** cleaning; **4** blue; **5** left;
> **6** powerful; **7** feel; **8** do; **9** interesting

Tracks 1.32, 1.33 and 1.36
Katie, Neil
Part 1
K: Hi Neil. Thanks for calling. Can you hear me?
N: Yes, I can. Loud and clear. How's it going over there? Having fun at the animal sanctuary?
K: Sure am, but it's hard work. But everyone's looking after me, and it's great to see the work in action. Anyway, you want to talk about the photos? I'm sorry there's no Internet connection here.
N: That's OK. Yeah, basically, I need to choose the pictures now and I wanted to discuss my ideas with you first.
K: Fine. Fire away. Which section are you talking about?
N: Well, it's the home page link to the animal rescue page. Basically, I've got two photos of whale rescues, and two of bird rescues.
K: OK.
N: So, first of all the whale rescue photos. In the first one, there are four whales that are close to the beach. Two men are pulling one of the whales off the beach, and there are loads of people in the background who are watching the rescue.
K: Fine, and the second one?
N: Well, in that one, on the left of the picture, we can see the large head of a whale. On the right, there are two people who are throwing water on the whale. I guess they're trying to keep it alive. It's a very unusual picture, the whale's head is massive. But, well, I think the first picture is the best one for the website because it shows a team of people that are working together. They look very professional and it's also more dramatic.
K: It certainly sounds good. What about the bird rescue pictures?
Part 2
N: Sure. The first one is on the beach, and there's a man in the water. He's passing a bird to someone who's standing on the beach. The second one shows some people who are cleaning a bird. On the right, there's a woman in a blue shirt who's holding the bird, so the bird's in the middle of the picture. Then, there's another woman on the left who's cleaning the bird. She's wearing a yellow coat.
K: OK, so in the first one, are the men rescuing the bird from oily water?
N: Uh-huh. And I like that picture, I think it's more powerful than the one about the cleaning, I think it really makes you feel the terrible situation.

continued…

K: Yes, I guess so, although it's hard for me to say without seeing it. What's good about the second one?
N: Well, it shows the work that our experts do, but it's not a very interesting picture. Overall, I recommend that we use the whale rescue picture.
K: The one of the team working together?
N: Uh-huh.
K: Well, that sounds OK. Go ahead with that for the moment, we could change it quite easily in the future, couldn't we?
N: Well, we could, but I need to get something up on the site today.
K: Sure, I understand. Use the whale one, and when I get back to the office, I'll let you know if there's a problem.
N: OK. You're the boss. I think you'll like this one anyway.
K: I'm sure I will. Your choices are usually spot on. Anyway, gotta go now, there's a monkey that's waiting to meet me.
N: Lucky monkey. Say hello from me! Bye for now.
K: Bye.

KEY LANGUAGE: describing photographs

This function is particularly important for students who are likely to take examinations with a Speaking component in the future, as all Speaking examinations include asking a student to talk about a picture.

1.32– 1.33

4a Students do activity as per Coursebook.

> **1** there; **2** in; **3** see; **4** who; **5** look; **6** passing;
> **7** shows; **8** in; **9** on

Tracks 1.32 and 1.33
See audioscript above.

4b Students do activity as per Coursebook.

> **1** present continuous; **2** adjective; **3** in the background, on the left, on the right, in the middle
> Other phrases could include:
> In the top/bottom right/left corner …
> Behind the …
> In front of …
> Underneath/Over the …
> Beside / Next to …

It may be a good idea for students to practise describing photos as soon as they have done this activity, rather than waiting for the extended speaking activity at the end of the lesson. Either bring in some suitable pictures or ask students in the previous lesson to bring in some and get them to describe the pictures to each other, using the language they have learned here.

E Students can do exercise 5 from the Extra practice activities on page 135 either in class or for homework.

pronunciation

1.34

5a Students do this activity as per Coursebook.

> **Track 1.34**
> In the **first** one, there are **four whales** that are **close** to the **beach**.

1.35

5b Students do this activity as per Coursebook.

> **Track 1.35**
> 1 a /strong/   a /weak/
> 2 that /strong/   that /weak/
> 3 of /strong/   of /weak/
> 4 to /strong/   to /weak/
> 5 some /strong/   some /weak/
> 6 are /strong/   are /weak/
> 7 can /strong/   can /weak/

1.36

5c Students do this activity as per Coursebook.

> **Track 1.36**
> See audioscript for Tracks 1.32 and 1.33.

6 Students do this activity as per Coursebook.

! Even native speakers can have trouble identifying the stress in sentences. Get students to practise saying the sentences over and over again to identify the stress clearly. Then get them to write their own sentences and practise stressing them correctly.

TASK: choosing photos for a website

Tell students they are now going to use the language they have learned in this lesson to do a role-play. Point students to the OTHER USEFUL PHRASES box (point out the comparatives) and also get them to run through what phrases we can use to describe pictures.

☼ If you have time, you might like to do an extra activity to practise the language of expressing opinions from the OTHER USEFUL PHRASES box. Use the pictures from the previous optional activity described under exercise 4b and get students to compare two pictures and express their preference.

7a Put the students into pairs (although you might also like to use monitors to listen in and report back to the class). Identify one student as A and the other as B. Student A turns to page 116 and reads the task. Give Student A a minute to think about what he/she is going to say. Then let them do the activity. If you choose to use monitors, give them the task of noting any good phrases used by students during the activity. When the first activity is finished, do a class feedback and if you have used monitors, get them to feed back good phrases and write the best on the board to improve the quality of utterances in the second role-play.

7b Students now swap roles. Do the same as in exercise 7a.

☼ If students are likely to take a Speaking examination in the near future, you may like to tell them that this is good practice.

8 Students do activity as per Coursebook. As a class, see which photos were chosen and have a class discussion to agree on the class choice.

E You can now do photocopiable activity 5B to revise comparatives and superlatives and the language of giving opinions.

HOMEWORK OPTIONS

Students do the exercises on page 32 of the Workbook.

5.4 STUDY AND WRITING SKILLS

Lesson topic and staging

This lesson looks at time management as a study skill. First, students are introduced to the concept of time through some common expressions. They are then asked to assess their own time management skills. They listen to a recording on the topic and are encouraged to plan how to improve their skills. They think about timing and planning a written composition, which they do by analysing a text. To conclude the lesson, students write a composition themselves on a topic they have already studied in the unit.

Objectives

By the end of the lesson, students should have:

- considered the issue of time management
- analysed their own time management skills and looked at ways to improve them
- considered the importance of timing and planning a written composition
- written a composition on a topic from the unit, using what they have learned about timing and planning

Timings

Although the project is optional, it is highly recommended if you really want students to improve their time management. The written composition can be done for homework, although it should really be done in class if you want to check that students can complete a good 150-word composition in 45 minutes. It will therefore need a separate lesson.

Exercise 6 can be omitted if there is not enough time.

STUDY SKILLS: time management

1 Students do activity as per Coursebook. Do the final question as class discussion.

sentences 2, 3 and 6

The final question could be done as a debate. At the end of the lesson, students could come back to the result of the debate and see if they have changed their minds.

2 Students do activity as per Coursebook. When each individual student has finished, they should compare notes with a partner. The final question should be done as a class discussion and may lead to a class or personal resolution.

P This project is highly recommended as it makes the skill of time management relevant and thus meaningful to the students. Students keep a record for the rest of the week of their time management and fill in the same chart with a second column (titled 'Actual'). You should leave about 15 minutes at the beginning of the next week's lesson for students to compare the results of their time management analysis. Were the results similar to their guesses? Were they better or worse? What are they going to do to improve them? This can lead to class or personal resolutions, which can be monitored throughout the rest of the course either invidually by students, or by you, or by the class as whole. You could also give a prize at the end of the course for the person who has the most improved time management skills.

3a Divide the students into groups of three or four. Ask students to look at the four problems and ask them to decide on the advice they would give. If there is a lack of time, only assign one or two problems to each group.

students' own answers

1.37

3b Students do activity as per Coursebook. You should check that they have identified the right pieces of advice. Students, still in their groups, should then compare the advice they came up with in exercise 3a with what they heard on the audio and decide which advice is best. The class as a whole can then decide on what they think is the best advice to give for each problem.

3c Students do activity as per Coursebook. This activity can be done individually or in pairs.

1c; 2f; 3a, d, g, h; 4b, e

3d Students do activity as per Coursebook. Students can discuss the second point in pairs and then larger groups. Make sure they are prepared to say why they find the two tips useful.

Track 1.37
Tutor, Students

T: Yes, that's a very good point, Nicole. OK, now, let's have a look at the next problem. OK, it says here: 'I'm often late for appointments, or sometimes I miss appointments completely.' Would anyone like to say something about this?

s1:   Yes, <u>keep a diary</u> which clearly shows all your appointments ... and classes.

s2:   That's right, but it's not enough just to have a diary. We need to make sure we look at it. <u>Check your diary</u> last thing at night and first thing in the morning.

T: Absolutely. You should also write all the homework you have to do in the diary – not on pieces of paper that you can lose easily. Good. Now, next problem: 'I spend a lot of time looking for my notes. I can never find anything.'

continued...

---

s1: Yeah, I was like that last year. The best thing is to <u>organise your files</u>, using colour codes and labels – so you can find things easily. I don't have any trouble any more.

T: Thanks, Riz. So … these things show how important it is to be well-organised. OK, let's take another problem. This one says: 'I sometimes study for a long time, but I don't feel I'm learning anything. I read the material but nothing's happening – it's not going in.' Right. Has anyone got any suggestions? Yes, Tim.

s3: Basically, <u>it isn't a good idea to study for long periods at a time without a break</u>. It's better to do a little at a time.

T: That's right. <u>Be nice to yourselves!</u> When you finish something, an essay, for example, give yourselves a break, do something for fun: go for a walk, or watch a film. This can make you work better before and after the break. And another thing – it's <u>important that you can concentrate</u> on your studies. You can't work well when the phone's ringing every five minutes. Don't forget, too, it's <u>important to know when you study best</u>. Do you study best in the morning, in the afternoon, in the evening, or late at night? Everybody's different. We need to study at a time that suits us.

s4: Oh, that's interesting. I've never thought of that.

s5: Yeah, maybe some people study at the wrong time of day for their body clock.

T: OK, let's take another one … 'I can't finish all the things I need to do in the day.'

s1, s5: <u>Prioritise!</u>

s4: Yes, decide what you need to do now, or later today, and what you can leave until tomorrow, or even next week.

T: Yes, good. Remember, too: maybe there are some things that aren't important at all. It's a bad idea to waste time on them. And it's important to allow time for things you don't expect, and for emergencies. Perhaps this is the moment to say something about making lists. You probably make shopping lists of things you need to buy. <u>Make a list of things you need to do</u> as well. When you reduce all the things to one piece of paper, it doesn't seem so difficult. When you've done the things on your list, cross them off. It's a nice feeling! However, be realistic! Don't put a lot of big things on your list when you know you can't do them all. So, read one chapter of your textbook, instead of three chapters. Putting smaller things on your list means that you can achieve them, and this makes you feel good. Alright, what's the next question …?

4a Students do this on their own and then discuss with their partners. Follow this with a class discussion.

4b Students do this on their own and then discuss with their partners. Follow this with a class discussion.

5 Point out to students that time management and planning are important for writing tasks, especially when having to write in an examination. Students then do activity as per Coursebook.

(!) Some students who are not taking an exam may feel this activity is not relevant. However, point out to them that it is still a useful example of how to manage their time and improve their ability to write.

> **2** (10 mins); **3** (30 mins); **1** (about 5 mins)

WRITING SKILLS: a comparative essay

6 Do the first two questions as a class discussion. Then let students work in pairs before checking as a whole class.

active (adj) – able to explode at any time

dormant (adj) – not active now but able to be active at a later time

erupt (v) – to explode, with smoke, fire and rocks coming out of it

eruption (n) – the time when a volcano becomes active and explodes

cone (n) – a hollow or solid object with a round base, sloping sides and a point at the top

7 Students do this activity as per Coursebook.

> 2

Ask students why title 2 is the answer (the concluding paragraph clearly compares and contrasts the two volcanoes; we know this because of the use of comparatives and *whereas*).

8a Students do activity as per Coursebook.

> The essay on page 47 is easier to understand because the information is organised into paragraphs.

8b Students do activity as per Coursebook.

> **1** introduction: paragraph 1; **2** main body: paragraphs 2 and 3; **3** (summary and) conclusion: paragraph 4

9a Students do activity as per Coursebook. Ask the class as a whole.

(i) The River Nile is regarded as probably the longest river in the world and flows through many African countries. The River Thames is in England.

> Yes, they mean the same thing.
> full stop before and comma after *in contrast*, no comma with *but*, comma before *whereas*

9b Students do activity as per Coursebook, individually.

i Mount Everest is in Nepal. Ben Nevis is in Scotland. The Pacific Ocean is between America and Japan/ China. The North Sea is between Northern England / Scotland and Germany/Scandinavia.

> **1** Mount Everest is 8,848m high. In contrast, Ben Nevis is 1,343m high. / Mount Everest is 8,848m high but Ben Nevis is 1,343m high. / Mount Everest is 8,848m high, whereas Ben Nevis is 1,343m high.
> **2** The Pacific Ocean is 11,022m deep at its deepest point. In contrast, the North Sea is 310m deep. / The Pacific Ocean is 11,022m deep at its deepest point but the North Sea is 310m deep. / The Pacific Ocean is 11,022m deep at its deepest point, whereas the North Sea is 310m deep.

10 Ideally this activity should be done in class so that students can properly time themselves without instructions.

• You may like to have a feedback session about how easy students find it to write 150 words in 45 minutes. For those students who find it difficult, assure them that with time they will find it easier providing they manage the time effectively.

HOMEWORK OPTIONS

Students can do exercise 9 from the Extra practice activities on page 135.

Students do the exercises on page 33 of the Workbook.

Society and family

6.1 FUTURE OPPORTUNITY

Lesson topic and staging

This lesson focuses on the subject of futurologists and the opportunities they give to business. The lesson begins with students discussing trends in their country. They then read a small advert for a firm of futurologists and listen to a meeting between a businessman and a futurologist. With the advert, students practise reading for gist and with the recording, they also practise looking for specific information. The vocabulary section presents ages. The grammar focuses on *will*, *might* and *may*, with the examples taken from the earlier recording. *Will* should be revision but this may be the first time students see *may* and *might*. They practise these forms in a freer spoken and written activity. There is also some recycling of comparatives in the speaking task.

Objectives

By the end of the lesson, students should have:

- discussed trends and futurology
- read for gist and deduced meaning from context
- listened for gist and for specific information
- learned vocabulary for describing someone's age
- learned and practised *will*, *might* and *may* for predictions
- completed a speaking and writing task on predictions

Timings

Exercise 6b can be omitted if these is not enough time. Exercises 5b and 5c can be given for homework.

Possible lesson break: after exercise 4.

SPEAKING

1 Students discuss these questions in groups. Then have quick class feedback. Don't provide any information on these issues as they are all covered in the listening.

READING

2a Students do activity as per Coursebook.

> 2 (business people)

2b Students do activity as per Coursebook. When this has been checked, ask students what they know about futurologists. To check they have understood *trend*, ask them how many trends there are on page 48 (four in exercise 1). For *prediction*, elicit from students the verb form. You can also check they understand the following words:

constantly (adj) – all the time or regularly

retire (v) – to stop work because you are old

profit (v) – to get something good or useful from a situation

consumer (n) – someone who buys or uses goods and services

> 1 futurologist; 2 trends; 3 predictions

LISTENING

`1.38`

3a Set the scene for the students. Ask them to predict which answers they expect to hear. Then they listen and check.

> She discusses 1, 2, 3 and 5.

3b Students do activity as per Coursebook.

- You can check students understand the meaning of the following words from the recording:

focus (v) – to give all your attention to one thing

connect (v) – to join two or more things together

vacuum cleaner (n) – a machine that cleans floors by sucking up the dirt from them

investment (n) – the use of money to make a profit or make a business successful, or the money that is used

cyber (adj) – related to computers or the Internet

click (n) – a short hard sound when you press or switch something

> 1 technology; 2 age; 3 third; 4 (much) longer;
> 5 under-25s; 6 cruise ships; 7 clean the house;
> 8 drive the car; 9 over the Internet; 10 goods;
> 11 services; 12 technology

Tracks 1.38 and 1.39

Patrick, Susan

P: Hello Susan. Good to see you again.

S: Hi Patrick. How are you?

P: I'm fine. Can I get you a drink? Coffee? Tea?

S: Oh, a coffee would be lovely, thanks.

P: Sure, I'll just ask Bob to do that. Bob, could you get us two coffees, please? So, what does the future hold for me?

S: Well, hopefully, good business opportunities. I've got the full report here, but I'll go through the main points first.

P: Fine. Go ahead.

S: Well, I think the two most important trends for you are about technology and age.

P: Age?

S: Yes, basically Britain is getting older. By 2025, more than a third of the UK's population will be over 55 years old. And these older people will live for much longer, we know that from the statistics. They might live until the're 95, or even 100.

P: But that definitely won't be good for business. They won't have jobs, so I'm sure they won't have much money.

S: Oh, it'll definitely be good for business. First of all, they'll retire a bit later than now, but the main point is that these people will definitely need things to do with this extra time, for sure, and, they'll need things that improve the quality of their lives.

P: OK. Any examples?

S: Well, we predict that older people will travel more, so there'll be more companies that specialise in holidays for them. At the moment, holiday companies focus on families or young adults. But, in 2025, there'll be more elderly people, the over-65s, than under-25s. So, the party and adventure holiday market may get smaller but, for example, holidays on cruise ships will increase. They may also want activity holidays, but that'll depend on their health and on how demanding the activities are – they probably won't go bungee-jumping, but they might go hiking and sailing.

P: OK. Er, what about daily life?

S: Well, this connects to the other trend I mentioned, technology.

P: You mean the Internet?

S: Yes, indeed, and not only that, but also robots.

P: Robots?

S: Exactly. Older people want things that make life easier. In the future, they might have a robot that cleans the house, they might have a robot that drives the car, they might have a robot that does the gardening.

P: You say *might*, rather than *will*. Why's that?

S: Well, we can't be definite about this because it all depends on the technology. At the moment, robots are very basic.

P: Yes, I think there's a robot vacuum cleaner and that's about it. Oh, and robot pets.

S: Exactly, so the technology needs to improve. Perhaps it will, perhaps it won't. But older people will definitely want robots.

continued…

P: Mmm, that's interesting. I guess the Internet will be important.

S: Of course, or something like it. And this is the other possible area for investment. In general people will order goods and services over the Internet, and they'll meet people over the Internet. In the future, people might have more cyber friends than real friends. So, for example, we think that there'll be many companies that'll offer Internet dating services for elderly people.

P: Internet dating? For the elderly?

S: Oh yes. Love is important, however old you are. People will definitely live for longer, and they'll have more relationships in their later years. Older people will get divorced more often, and they'll probably meet new partners online, or perhaps on their cruise holidays.

P: Really?

S: Why not? You're 60 years old, your children are adults, you have 40 more years to live, a new life will be just a click away.

P: Interesting. So, basically, I should look for companies that provide goods and services for the elderly.

S: Exactly, especially those businesses that are planning to use technology in some way. The middle-aged people of today are happy to use technology, and they'll be even happier to use it in twenty years' time.

P: Well, that's all very interesting. Now, where have those coffees got to? Perhaps I need a coffee robot!

▎VOCABULARY: ages

4 Students should guess what they think in pairs and then answer as a class. To check, you can ask them about people they know (or famous people) who are that age. Do the questions together as a class.

i Note these figures are approximate as the age range changes according to cultural opinions.

an adolescent – 13–19

a middle-aged person – over 40

a young adult – 18–30

a thirty-something – 31–39

a child – 3–12

an elderly person – 60+

a teenager – 13–19

a retired person – 65+ (depends on law of the country)

> **Sample answer:** I think life is quite difficult for middle-aged people. They have a lot of responsibilities. They go to work every day. They often have a family. I think they spend their money on their houses and family, and on cars!

GRAMMAR: *will, might* and *may* for predictions

`1.39`

5a Students should attempt to fill in the blanks before they listen. When they have listened, let them check with a partner.

> **1** will; **2** might; **3** definitely; **4** won't; **5** definitely; **6** may; **7** probably

> **Track 1.39**
> See audioscript for Track 1.38.

5b Tell students to look back to the sentences in exercise 5a to do 5b. Students do activity as per Coursebook.

• When students have completed this activity, make sure they look at the Language reference and especially the difference between *may* and *might*, and their use in questions about the future in comparison with *will*.

Ⓔ When students have finished 5b, they can do exercises 1 and 2 from the Extra practice activities on page 137 either in class or for homework.

> **1** sentences 1, 3, 4 and 5; **2** sentences 2, 6 and 7; **3** the infinitive form; **4** after *will*, before *won't*

5c Students do activity as per Coursebook.

> **1** He might live to the age of 90.
> **2** Many people will probably work from home.
> **3** I will definitely live in my own country.
> **4** There probably won't be big families.

SPEAKING

6a Students do the activity as per Coursebook individually. There are no right answers as these are students' opinions.

6b Put students into pairs and let them discuss the predictions. Make sure they justify their opinions. Students should try and come to an agreement over the issues. Then split the pairs and put them into separate groups, where again they try and come to an agreement.

WRITING

7 This can be done in class or for homework. Students should write about their own opinions, not opinions they agreed on in class.

HOMEWORK OPTIONS

Students can do exercise 6 from the Extra practice activities on page 137.

Students do the exercises on pages 34–35 of the Workbook.

6.2 THE FAMILY

Lesson topic and staging

The topic of this lesson is 'the family', particularly causes and effects of low birth rates. Students begin by discussing the general issue of families. They then read a text, for gist and for specific information, on the causes and effects of low birth rate in Germany. Students then learn and practise the use of the prefix *un-* and the suffix *-less*. The first conditional (a grammar point which might just be revision for some students) is presented in the reading text. Students practise the new tense and, after listening to a model conversation on the recording, use it in a free speaking activity which also involves learning the pronunciation for the phrase *What'll you do if ...*

Objectives

By the end of the lesson, students should have:

- discussed the issue of families
- learned some vocabulary on families
- read for gist and for specific information
- learned and practised the prefix *un-* and the suffix *-less*
- learned (or revised) and practised the first conditional
- listened for gist and specific information
- completed a speaking activity requiring the first conditional and the use of *What'll you do if ...* with the correct pronunciation

Timings

Exercise 2b and/or 4b can be omitted if there is not enough time. Exercise 6a can be done for homework.

Possible lesson break: after exercise 4b.

SPEAKING

1 Students do activity as per Coursebook. Do class feedback. If you have a mixed nationality class, you might like to compare opinions for questions 1 and 2. For question 3, you can make two columns on the board and have a vote for inclusion of class-accepted advantages and disadvantages.

READING

2a Students do activity as per Coursebook. Before doing feedback, you can ask your students to find the sentences where these words are used in the text and see if they can work out the meaning from context.

> 1 old-fashioned; 2 responsible; 3 employer;
> 4 suitable; 5 childcare; 6 birth rate

2b Students read the whole text. Give students no more than two minutes to do this, otherwise they will read intensively rather than for gist.

> **Suggested answer:** This article is about the low birth rate in Germany.

2c Again, students are reading for gist so keep the timing tight on this activity. Students can do this individually and then check in pairs.

> 1d; 2a; 3b; 4c

2d This exercise involves students reading for specific information, so they will need more time. Students do activity as per Coursebook.

> 1 false (40% of German female graduates have not had children); 2 true; 3 true; 4 true; 5 false (the government will pay each family 1,800 euros); 6 true

3 Do this as a quick class activity. When students state opinions, elicit the reasons why they feel this way and get them to quote from the text. The skill of using the text to support opinions is an important skill, especially in an academic context.

VOCABULARY: negative adjectives

Put the words *happy* and *power* on the board. Ask students if they know how to make these words negative. Get students to read the explanation of the use of *un-* and *-less*. Ask students to find examples in the reading text (there are four: *childless, uncertain, unsure* and *unhappy*). Then elicit how *-less* and *un-* are used (*un-* as prefix, *-less* as suffix).

4a Students do activity as per Coursebook.

Write the following sentences on the board and ask students to provide the right word.

My brother is very _____ so he makes a lot of mistakes. (careless)

His father was very _____ and threatened him badly. (unkind)

The website is full of _____ information. (useless)

The child complained a lot because her new car seat was very _____ . (uncomfortable)

> careless; uncomfortable; hopeless; unkind; unlucky; useless; unusual

4b Students do this task individually and then in pairs. You should check the questions with students before they ask each other as they may not be appropriate, e.g. *Are you useless?*, or too general, e.g. *What is uncomfortable?*

Ask students to choose three negative adjectives and write them across the top of a sheet of paper. Then ask them to write any things or events they associate with the negative adjective. They should write no more than two for each, e.g. *useless – the new washing machine I bought.* Students then play '20 Questions' in pairs to guess the things or events associated with the negative adjective.

GRAMMAR: first conditional

This should be revision. Before doing exercise 5a, write up the following sentence from the text on the board:

If a man takes time off work, his career will be over.

Tell students that this is an example of the first conditional. Elicit from students why we use it. Then, to confirm, ask students to read the two lines under the Grammar heading.

5a Students do activity as per Coursebook.

> 1c; 2a; 3b

5b Students do activity as per Coursebook. Read through the grammar tip with the students and then ask them to re-write the sentences in exercise 5a with the main clause before the *if*-clause. Make sure they leave out the comma.

- Students can then check the Language reference and do exercises 3 and 4 on page 137. Alternatively, you might like to save exercise 4 until after the grammar tip for 6a.

> yes

6a Students do activity as per Coursebook.

> **1** see, 'll tell; **2** 'll be, doesn't rest; **3** will you do, don't pass; **4** won't arrive, don't hurry; **5** move, 'll be; **6** 'll do, have

6b Students can do this activity in pairs. Then do classwork and find out what students are thinking of doing today, tomorrow or at the weekend. This allows other students to comment on people's ideas and bring the structure to life.

SPEAKING

1.40

7a Read through the instructions with the students, who then listen and do the activity as per Coursebook.

> **1** brother and sister; **2** an International Business course in the United States

7b Students do activity as per Coursebook. Ask students what they think of Shane's problem. Do they agree with Evelyn or Shane? Why?

> **1** Their parents might not like the idea. The course might be really difficult. He might not like the other students. **2** He'll persuade them. He'll get help from his teachers and the other students. He'll find a nice American girl. **3** She doesn't think it's a good idea.

Track 1.40
Shane, Evelyn
s: You know, Evelyn, I'm thinking about doing a course in the United States.
e: What, you want to study in America?
s: Yeah, I think it'll help my career.
e: What kind of course?
s: International Business.
e: Oh. Well … What'll you do if Mum and Dad don't like the idea?
s: Oh, it's OK. I'll persuade them.
e: Really? I don't think Dad will like the idea.
s: Oh, he'll be OK about it. You wait and see.
e: I hope you're right. And what'll you do if the course is really difficult?
s: Easy. I'll get some help from my teachers and other students.
e: You seem very confident. What'll you do if you don't like the other students?
s: I'm sure I'll find a nice American girl!
e: Oh really! Shane, I don't think this is a good idea, you know. There are lots of good courses here in Australia …

pronunciation

1.41

8 Before starting this exercise, ask students to turn to the audioscript on page 156. Ask them to underline when Evelyn suggests problems with Shane's ideas. Check this. Elicit from students that we use *What'll you do if …* when we want someone to consider a possible problem or situation. Students then do activity as per Coursebook.

Track 1.41
1 What'll you do if your parents don't like the idea?
2 What'll you do if the course is really difficult?
3 What'll you do if you don't like the other students?

---

9 Put students into pairs. Students read through the tasks on page 117. For the first task, Student A has the issue and Student B will ask the questions. For the second task, the roles are reversed.

🔧 To make the task more challenging, when students do the role-play, have Student A act it out with a Student B from another pair. This means Student A will need to come up with his/her own replies.

HOMEWORK OPTIONS

Students can do exercise 7 from the Extra practice activities on page 137.

Students do the exercises on pages 36–37 of the Workbook.

6.3 SCENARIO: FAMILY MATTERS

IN THIS LESSON

Lesson topic and staging

The topic for this lesson is family matters and in particular, people's opinions on how children should be brought up. The lesson begins with an open discussion on family life to set the scene. Students then listen to a talk show discussing whether mothers should stay at home and whether children should watch TV. Students listen for gist and then for specific information. They finally listen to identify key phrases for expressing opinion and check they have understood the purpose of these phrases. Students then practise how to link words in speech. Before starting the final task, 'Speaking on a talk show', students revise the vocabulary they need. To complete the task, they use the language of expressing opinions, word linking, the revised vocabulary and the phrases in the 'Other Useful Phrases' box.

Objectives

By the end of the lesson, students should have:

- discussed issues related to the family
- listened for gist and specific information
- identified , understood and practised the language of expressing opinions
- practised word-linking in speech
- revised key vocabulary
- completed a spoken task based on speaking on a talk show

Timings

If your students have few problems with word linking, you may omit exercises 4a, 4b and 4c. Exercise 5 from the Extra practice activities can be given for homework, as can exercise 6a, if there is not enough time.

Possible lesson break: after exercise 3b or 4c.

Common European Framework

Students can use language effectively to present opinions and justify them, and also to agree and disagree with other speakers.

PREPARATION

1   Students work in pairs and discuss the four questions. Follow this up with class discussion.

SITUATION

- Read through the introduction with the students. You can ask the following questions:
  - *What is a talk show?*
  - *Why do we have talk shows on TV?*
  - *What do you think of them?*

i A talk show (or chat show) is a TV or radio programme where a group of people come together to discuss various topics introduced by a talk show host. Often, talk shows feature a panel of guests, including some who are learned or experienced in the issue being discussed on that day. Some talk shows take live phone calls so anyone can take part. These have existed since the beginning of radio and TV but have recently become more and more controversial. Talk shows are now appearing on the Internet.

1.42

2a Ask students to read the issues. You can ask for your students' initial opinions on each one to make sure they understand the problems.

Ask students to look at the pictures of the four families on the page. Ask them what they think these families' opinions on the issues would be.

- Students then listen and identify the issues. They should only listen once.

They discuss issues 1 and 3.

2b Before students listen again, ask them to try and remember the order from the first listening and then listen again to check (option: they could also check with their partners before listening again). This shows your students that they may have understood more than they expected from the first listening.

1b; 2a; 3d; 4c; 5f; 6e; 7h; 8g

2c Do this activity as classwork. Ask students who they agree with and why.

Track 1.42
Robert, Sheila, Grace, Brian, Henry, Kate
R: OK, so that's the expert's view, let's see what you, the public, think. Now, what's your name?
S: Sheila.
R: OK, Sheila, are you a mother?
S: Yes, I am. I've got two young girls.
R: Great, so what do you think?
S: Personally, I think mothers should stay at home. I look after my kids and I think that's best for them and for me.
R: In what way?
S: Well, you know, kids should be with their mother, they need my love and, well, I know what they like and don't like. You know, it's natural.
R: OK, so does anyone disagree? Yes, you, what's your opinion?

continued...

G: **Well, I understand her_opinion, but** sometimes mothers have no choice, they have to work. Surely it's better for the family to have money to buy food and stuff. I mean, what's the point of staying at home with your kids if you can't put food on the table? We're not all in happy families with two parents, are we?

R: Indeed. What do you say to that, Sheila?

S: Well, that's a good point, but I think some mothers work because they want to, not because they need to. They prefer to work rather than look after their children, and I think that's wrong, I really do.

R: OK. Does anyone else have anything to say on this?

B: Er, I do, Robert.

R: Yes?

B: I agree with Sheila. I know loads of mothers who work just because they like to have a job, not because they need to. And that's a real pity, because they're missing out on the best time in their children's lives. You can work anytime, but your children are only young once.

R: OK, well, while we're on the subject of children, let's look at another question. Basically, should we limit the amount of TV young kids watch? Are they watching too much TV these days? What's your name and what's your opinion?

H: Hi, I'm Henry and I'm a dad.

R: OK, then Henry, what's your view?

H: Well, **what_I think_is that** they shouldn't watch any TV.

R: What, none at all?

H: None at all. I never watched TV when I was a kid, and I don't think my kids need to watch it now, especially when they're young.

R: Right, well, I'm sure many people will disagree with you. Let's see. Yes, madam, yes, you in the red dress.

K: Well, personally, I completely disagree. TV is part of the modern world, like computers and phones. We can't hide TV from our kids. I think it's better if they know that TV is a normal thing, as normal as having dinner, or whatever.

R: Henry?

H: **Well, that's_an interesting_idea, but** TV is different to phones, and having dinner. The kids just sit there, like vegetables. It's not good for them, not good at all.

K: But why not just control how much they watch? You know, have a maximum of two hours a day or something.

H: Well, I know we won't agree, but the best control is to sell your TV. If you do that, they'll do something else.

K: That's just silly.

H: You're the one that's silly.

R: OK, OK, calm down everyone. Let's take a break now, and after the ads we'll look at the role of the father in the family.

KEY LANGUAGE: expressing opinions

1.42

3a Point out to students the objective of this exercise. Ask them to try and fill in the blanks first without listening and then listen to check.

> **1** Personally; **2** opinion; **3** point; **4** with; **5** what; **6** completely; **7** better; **8** idea

3b Students do activity as per Coursebook. Ask students to tell you why they think each sentence is either showing agreement, disagreement or opinion.

> **a** 4; **b** 2, 3, 6, 8 ; **c** 1, 5, 7

pronunciation

1.43

4a Word linking is very important for your students. When we speak naturally, we automatically link words. However, when they learn new language, students try to pronounce each word in isolation. These activities are to help them with their fluency and to make them sound more natural when they speak.

- Before they repeat, get students to listen to the phrase. See if they can identify the word linking. Ask students if they think the phrase sounds natural. Check that students understand the meaning of *vowel* and *consonant*. Then do activity as per Coursebook.

> **Track 1.43**
> Well, that's a good point, but …

1.44

4b Students do activity as per Coursebook. This means predicting before listening. Ask students to identify the linking consonants and vowels for each phrase, and then to listen.

> **Track 1.44**
> See audioscript for Track 1.42.

4c Mix choral drilling with individual drilling.

⊙ Students can make their own natural sentences including word linking which they can get other students in the class to try out.

5 Students work in pairs for this activity. Model 1 with a student at the front of the class. Model more than one reply showing agreement and disagreement.

- Students then work in pairs and do 2 and 3 with the partners taking it in turns to defend the 1st idea and the 2nd idea. You can also get students to come up with their own ideas which they can share with the rest of the class.

E Students can now do exercise 5 in the Extra practice activities on page 137.

TASK: speaking on a talk show

6a Tell students that this activity focuses on some words they will need for the task. Students do activity as per Coursebook. Then try and elicit definitions for each of the words and phrases.

> **1** pay; **2** house husband; **3** permission;
> **4** pocket money; **5** elderly

To further practise expressing opinions, ask students what they think of the idea of a house husband.

6b Students read the question. Make sure they know that the *For* and *Against* arguments are in response to statement 1 in exercise 6a. Put students into pairs and ask them to come up with one more set of for and against arguments for statement 1, as well as for and against arguments for statements 2–5.

7a Break up the partners so that they do not join the same group and form groups of three or four students. Allocate one student to the role of presenter, then students act out the talk show using one of the statements in exercise 6a as a starting point. Make sure the presenter understands and uses the language in the OTHER USEFUL PHRASES box.

7b Do activity as per Coursebook. When this is finished, do the programme as a class with you as a presenter and see how many arguments for and against you get. Do this just with one or two statements.

E You can now do photocopiable activity 6A to revise and practise *will*, *might* and *may* for future predictions, first conditional and the language of giving points of view.

HOMEWORK OPTIONS

Students do the exercises on page 38 of the Workbook.

6.4 STUDY AND WRITING SKILLS

IN THIS LESSON

Lesson topic and staging

The topics for this lesson are how to correct writing and how to write an article. The first half focuses on the study skill of correcting writing, the second half on how to write an article.

In the first half, students begin by reflecting on how they feel about correction. They then look at different types of correction and learn a correction code for writing. This part of the lesson also indirectly revises word order and punctuation.

In the second half of the lesson, students discuss competitions and then analyse an article on society written for a competition. Students revise and practise the use of linkers and how to divide articles into paragraphs. Finally, they write an article using the template and linkers and are also given the opportunity to use their newly-acquired correction skills.

Objectives

By the end of the lesson, students should have:

- thought about correction
- identified and understood different types of writing mistakes
- revised and practised word order and punctuation
- learned and practised using a writing correction code
- analysed an article for a competition
- revised and practised linkers
- written an article and corrected someone else's article

Timings

Exercise 5a can be omitted if there is not enough time. Exercise 9 and/or 10 could be given for homework.

Possible lesson break: after exercise 4b.

STUDY SKILLS: correcting your writing

1 Before beginning this activity, ask students to read the title of this section. Ask them if they think their writing should be corrected. Elicit from them why correcting writing is beneficial. Divide students into groups, get them to discuss the five statements and encourage them to express their opinions (they could use the language from Lesson 6.3 for this). Then do a quick class feedback session on this, getting the majority opinion.

Explain why it is important for students to correct their own writing. You could write the following adaptation of a Chinese proverb on the board:

Tell me and I will listen (or read).

Let me do it and I will learn.

Ask them for their opinions on this proverb. Try not to shorten this activity because the success of this part of the lesson largely depends on students accepting that self-correction is an important dimension of learning .

2 Before starting this activity, tell students that they are now going to identify different types of mistake. Check that they understand all the words in the box. Then students do activity as per Coursebook.

> **1** punctuation; **2** grammar; **3** word order;
> **4** leaving words out; **5** vocabulary; **6** spelling

3a Explain that students often get word order wrong in writing. You can revise this in the following way. On the board, write:

Paul wants a car.

Elicit subject, verb and object from the students. Then elicit from students where to put the adjective *new*. Elicit the type of word this is, then change *wants* to *has wanted* and elicit the auxiliary and main verb. Finally add *always* and identify the adverb. You should finish with:

Paul has always wanted a new car.

Students then do activity as per Coursebook.

> **1** More people will probably live alone in the future.
> **2** Bob hopes that there will be good business opportunities for him in the future.
> **3** Everyone in my family has got unusual eyes, except for me.
> **4** What will she do if he doesn't arrive on time?

3b Students do activity as per Coursebook. Make sure they refer to the corrected sentences from exercise 3a to work out the word order.

> **1** People **are** living longer than before.
> **2** If men spend more time at home, children might **be** happier.
> **3** The majority of young people will go **to** university.
> **4** Older people will meet on **the** Internet.
> The missing words are all short words.

3c Refer students back again to exercise 3a and elicit the basic word order for sentences (subject – verb – object).

• Write the following text on the board:

people live in small houses they build the houses from wood these houses are very strong

• You are going to show students how to turn it into:

In small villages, people live in small houses. They build the houses from wood, stone and metal. These houses are very strong and they last for years.

• Elicit the rules from students:

- there are three main verbs in the original line, which means three sentences and three full stops;

- add *and they last for years* at the end – two main verbs can be linked with linkers such as *and* or with relative pronouns (don't spend too much time on this as students will do linkers later in the lesson);

- when adding *stone and metal*, you put a comma before *stone* as commas split lists of things until the last two items, when you place *and* between the words;

- *in small villages* goes at the beginning and is followed by a comma, as commas come after prepositional phrases which give the context of the sentence.

• Students then do activity as per Coursebook.

(!) Commas are used in different ways and not always consistently. Just deal with the use of commas here and don't explain any more uses of commas for now.

> In my country, family life is very important. We spend a lot of time with our families and we always have lunch together on Sundays. There are also a lot of family businesses.

4a Make sure students understand the meaning of the correction code. They do the activity individually and then check in pairs. End with a class check.

> One problem in my country is that rich people are getting richer and poor people are getting poorer. If the gap between them becomes very big, it will create serious problems.

4b Students do the exercise individually and then in pairs before checking on page 117.

> Violence will increase. We will be frightened to leave our homes. What can we do? I believe that rich people should pay more tax and the government must provide more opportunities for poor people.

(☼) Another way is to write the text (or another uncorrected text) on the board. Appoint a corrector. Students tell the corrector which corrections to make. When they think it is finished, you can check and tell them which corrections are appropriate and how many they still need to find. You can then give clues to help them finish the correction. This is a good activity because it gives the whole class a feeling of success.

5a Students discuss the questions. Do this as quick classwork to set the scene.

5b Students do activity as per Coursebook. You can also ask the following questions:

What is the topic of the article? (What makes you proud of your society today?)

How many words should you write? (200)

What's the prize? (£250 and article will appear on the Council's website.)

> 20

6 Give students a few minutes to read individually and take notes. You can teach the following words and phrases:

proud (adj) – feeling pleased because you think that something you have achieved or are connected with is very good

creativity (n) – the ability to think of new ideas

race (n) – a way of grouping people according to the colour of their skin and physical appearance

out of sight – if it is out of sight, it cannot be seen

voluntary (adj) – not being paid, especially work to help people

cause (n) – an organisation or an aim that people support or fight for

contribute (v) – to give money, help or ideas, etc. to something that other people are involved in

• Students discuss the text in small groups. Have a class feedback, noting on the board what students say.

> It starts with a question which is a good way to get the reader's attention. It's clear and well-written. There's good development of the ideas, with clear examples of the concepts (multiculturalism and voluntary work). There are no silly mistakes, e.g. spelling. The vision of society is modern and positive; she shows herself to be a mature and caring young person with a feeling for other people. The only real problem is the lack of paragraphing. Some of these points are in exercise 9.

7a Elicit from students the meaning of *paragraph*, and the reason why we divide texts into paragraphs (different topic areas). Students then do activity as per Coursebook.

> **paragraph 1:** starting *What to choose?*
> **paragraph 2:** starting *First, our big cities are very multicultural;*
> **paragraph 3:** starting *The second thing is less obvious;*
> **paragraph 4:** starting *Because of these things*

7b Students do activity as per Coursebook.

> 2c; 3b

8 Read the instructions together with the students. Look at the two paragraphs and elicit how the three sentences in the first one have been joined together (they can be linked together with commas and *and* because they share the same subject, *they*). See if students can see the connection with the use of commas in exercise 3c.

(!) Make sure students understand they can do this because all three sentences share the same subject. If there was a different subject, you could not link the sentences in this way.

• Students then do activity as per Coursebook.

> **1** Silvia studies business at university, lives with her parents and helps in her parents' shop at weekends. **2** Her sister studies at school, likes boy bands and wants a car.

9 Students first underline the uses of *so, as, however* and *because of* in the text. Elicit from students how they are used to link sentences. Make sure students also note the use of commas with these linkers. Students then do activity as per Coursebook.

> **1** so; **2** However; **3** as; **4** so; **5** however; **6** because; **7** as; **8** However

10a Students now do activity as per Coursebook and write their composition.

10b Students look at their partner's article and correct it using the codes from the first half of the lesson. This can be passed back to the writer to correct. You can monitor how students do this. Although this activity does take time, it is worthwhile as students do something useful for their learning, other than just writing a text and receiving a mark.

(💡) Before students attempt exercise 10a, divide the class into three groups and the board into three columns. Students write a short article (up to 50 words), one per group. Give students about five minutes' preparation and ten minutes' writing time. One student from each group writes the text on the board. Give students an extra three minutes to make any corrections and changes and then, using the codes from the first half of the lesson, show the mistakes. Give students another three to five minutes to make the corrections and then check again and declare the winner (the team with the text which has the best content and the least number of mistakes in the final correction). Students like this activity as it involves all of them in the process and adds competitive motivation.

(E) You can now do photocopiable activity 6B to revise vocabulary from the whole unit.

| HOMEWORK OPTIONS |

Students can do exercise 8 from the Extra practice activities on page 137.

Students do the exercises on page 39 of the Workbook.

Review

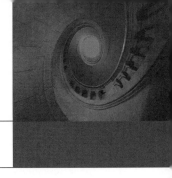

UNITS 4–6

GRAMMAR

1

> **First text:** from a travel brochure or advert for a holiday company
> **Second text:** from the Internet

2

> **1** true; **2** false – Iceland is larger than England and Wales. **3** true; **4** false – London feels less crowded than Reykjavik on Independence Day. **5** false – Iceland has been independent since 1944. **6** false – Mount Hekla has erupted sixteen times. **7** false – Reykjavik is the smallest capital city she's ever seen. **8** true; **9** false – If the weather's good, they'll stay in Reykjavik and go whale-watching. **10** false – They might hire a car at the weekend.

3

> **1** European cities are less peaceful than Iceland. **2** Few people live in Iceland. **3** Iceland has been independent since 1944. **4** Reykjavik is further north than any (other) capital city.

VOCABULARY

`1.45`

4

> **1** an environmentally-friendly holiday;
> **2** Murchison Falls and Queen Elizabeth

5a

> **A** Bwindi; **B** Murchison Falls; **C** Queen Elizabeth; **D** Mgahinga

5b

> **1** forests; **2** gorillas; **3** river; **4** elephants; **5** giraffes; **6** lakes; **7** leopards; **8** volcanoes; **9** monkey

---

Track 1.45
Jane, Andrea
J: Hello, Jane Barton here.
A: Jane, it's Andrea. Listen, you know we were talking about an environmentally-friendly holiday this year?
J: Yes, why?

continued…

A: Well, I've got some details from a great company – holidays in Africa, Uganda. Shall I tell you about them?
J: Yeah ... but I'm working, so I can't talk for too long.
A: OK, no problem. Right, I've looked at the information and there are four tours that look good. Oh, they're all in national parks. I think we should get more details on a couple of them.
J: OK, good idea.
A: First one, mmm, I don't know how to pronounce this. It's Mgahinga National Park – there are about nine volcanoes in ...
J: Volcanoes!
A: ... six are extinct, so don't worry.
J: I am worried!
A: Anyway, it's mainly forest, with lots of different plants and birds ...
J: And animals?
A: It mentions the golden monkey, that's all.
J: No, I don't like the sound of that one.
A: OK, number two, Bwindi National Park. Listen ... 'over half the world's population of mountain gorillas live in Bwindi's forests ...'
J: That sounds good.
A: Yes, but the others are too. Number three, Queen Elizabeth National Park – open grassland, rainforest, lakes, with over 100 types of animal including elephants, leopards, lions and buffalo.
J: I like that one.
A: OK, and the last one, the Murchison Falls National Park. This one's by the River Nile, and there are river animals and birds, and other animals like elephants, giraffes and buffalo again. I like this one.
J: OK, well, why don't we get details on the last two – Queen Elizabeth and Murchison Falls?
A: Yes, I'll do that ... and shall I ...
J: My boss is coming – I have to go. Bye, I'll speak to you later.

KEY LANGUAGE

`1.46`

6 Students do the activity in pairs. Do class feedback to make sure students are on track.

7 Students do activity as per Coursebook.

> **1**a; **2**h; **3**b; **4**c; **5**d; **6**f; **7**e; **8**g

Track 1.46

Tom, Shula

T: ... and this photo is from my job in India, years ago. That's the clinic on the left.

S: Oh, it's lovely. Who's the little boy on the right with the two women?

T: He helped the doctors and nurses, you know, made tea, fetched things.

S: It's interesting that the photo is in black and white.

T: Yes, personally, I believe that you get better photos this way.

S: Yes, I agree. The mountains in the middle look amazing – so impressive.

T: I know. I loved the mountains. In fact, I loved everything there!

S: Really, why?

T: Well, because the weather was good, the food was wonderful, the people were really friendly. I'd really like to go back to see them all again.

S: You should do that! You can take three months off from this job, you know.

T: That's a good point, but I couldn't leave my family for that long. I think it's better if I wait till the children are older.

LOOK BACK

9 Students do the exercise in small pairs or groups.

- listen to extracts from podcasts: 4.1, exercise 3;
- learn how to give reasons for an action: 4.3, exercise 5;
- write a thank you email: 4.4, exercise 12;
- compare two places you know well: 5.1, exercise 7;
- read about animal invaders: 5.2, exercise 2;
- learn about managing your time: 5.4, exercises 2 and 3;
- talk about the different stages in life: 6.1, exercise 4;
- learn how to express conditions that affect future actions: 6.2, exercise 5;
- discuss family issues for presentation on a TV show: 6.3, exercise 7

LANGUAGE CHECK

8

2, 4, 7, 9 correct

3 There's a problem with lack **of** motivation.

5 This is **the** least impressive part of the country.

6 Humans have caused a lot **of** problems to the environment.

8 Elderly people might **be** healthier in the future.

10 I'm not sure. I think I agree **with** Angela.

Science

7.1 CRIME LAB

IN THIS LESSON

Lesson topic and staging

This lesson focuses on what science can contribute to criminal investigations. Students begin with reading activities, first reading for gist and for specific information, then deducing the meaning of some verbs from the context. Students then listen for gist and for detailed information as they learn more about the use of science to solve crimes. The reading and listening passages provide examples of *must* and *have to*, which should be revision for most students. Students do grammar discovery exercises and then controlled practice tasks before using the structures in a freer speaking and writing activity.

Objectives

By the end of the lesson, students should have:

* found out how science is used to solve crime
* read for gist and specific information
* worked out the meaning of verbs from context
* listened for gist and specific information
* studied the use of *must* and *have to* in affirmative, negative and question forms
* practised *must* and *have to* in controlled and free practice

Timings

You can omit exercise 5 if there is not enough time.

Possible lesson break: after exercise 4b.

READING AND VOCABULARY: science and crime

1 Direct students' attention to the three pictures and the title of the lesson. Ask them what they think the lesson is about and what people are doing in each picture. Then do activity as per Coursebook.

> 1A; 2B; 3C

2a Write *documentary* and *drama* on the board and check students remember what they mean. Give students just a minute to complete the activity so that they don't have time to read intensively.

> Crime lab: drama; CSI – the reality: documentary

2b Students do the activity individually. Give them five or six minutes to do this, then let them check their answers in pairs. You can also ask the following questions to early finishers:

What does CSI stand for? (Crime Scene Investigation)

Why does Karen's boss want her to leave the investigation? (Because she found her sister's DNA at a crime scene.)

Why does Dan Turner need to use a new machine? (The burglar hasn't left any fingerprints.)

> 1 *CSI – the reality*; 2 three; 3 DNA molecules

3 This is a 'meaning from context' activity. Ask students to read the definitions first. Make sure they understand they are looking for verbs. Ask them where they will find verbs (after a subject). Give students three or four minutes to do this activity and then check in pairs. When they have completed the activity, ask pairs to write sentences using the verbs to show they have understood the meaning.

🔧 If this activity is too difficult for your students, you could put the answers mixed up on the board and get them to match the word to the definition by checking its use in the text. First ask students to find the verbs in the text and check the context before matching them with the definitions.

* Once you have finished work on the reading text, you may also want to check the following words have been understood:

investigation (n) – an official attempt to find out about something, especially a crime or accident

burglary (n) – the crime of going into a building in order to steal things

forensic (adj) – using scientific methods to solve crimes

vital (adj) – extremely important or necessary

fingerprints (n pl) – the marks made by the pattern of lines at the end of someone's finger

hardly (adv) – almost not or almost none

> 1 solve; 2 discover; 3 reveal; 4 analyse; 5 commit (a crime)

LISTENING

> 1.47

4a Read through the instructions and the topics with the students. Elicit from students the meaning of *researcher*. Students then do activity as per Coursebook.

> 1c; 2a; 3g; 4b; 5d; 6e – Item f is not needed.

4b Put students into pairs and then ask them to fill in in the gaps before listening. When they have finished, check what they have written before listening again. When the activity is finished, get students to feed back on how well they did before listening. The objective of doing this is to give students more confidence in what they can hear from one listening.

> **1** analyse the evidence; **2** are experts on everything; **3** are murders; **4** they have to wait 20 days; **5** has increased

---

Track 1.47

Researcher, Iris

R: Well, first of all, thank you for meeting me.

i: Not at all. I hope I can help.

r: Well, as you know, we're doing some research for a documentary series about forensic science – we want to call it *CSI – the reality*. I must tell you that, at the moment, we're most interested in the differences between the TV dramas and the reality of a crime lab.

i: That's fine, I can talk about that.

r: Great. So, first of all, how do you organise the work here?

i: Well, basically, we work in two teams. In the first team, we have the crime scene analysts. They're the people who collect the evidence from the crime scene. In the second team, we have the forensic scientists, people like me, who actually do the scientific tests in the lab. The important thing is that these forensic scientists are experts in different fields, so, for example, we have an expert on guns and bullets, a fingerprints expert, and so on. I'm a DNA expert.

r: I see. That seems a little different to the TV show.

i: Yes, you're right. On the show, the crime scene analysts also work in the lab, and they often know about everything, from bullets to fingerprints.

r: Exactly. So, when the crime scene analysts are at the crime scene, what do they have to do?

i: Well, first of all, the photographer takes hundreds of pictures of the crime scene, and at the same time, someone interviews any witnesses. Then, they collect any evidence, and this is when they have to be very careful. They have to wear rubber gloves because they mustn't damage any of the evidence. Basically, they look for fingerprints, hairs, perhaps blood. It all depends on the crime really. Also, they have to take very careful notes. This is important because we, the scientists in the lab, have to know exactly where all the evidence has come from.

r: Right. Now, on TV, most of the crimes are murders. Is that true for you?

i: Oh, no, not at all. Ninety percent of our work is with burglaries or stolen cars, you know the kind of thing.

r: Really? OK, so what about the lab work? Do you have to do anything special?

i: Well, first of all, we always tell the police that they must be patient because our work in the lab takes time. On TV, a police officer doesn't have to wait very long to get test results, perhaps just a few hours. In reality, an officer has to wait twenty days to get a DNA test result. Secondly, we work in a lab, so there are certain lab rules. We have to turn our mobile phones off, and we mustn't eat or drink in the lab, that kind of thing.

continued...

R: OK. Any more differences?

I: Well, I must be honest here, unfortunately, scientists sometimes make mistakes, but, on TV, the scientists never make mistakes! Amazing!

R: Indeed. And, now that we have these dramas about forensic scientists, have there been any changes in your work?

I: Well, there's been a positive change in our image. For once, science is an interesting or glamorous profession. It's incredible really, so many young people are now applying to work in crime labs. There's been a 500 percent increase in applications to university courses, for example. And many of these people are young women. And the thing is, we're scientists not police officers, so you don't have to study law. Instead you have to study chemistry or biology. So, although the TV shows are basically police dramas, more people are now studying science subjects, which is great.

R: Interesting. So, erm, can I have a look around your lab?

I: Well, I'm not sure. My boss says all visits must only be for work reasons.

R: Well, this is kind of work related, I mean, we must get the documentary right.

I: I suppose so. Well, OK, but you must turn your phone off and you must be quiet, or my boss will kill me!

R: Hmm ... murder in the crime lab. Could be a good story for the TV show ...

---

5 Divide students into groups and ask them to discuss the three questions. When completed do a class discussion. For question 2, you can also add the following items: *fingerprints, lie detectors, criminal psychology*.

▌ GRAMMAR: *must* and *have to*

For most students, this should simply be revision.

6a Start by looking at sentences 1–4. Ask students to read them and tell you which verb forms are being used (*must* + infinitive, *have to* + infinitive). Then ask students if they know how and why they are used. Do this before looking at A–C. This should trigger their memory of this structure. When you have done this, ask students to match sentences 1–4 with A–C.

> **A** 3, 4; **B** 2; **C** 1

(!) Although exercise 6a does draw a distinction between *mustn't* and *don't have to*, it may need to be emphasised further before it sticks in your students' minds. In this case, put particular emphasis on the respective uses of the phrases when doing exercise 6b.

6b Students do the activity individually by turning to the audioscript on page 157. Then go through it as a class, particularly emphasising the difference between *mustn't* and *don't have to*.

• When this activity is completed, read through the grammar tip with your students. Tell them that this is not a rule, pointing out the use of the words *usually* and *often*. Invite students to find examples of this usage in the audioscript (e.g. *they have to be very careful* and *they must be patient*).

- At this stage, students can check the Language reference to confirm they have understood everything.

E Students can do exercises 1 and 2 from the Extra practice activities on page 139, either in class or for homework.

> **Answers:** see audioscript for Track 1.47.
> *Do/Does* + subject + *have to* + infinitive … *?*

7a Students do activity as per Coursebook.

> **1** She has to check the evidence carefully. **2** We mustn't eat or drink in here. **3** As I'm a DNA expert, I don't have to know about guns. **4** He must do what I say.

7b Students do activity as per Coursebook.

> **2** doesn't have to have; **3** doesn't have to wear; **4** must wear / has to wear; **5** mustn't make; **6** mustn't lend

SPEAKING AND WRITING

8a It's probably best to model this activity first. Tell students a little about your life and job (or make it up). Brainstorm with students what they think you have to or mustn't do in your daily life. Build this list on the board. When you are all happy with your list, get students to write their own list of ten things.

8b Put students into pairs. Students compare the sentences about their lives and choose the five most annoying things.

- Option 1: students can choose an aspect of their life (e.g. job, hobby, etc.) and write *have to* or *mustn't* sentences. Their partner has to guess what this aspect of their life is.

- Option 2: students could keep changing pairs and look for similarities between people's lives. Then in class feedback, they could draw conclusions about the character of the class.

E You can now do photocopiable activity 7A to revise vocabulary for science and *must / have to*.

HOMEWORK OPTIONS

Students can do exercise 6 from the Extra practice activities on page 139.

Students do the exercises on pages 40–41 of the Workbook.

7.2 A BRIEF HISTORY OF STEPHEN HAWKING

IN THIS LESSON

Lesson topic and staging

The main topic of this lesson is the life of the scientist Stephen Hawking. It starts with students revising some school and academic subjects and classifying them as to how scientific they perceive them to be. Students also discuss the question of science as a school subject. This introduces Stephen Hawking, who attempted to make science more accessible to the common person. Students read a text for gist and specific information and give their personal response to the passage. The reading acts as a platform to two language objectives. Firstly students look at and practise combinations of nouns, adjectives and verbs with prepositions. Then they learn and practise the use of *had to* and *could*. Finally, students discuss their own attitudes to science.

Objectives

By the end of the lesson, students should have:

- revised the names of academic subjects
- considered the importance of science to people
- learned about the life of Stephen Hawking
- read for gist and specific information
- studied and practised using nouns, adjectives and verbs with prepositions
- learned and practised the use of *had to* and *could*
- considered and discussed their own attitudes to science

Timings

Students could do exercise 5b for homework. Exercise 4c can be omitted if there is not enough time.

Possible lesson break: after exercise 4b or 4c.

SPEAKING AND VOCABULARY: science

1 Begin by directing students to the box. Explain that these are academic subjects and elicit their meaning. Then students answer the first question in pairs. Before moving onto 2, get class feedback on this.

i A survey of EU citizens (2005) gave this order: Medicine, Physics, Biology, Mathematics, Astronomy, Economics, History.

- Students discuss the two remaining questions in pairs and then as a class. You can also ask the following questions:

  Do people know enough about science?

  Are there programmes about science on TV? Are they interesting?

E Students can do exercise 5 from the Extra practice activities on page 139 either in class or for homework.

READING

2a Ask students if they know who Stephen Hawking is. What do the pictures tell us? Collect as much information as you can from students before starting the reading. Ask them to read quickly and find out why he is famous.

> He is famous for his work on black holes.

2b Students do activity as per Coursebook, first individually and then in pairs for checking.

(!) Make sure students see the explanation for *black holes*.

• When you have finished, check students' understanding of the following words or phrases:

birth (n) – the time when a baby comes out of its mother's body

separate (adj) – different, not the same

version (n) – one form of something that is different from other forms

fortunate (adj) – lucky

in spite (n) *of* – although something exists or is true

consider (v) – to think of someone or something in a particular way

> **1** born; **2** discovered; **3** job; **4** Mathematics; **5** speak; **6** *Brief*; **7** unlucky; **8** help

3 Students discuss this in pairs and as a class. You can also ask the following questions:

Which year do you think was the most important for Hawking?

Think of three adjectives to describe Hawking. (You might like to refer students back to Lesson 2.1 for this.)

Which information about Hawking in the text would you like to know more about?

(i) *A Brief History of Time* is a popular science book written by Professor Stephen Hawking and first published in 1988. It rapidly became a best-seller, and had sold 9 million copies by 2002. It was also on the London Sunday Times best-seller list for a record-breaking 237 weeks. The book attempts to explain a range of subjects in cosmology, including the Big Bang and black holes, to the non-specialist reader. Its main goal is to give an overview of the subject but, unusually for a popular science book, it also attempts to explain some complex mathematics. The author notes that an editor warned him that for every equation in the book the readership will be halved, hence it includes only a single equation: $E = mc^2$. The book is considered by many to be an 'unread bestseller', i.e. a book many people own but few have finished.

4a Read the title of the section with the students. Elicit examples of nouns, adjectives and verbs with prepositions before starting this activity (they should already know quite a few). Students fill in the blanks and then check by finding the phrases in the text on page 60. Check students have understood the meaning and finally, brainstorm other prepositions they know.

> **1** from; **2** of; **3** in; **4** to; **5** from

`2.2`

4b Students first do this activity individually. They then check in pairs and finally confirm by listening.

> **1** in; **2** with; **3** of; **4** of; **5** to; **6** on; **7** to

> **Track 2.2**
> **1** What are you interested in?
> **2** DO YOU HAVE A GOOD RELATIONSHIP WITH EVERYONE IN YOUR FAMILY?
> **3** WHAT ARE YOU AFRAID OF?
> **4** WHAT ARE YOU PROUD OF?
> **5** WHAT'S THE BEST THING THAT'S EVER HAPPENED TO YOU?
> **6** WHAT DO YOU SPEND YOUR MONEY ON?
> **7** Do you belong to any clubs or organisations?

4c Students do activity as per Coursebook.

E Students can now do exercise 7 from the Extra practice activities on page 139 either in class or for homework.

GRAMMAR: *had to* and *could*

Although this is probably the first time students have studied *had to* and *could*, they should have few problems as they should already know *have to* and *can*.

5a Start by eliciting a sentence with *have to* and a sentence with *can* from the class, and the difference in meaning. Explain that they are now going to look at the use of these forms in the past tense. Students then do activity as per Coursebook.

• Elicit from students which structure, similar in meaning to *have to*, is missing. Then direct them to the grammar tip. Explain to them that as *must* is not used, the past form is easier then the present.

> **1**b; **2**c; **3**d; **4**a

☼ Once students have finished exercise 5a, they can do either or both of the following activities:

• Tell students that scientists have changed our lives in many different ways. In pairs, ask students to discuss how people lived before the invention of these things: computers, electricity, television, telephones, trains, cameras.

You can put the following examples on the board:

Before the invention of electricity, people had to read by candlelight.

Before the invention of computers, they couldn't send emails.

- Students then talk with their partners about what they could / couldn't do at the ages of five and ten (*I couldn't … Could you … ?*). Tell students that they should find out about their partner's life as a young teenager (*Did you have to … ? Could you … ?*).

5b Students do activity as per Coursebook.

> **1** could; **2** could; **3** had to; **4** had to; **5** could not; **6** could; **7** had to; **8** could; **9** had to; **10** could; **11** had to; **12** had to

E Students can now do exercise 3 from the Extra practice activities on page 139 either in class or for homework.

SPEAKING

6 Divide students into group of three or four students. Read through the statements with the students. Then explain that they should discuss the statements and decide which ones, as a group, they agree with and why. Give students a good amount of time to do this and then split the groups so no two students are in the same group and do the activity again. Then do class feedback. Find out if any students felt they changed their mind because of the other group members' opinions.

You might like to add the following extra statements:

I read articles about science in newspapers, magazines and on the Internet.

I've never been to a science museum.

Because of their knowledge, scientists have a power that makes them dangerous.

I think experiments on animals are wrong.

Write the statements from the Coursebook onto small pieces of card. Give one card to each student and then tell them their task is to try and convince other people to agree with them.

HOMEWORK OPTIONS

Students do the exercises on pages 42–43 of the Workbook.

7.3 SCENARIO: IDEAS AND INNOVATIONS

IN THIS LESSON

Lesson topic and staging

This lesson focuses on people's inventions, theories and discoveries. Students start by learning the vocabulary for a number of inventions, theories and discoveries and discuss others they may know about. Students hear an intellectual discussion from the radio and listen for gist and then specific information. While they do this, they also learn one style of note-taking. Next, students listen to identify the language for developing an argument and then practise that language. Before moving onto the final task, students learn to differentiate between voiced and unvoiced consonants and they practise those sounds. Finally, students discuss inventions and discoveries, using the language for developing an argument and other useful phrases.

Objectives

By the end of the lesson, students should have:

- thought about specific inventions, theories and discoveries
- listened for gist and specific information
- learned and practised the language for developing an argument
- learned to discriminate between and pronounce voiced and unvoiced consonants
- completed a task to choose an invention, using the full range of language presented in the lesson

Common European Framework

Students can use language effectively to give opinions and develop an argument, using cause and effect.

Timings

Exercises 1b and/or 4b can be omitted if there is not enough time.

Possible lesson break: after exercise 5.

PREPARATION

1a Point students to the boxed list of inventions, theories and discoveries. Elicit the meaning of each and check that they also understand the meanings of the science subjects. Students match the ideas and innovations in the box with the subjects.

> **1** biology and chemistry: molecules, genetics; **2** engineering and mechanics: the printing press, levers and pulleys; **3** physics and mathematics: the theory of relativity, infinity; **4** medicine and psychology: vaccinations, psychoanalysis

ⓘ **Theory of relativity:** created by Galileo in the 1600s and further developed by Einstein. There are two theories: Special Relativity says that every person has their own time. One person's clock is different from someone else's. General Relativity says that space and time are joined together.

Molecules: the smallest amount of a chemical substance that can exist. Molecules cannot be split and stay the same.

Infinity: this is not a number. This is what is larger than any number that can be possibly imagined. Infinity cannot be counted.

The printing press: created by Johannes Guttenberg. It is used to make many copies of anything written on paper, for instance books and magazines.

Vaccinations: this means giving someone a substance that helps their immune system (the body's own protection system) fight against illness and disease. The first vaccinations were given by Edward Jenner in 1796.

Genetics: the study of how the qualities of living things are passed on in their genes, including the controversial question, 'Can we change DNA to make healthier better people?' The father of genetics is Gregor Johann Mendel whose study of the genetics of plants was published in 1865.

Levers and pulleys: a lever is something that can be used in many ways but most commonly for lifting things, as with a seesaw. A pulley is used to lift heavy weights by means of a rope being pulled around a small wheel.

Psychoanalysis: the study of people's minds, originally devised by Sigmund Freud in the 1890s to help people with psychological problems.

1b Brainstorm this activity with the whole class. Put everything on the board and ask students to explain their ideas.

SITUATION

Students read through the introduction. Check their understanding. You can ask *What type of programme is it?* and *What's the topic?*

`2.3`

2 Students read the options and predict which of the reasons David will discuss. They then listen and check.

> He discusses reasons 1, 2 and 4.

3 Students first do the activity individually as per Coursebook. Students then check in pairs before class feedback. Explain that this is one way of making notes for a talk. Ask the students to read the notes carefully and elicit what *PP, pdctn., imp., v.imp.* and *educ.* stand for (*printing press, production, important, very important, education*). Tell students that they should use this as a template when they prepare their argument later in the lesson.

> **1** 1457; **2** numbers; **3** changes; **4** education;
> **5** work; **6** writers; **7** professional; **8** society; **9** 400

Tracks 2.3 and 2.4
Presenter, David

P: SO, JULIAN, COULD YOU TELL US ABOUT ONE OF YOUR CHOICES PLEASE, AND PLEASE JUST GIVE A FEW REASONS FOR YOUR CHOICE. UNFORTUNATELY OUR TIME IS LIMITED …

J: RIGHT, WELL, ONE OF MY CHOICES IS THE PRINTING PRESS. NOW, GUTTENBERG INVENTED THE MODERN PRINTING PRESS IN 1457 AND I THINK THIS CAUSED A REVOLUTION IN KNOWLEDGE, SOCIETY … AND, WELL, IN EVERYTHING REALLY.

P: IN WHAT WAY?

J: WELL, THE MAIN REASON I THINK IT'S IMPORTANT IS THAT THE PRINTING PRESS MEANT WE COULD PRODUCE BOOKS AND NEWSPAPERS IN LARGE NUMBERS AND VERY QUICKLY. BEFORE THEN, WRITING WAS A SLOW PROCESS AND EACH COPY OF EACH BOOK TOOK WEEKS TO MAKE. SUDDENLY, WE COULD MAKE A HUNDRED COPIES OF A BOOK IN A DAY. THIS MEANT THAT IDEAS COULD SPREAD MUCH MORE QUICKLY THAN BEFORE. THIS CAUSED GREAT CHANGES IN SOCIETY, TOO MANY CHANGES TO TALK ABOUT NOW. ANOTHER REASON THE PRINTING PRESS IS IMPORTANT IS THAT IT LED TO EDUCATION FOR EVERYONE. THIS IS CONNECTED TO THE FAST PRODUCTION OF BOOKS BECAUSE IF YOU HAVE BOOKS, YOU CAN HAVE A SCHOOL. AS WELL AS THAT, THE IDEA OF EDUCATION FOR ALL IS ALSO CONNECTED TO THE DEM AND FOR READING SKILLS. THE WRITTEN WORD BECAME IMPORTANT AT WORK, AND SO PEOPLE HAD TO READ, AND SO THEY NEEDED EDUCATION.

P: OK THEN. A KEY REASON FOR CHOOSING THE PRINTING PRESS IS THAT IT MEANT THAT IDEAS COULD SPREAD QUICKLY AND THIS CAUSED MANY CHANGES IN SOCIETY. SECONDLY, YOU CLAIM THAT IT LED TO EDUCATION FOR ALL. ANYTHING ELSE?

J: WELL, YES. THE OTHER THING IS THAT THE PRINTING PRESS MEANS THAT WRITERS CAN MAKE MONEY, WHICH, AS I'M A WRITER, IS SOMETHING I'M RATHER PLEASED ABOUT.

P: HA HA!

J: BUT SERIOUSLY, WITHOUT THE PRINTING PRESS, YOU CAN'T MAKE THOUSANDS OF COPIES AND THEREFORE YOU CAN'T MAKE ANY MONEY. THE PRINTING PRESS MEANT THAT PEOPLE COULD BECOME PROFESSIONAL WRITERS AND JOURNALISTS, WHICH I THINK HAS BEEN VERY GOOD FOR SOCIETY, DON'T YOU?

P: WELL, YES I DO, I SUPPOSE. HOWEVER, I'M NOT COMPLETELY CONVINCED BY YOUR ARGUMENT ABOUT EDUCATION. AFTER ALL, WE DIDN'T HAVE GENERAL SCHOOLS UNTIL ABOUT 400 YEARS AFTER THE INVENTION OF THE PRINTING PRESS. IS THERE REALLY A CONNECTION?

J: WELL, ER, THAT'S A FAIR POINT, ALTHOUGH I STILL SAY THAT THE MASS PRODUCTION OF BOOKS CAUSED CHANGES IN THE WAY PEOPLE WORKED AND THIS LED TO WIDER EDUCATION.

P: MMM. OK, WE'LL LEAVE THAT DISCUSSION THERE FOR THE MOMENT AND LET'S MOVE ON. SANDRA, WHAT HAVE YOU CHOSEN?

KEY LANGUAGE: developing an argument

`2.4`

4a Read the first sentence of the instructions together. Ask students to find all the arrows in the notes. Check they have done this. Ask them if they can substitute words for the arrows. Do this because some students may already know the phrases here. Students then do the activity as per Coursebook, first individually and then checking in pairs.

> 1 caused; 2 meant that; 3 led to; 4 is connected to; 5 so; 6 means that

Track 2.4
See audioscript for Track 2.3.

4b Students do activity as per Coursebook.

💡 Ask students to mark each use of these phrases with an arrow to show how things are connected. This will allow you to be sure that students have understood how these phrases are used.

E Students can do exercise 4 from the Extra practice activities on page 139 either in class or for homework.

> **Answers:** see audioscript for Track 2.3.

5 Students do this individually and then in pairs. Then do a class check to ensure students are using the structures correctly.

pronunciation

`2.5`

6a Students listen to the sounds and try and answer the question. You can make the sounds in isolation to make it clearer to them. Students then follow the instruction and try to make the sounds, working in pairs. Go around the class and find the best examples. Suggest that they put the thumb and first finger on either side of the trachea and then make the sounds. If the trachea vibrates it means they are making a voiced sound. If not, they are making an unvoiced sound.

Track 2.5
the theory of relativity

`2.6`

6b Students do activity as per Coursebook.

💡 Ask students to find common words in English that begin with the voiced and unvoiced consonants.

> 1 /b/; 2 /d/; 3 /g/; 4 /v/; 6 /z/; 7 /ʒ/; 8 /dʒ/

Track 2.6
1 /p/ AND /b/
2 /t/ AND /d/
3 /k/ AND /g/
4 /f/ AND /v/
5 /θ/ and /ð/
6 /s/ AND /z/
7 /ʃ/ and /ʒ/
8 /tʃ/ and /dʒ/

`2.7`

6c Students do activity as per Coursebook.

> 2 /p/; 3 /k/; 4 /d/; 5 /k/; 6 /s/; 7 /t/, /f/; 8 /k/, /p/, /t/; 9 /t/, /v/, /ʒ/; 10 /k/, /s/, /t/; 11 /f/, /dʒ/; 12 /t/, /t/

Track 2.7
1 nuclear energy
2 aeroplanes
3 the car
4 DNA
5 the clock
6 the printing press
7 the telephone
8 the computer
9 television and radio
10 electricity
11 the refrigerator
12 the Internet

TASK: choosing the best invention

7a Read through the instructions with the students. Check they've understood, asking, e.g.:

Where can you find the top 12 inventions and discoveries? (in exercise 6c)

How many do you have to choose? (four)

Students then work alone. Give them about six or seven minutes to prepare. Make sure they take some notes as prompts. You can tell them they can use the notes from exercise 3 as an example to prepare their arguments.

7b Direct students to the OTHER USEFUL PHRASES box before they start working with a partner. Look at the first three phrases in particular. Use an example not in the list of 12, e.g. *trains*, and elicit example sentences using these first three phrases. Students then do activity as per Coursebook. If you have a large class it would be better to then form groups of four before doing exercise 7c.

7c Students do activity as per Coursebook. Allow students to ask questions after each mini-presentation. Then take a classroom vote.

☼ Either in class or for homework, ask students to now write a composition about what they believe to be an important invention or discovery. It must be one that is not mentioned in the lesson.

E You can now do photocopiable activity 7B to revise the language for developing an argument.

HOMEWORK OPTIONS

Students do the exercises on page 44 of the Workbook.

7.4 STUDY AND WRITING SKILLS

IN THIS LESSON

Lesson topic and staging

In this lesson, students are learning more about the study skill of note-taking from reading and the skill of reading charts and writing about them.

In the first half of the lesson, students discuss the importance of note-taking. They then hear a discussion between students about note-taking and listen for specific information. Students follow this up by reading an article on problems for women in science, first for gist and then for detail. They study different notes taken by students on the text and personally evaluate the notes. They finish this part of the lesson by practising their note-taking themselves.

In the second half, students start by studying a chart for general information and then for specific information. Students then learn and practise some of the language needed for analysing charts or graphs. In the final activity, they use what they have learned to analyse and write about a chart.

Objectives

By the end of the lesson, students should have:

- discussed when and why note-taking happens
- listened for specific information
- read for gist and specific information
- studied different types of note-taking and personally evaluated them
- practised note-taking
- studied and analysed charts
- learned and practised the language of increases and falls
- written about a chart themselves

Timings

Students can do the first part of exercise 5 and exercise 10 for homework if there is not enough time.

Possible lesson break: after exercise 5.

STUDY SKILLS: making notes

1 Students work in pairs or in small groups initially. Do a classroom feedback session, if possible eliciting the example answers suggested below.

> **Suggested answers:** to think about and understand what you have read, to give a talk, to prepare for an exam, to reduce the amount of information you have to handle

2.8

2 Read the first two lines of the instructions with the students. Ask students what advice they think Anisha might give to Shannon. Put their suggested answers on the board and refer back to them after the activity is completed to see if they correspond with what Anisha actually said. Students then read the rest of the instructions and do activity as per Coursebook.

You can write the following gapped sentences on the board. Students listen again and fill in the blanks.

First of all, you should _____ you're reading and making notes. (remember why)

The _____ I read the text, I don't make any notes. (first time)

After that, I read it again and highlight _____. (the main ideas)

When I make notes, I summarise the information, using a few key _____. (words or phrases)

I also make the notes using _____, not the same words as in the text. (my own words)

This task confirms that students have taken in the main points of the listening.

> **1** Remember *why* you're reading and making notes.
> **2** Only make notes if the information can help you to answer the essay question.
> **3** First read: don't make any notes – just read it and try to understand it.
> Second read: read it again and highlight the main ideas. Then make notes of the information highlighted. Don't copy out the information – summarise the information, using a few key words or phrases. Also use your own words.
>
> Shannon thinks it's useful advice.

> **Track 2.8**
> *Shannon, Anisha*
> S: MORNING ANISHA.
> A: HI SHANNON! HOW'S IT GOING? EVERYTHING ALRIGHT?
> S: WELL, I SUPPOSE SO.
> A: YOU DON'T SOUND VERY HAPPY.
> S: WELL, I'M HAVING A BIT OF TROUBLE WITH MY READING AND NOTE-TAKING.
> A: OH. WHY?
> S: WELL, I CAN'T TAKE VERY GOOD NOTES. THEY'RE USUALLY VERY LONG. I WRITE DOWN A LOT OF STUFF – PAGES AND PAGES. IT TAKES ME AGES. AND SOMETIMES I THINK I WRITE DOWN THE WRONG INFORMATION, TOO. I DON'T REALLY KNOW WHAT I'M DOING WRONG.
> A: OK. WELL, I CAN TELL YOU WHAT'S WORKED FOR ME. FIRST OF ALL, YOU SHOULD REMEMBER *why* you're reading and making notes. What will you use the notes for? Are they for an essay? A presentation? An exam? If they're for an essay, what's the essay question? Only make notes if the information can help you to answer the essay question. Don't make any notes if the information is about another topic. If you keep that in mind, it'll help you. You know what I mean?
> *continued…*

> S: YEAH, SURE.
> A: RIGHT, LET'S IMAGINE I'M READING AN ACADEMIC PAPER. IT'S ABOUT EIGHT PAGES LONG. IF I'VE GOT TIME, THIS IS WHAT I DO. THE FIRST TIME I READ THE TEXT, I DON'T MAKE ANY NOTES. I JUST … READ IT – STRAIGHT THROUGH. I JUST TRY TO UNDERSTAND IT, YOU KNOW. AFTER THAT, I READ IT AGAIN AND HIGHLIGHT THE MAIN IDEAS. I ALSO HIGHLIGHT OTHER POINTS IN A DIFFERENT COLOUR. THESE ARE IMPORTANT POINTS, BUT LESS IMPORTANT THAN THE MAIN POINTS.
> S: I'VE GOT IT.
> A: THE NEXT THING I DO … IS MAKE NOTES OF THE INFORMATION I'VE HIGHLIGHTED. BUT I DON'T JUST COPY OUT THE INFORMATION. WHEN I MAKE NOTES, I SUMMARISE THE INFORMATION, USING A FEW KEY WORDS OR PHRASES. AND I ALSO MAKE THE NOTES USING MY OWN WORDS – NOT THE SAME WORDS AS IN THE TEXT. LIKE THIS, I REALLY UNDERSTAND THE NOTES I'M MAKING. IF YOU JUST COPY OUT SENTENCES, IT'S POSSIBLE YOU DON'T ACTUALLY UNDERSTAND ANYTHING. AND … ER … WELL, THAT'S ABOUT IT, REALLY. I DON'T THINK I CAN TELL YOU ANYTHING ELSE.
> S: WELL, YOU'VE GIVEN ME SOME GOOD IDEAS. THANKS ANISHA.
> A: ANYTHING ELSE?
> S: ER … WELL … THERE *is* something else … yeah …

3a Students discuss the issues they expect to read about in pairs and then do classroom feedback before reading.

3b Students now turn to page 118, read and check if the article corresponds with their predictions.

4a Read through the instructions with the students. Make sure they realise this essay will be written using notes taken from the article on page 118. Then read through the notes with the class. Ask students which of the following sentences are true or false:

Notes can be long.

You can use whole sentences from the text.

You can use parts of the texts occasionally with quotation marks.

Students then do activity as per Coursebook.

> **A:** hard to compete with **men** who have written academic papers; **B: no** difference between men's and women's brains; **C: 50%** women in Paris lab

4b Ask students to study the notes and do the activity. They do it individually to start with and then check in pairs. Make sure students are aware of the note at the bottom of page 64, to the effect that there is no right or wrong style for notes.

> **1** good organisation: A and B; bad organisation: C;
> **2** all of C; **3** most of A is written in student's own words; **4** C: worked in Paris lab – 40% women;
> **5** *neg* – negative, *s.o.* – someone, *e.g.* – for example, *pos* – positive, *+* – and, *→* – which means that, *diff* – difference, *prob* – problem; **6** A – unsure about (their) career + life; B must change (the) way schools teach science, (they) don't go back to work, (someone) need(s) to give them confidence

5 Students turn back to the text on page 43. They have used this text before so should know it well. Give students about ten minutes to prepare their notes and then check them with a partner. Ask them to use the list in exercise 4b to check (e.g. *Is it clearly organised? Are there enough details of the topic/idea? Did you use your own words?*).

☼ Notes only have any validity if they can be used. You can ask students to give their notes to a partner who has to try and recreate the relevant section (invasive species in the UK) of the original text. They can then go to page 43 and check. Students then evaluate how successful the notes were.

WRITING SKILLS: describing charts

Read through the notes together with the students. Make sure students know what GCSEs are.

ⓘ The General Certificate of Secondary Education (GCSE) is the examination at the end of the courses that students between 14 and 16 take in England, Wales and Northern Ireland. GCSE courses can be taken in a variety of topics which the students choose themselves between the ages of 13 and 14. GCSEs are not compulsory but are the most common qualifications and virtually everyone takes English, Mathematics and Science. The final grade for the course usually includes an exam plus one or more completed assignments during the course.

• Ask the class the following questions in order to raise awareness of the topic:

Did you take any school exams at the age of 15/16? If yes, in which subjects?

Did you study Chemistry at school?

Did you like it?

When did you stop studying it?

Did you pass any exams in Chemistry?

6 Point students to chart A on page 65. Students then do activity as per Coursebook.

  information 2 and 4

7 Students do activity as per Coursebook.

  1 girls; **2** Chemistry; **3** England; **4** 2005; **5** grades

8 Before starting this exercise, elicit from students the meaning of X-axis (across) and Y-axis (up and down). Elicit from students what the X-axis and the Y-axis represent in this chart. Students then do activity as per Coursebook.

  1 passed the exam with grades A to C; **2** took the exam; **3** 13,000; **4** 15,000

9a Students do activity as per Coursebook.

  1 nouns: an increase, a rise, a decrease, a fall; verbs: fell, decreased, rose, increased
  2 going up: an increase, a rise, rose, increased; going down: fell, a decrease, decreased, a fall
  3 an increase – a rise; fell – decreased; a decrease – a fall; rose – increased

9b Students do activity as per Coursebook.

  1 a decrease / a fall; **2** fell / decreased; **3** a rise / an increase; **4** a rise / an increase; **5** rose / increased; **6** rose / increased; **7** a rise / an increase

10 This activity could be done in class or for homework. If you decide to do it in class, you might like to do it in three or four groups with the students writing up the text on the board and then correcting it together.

Ⓟ Ask students to do their own research and survey and write the text to go with it. Get students to bring these into class. Then disseminate the texts and the graphs separately around and ask students to match the charts with the relevant reports.

HOMEWORK OPTIONS

Students do the exercises on page 45 of the Workbook.

The night

8.1 SLEEP TIGHT!

Lesson topic and staging

The topic of this lesson is sleep, how we sleep and how important sleep is. Students start by discussing sleep and revising relevant vocabulary. They then read for gist and for specific information two emails about a talk that a student will give on sleep. Students then listen to this talk, looking for specific information. Both the reading and the listening provide examples for the grammar focus on verb patterns (revision of verb + infinitive, verb + -ing and introduction of verb + preposition + -ing). Students study and practise these structures and finish the lesson by doing a quiz on sleep, an opportunity to use both the vocabulary and the grammar of the lesson.

Objectives

By the end of the lesson, students should have:

- learned more about sleep and its importance to us
- revised vocabulary connected with sleep
- read for gist and for specific information
- listened for specific information
- revised and practised the patterns verb + infinitive and verb + -ing
- learned and practised the pattern verb + preposition + -ing
- combined all the language in a speaking activity on sleep

Timings

Exercise 4c can be given for homework if there is not enough time.

Possible lesson break: after exercise 3c.

SPEAKING AND VOCABULARY: sleep

1 First ask students to read the title and to tell you what they think the lesson will be about.

i The title of this lesson is part of something parents say to children before they go to bed: *Night night, sleep tight.* It is sometimes followed by the line *Don't let the bedbugs/feefees bite.* Nobody seems to know what a *feefee* is.

- Before students start the activity, you might like to check they know the meaning of the following words/phrases:

  sleep in (v) – to sleep deliberately later than usual

  doze (v) – to sleep lightly, usually for a short time

- Students respond to the statements individually, before sharing their responses with a partner. Finish by having a quick class discussion.

READING

2 Students do activity as per Coursebook individually and then check as a class. If students ask why some of the text is highlighted, tell them you will come back to that later. You may also like to ask the following questions:

Did Abolaji know about the conference in Oslo before he received Dr Wilson's email? (yes)

When will Dr Wilson next see Abolaji? (Tuesday)

Why do you think Abolaji has chosen this topic for his presentation? (students' personal answers)

> **1** He wants some advice for his end-of-course presentation. **2** lecturer/tutor and student; **3** students' own answers

---

LISTENING

2.9

3a Read the instructions with the students, who then listen and afterwards check their answers in pairs.

> **1** false; **2** true; **3** true; **4** does not say; **5** true; **6** does not say

💡 In the first part of his talk, Abolaji uses fractions. Write the following on the board:

a half a third a fifth ($\frac{1}{2}$, 0.50; $\frac{1}{3}$, 0.33; $\frac{1}{5}$, 0.20)

Ask students to come to the board and write these as fractions and as percentages (if students don't know what a fraction is, give an example with *a quarter*).

Then write the following percentages on the board and ask students to name and write them as fractions:

40% 60% 66.6% 80%

(two-fifths, three-fifths, two-thirds, four-fifths)

Track 2.9

Dr Wilson, Abolaji, Students

DR W: Alright, Abolaji, you're next. Are you ready?

A: Yes.

DR W: OK then, start when you like.

A: Good morning everybody. Let me start with a question. Do you <u>like sleeping</u>?

S: Yes! No! [LAUGHTER]

continued...

A: Today I'm going to talk to you about sleep. I <u>hope to show</u> you that sleep is a very important and interesting subject. But please stay awake – don't fall asleep during my presentation!

Scientists <u>are starting to understand</u> sleep much better than before, and I'll mention some new research in my talk. Because of the limited time, I'll cover three areas:

1 how much sleep we need
2 the types and stages of sleep, and
3 some problems with sleep in today's society.

So, let's look first at how much sleep people need. Most people spend around a third of their lives asleep, although the need for sleep decreases with age. A one-year-old baby needs about fourteen hours of sleep a day, a child of five needs about twelve hours, and an adult about seven to eight hours. However, different people need different amounts of sleep. Some adults <u>need to sleep</u> for ten hours or more a day, while others only need half that amount or less. Elderly people <u>tend to sleep</u> less than younger adults at night, but they doze more during the day.

Let's turn now to the different types of sleep, and I <u>apologise for using</u> some rather technical language here. There are two types of sleep, known as REM sleep and NREM sleep. REM means rapid eye movement. NREM means non-rapid eye movement. Most of our sleep – about 80 percent of the sleeping pattern – is NREM sleep; during this time, brain activity falls to its lowest level. In REM sleep, the brain suddenly becomes more active – like the brain of a person who's awake. The eyes move rapidly and dreams occur. REM sleep is about one half of sleep time in babies, and about one fifth of sleep time in adults.

2.10

3b Ask students to use the chart at the bottom of page 67 to predict the answers. Then students do activity as per Coursebook and finally check the answers in pairs.

> 1 five; 2 makes memories stronger; 3 street lights and security lights; 4 our days are becoming longer and our nights shorter

Track 2.10
Abolaji
OK. Turning to the stages of sleep, we can identify five stages in a night's sleep, as you can see on the slide. In different stages of sleep, our brains put together thoughts and experiences, then store them in an organised way, giving us clearer memories. According to Robert Stickgold, a sleep researcher at Harvard Medical School in Boston, it seems that different kinds of sleep improve different kinds of memories, and this might be why we have the five different stages of sleep. Recent experiments suggest that the final stage of sleep, REM sleep, is very important for *organising* our memories and <u>helps to improve</u> our learning. NREM sleep is important for making our memories *stronger*.

continued…

Experiments have also shown that the brain works in a different way after we've had a good night's sleep. The final area I <u>want to talk</u> about are things that can <u>stop us sleeping</u> well. One of them is too much light. Street lights and security lights mean that even when we're asleep, it's never completely dark. And the evidence suggests that the quantity and quality of darkness in our lives affects our health. Another problem is the 24/7 world, with the Internet, 24-hour shopping, global travel, etc. Because of this, our days are becoming longer and the nights shorter – and this could also damage our health, as we're not getting enough sleep.

To sum up, I hope I<u>'ve succeeded in showing</u> you that sleep is a very important and interesting subject. We sleep less as we get older, but everybody's different – some people need more sleep, others less. There are two types of sleep – NREM and REM; most sleep is NREM, but REM is when dreaming happens. During the five different stages of sleep, our brains organise our memories and make them stronger. But too much light and our modern way of life can have a negative impact on our sleeping patterns and, as a result, on our brains and our health. Thank you for listening. Are there any questions? Is anyone still awake?

3c Students do activity as per Coursebook. If they have problems, you can refer them to the audioscript on pages 158–159.

🔧 If you have a strong class, you might like to ask them to make a summary of the talk before they see the one in this exercise. They can then check it with the gapped summary.

> 1 less; 2 types; 3 brain; 4 dreams; 5 organising; 6 darkness; 7 damage

☀ If you have time you might like to discuss the following questions with your students:
Are you getting enough sleep?
Do you sleep less than when you were younger?
How much light is there in your bedroom when you are asleep?

GRAMMAR: verb patterns

4a Refer students back to the texts on page 66, especially to the highlighted text. Elicit from the students why they think it has been highlighted. Ask them to fill in the table. When you have checked this, tell them that these are examples of verb patterns. Explain that there is no rule or reason why one verb uses one pattern and not another. Generally they just have to be learned. Elicit from students other examples that they may know for each of the three columns.

4b Students then go to the audioscripts for Tracks 2.9–2.10 on pages 158–159 and find other examples. When students have finished and you have checked, read through the grammar tip together.

- Remind students to look up the Language reference for this (page 140) if they have any problems.

> **verb + infinitive with *to*:** seem (manage, decide, hope, start, need, tend, help, want)
> **verb + *-ing*:** keep (like, stop)
> **verb + preposition + *-ing*:** think about (apologise for, succeed in)
> See also audioscript for Tracks 2.9 and 2.10.

4c Students do activity as per Coursebook.

> **1** seemed to have; **2** succeeded in keeping;
> **3** Keep working; **4** are starting to develop;
> **5** managed to cover; **6** needed to say;
> **7** tended to speak; **8** kept reading

E Students can do exercise 1 from the Extra practice activities on page 141 either in class or for homework.

5a This is a freer activity. Make sure students realise that in this exercise, there are six questions that use verb patterns. Tell students to complete the questions with verb patterns so that you can find out things about other students in the class. Students should do this individually. Check students' questions are correct before going on to exercise 5b.

5b Students can now go round the class asking questions. Make sure that students don't ask each person more than one question. When you do feedback, students can tell different things about different students.

SPEAKING

6 Divide the class into groups of four. Students work together to complete the quiz on page 118, then turn to page 121 to check their answers.

- Alternatively, take copies of the answers. Blank out the numbers and then cut up each answer into a strip. When students have finished guessing the answers, they can match the answers to the questions.

- Another way of delivering the activity would be for you to divide the questions and the answers up into four and then recopy. In the lesson, divide the class into groups of four students. Then give each student in the group a quarter of the questions with a quarter of the answers, making sure none of their answers correspond to their questions. Students then have to ask each other questions to find out the answer. To test the structure and make it more difficult you could turn the fully-formed questions into prompts for questions so students have to make the questions themselves.

HOMEWORK OPTIONS

Students can do exercise 5 from the Extra practice activities on page 141.

Students do the exercises on pages 46–47 of the Workbook.

8.2 THE NIGHT SHIFT

IN THIS LESSON

Lesson topic and staging

The topic of this lesson is the jobs that people do that require them to work at night. Students begin by guessing which jobs require work at night and then discuss them in more detail. Next, students look at a text on night jobs, which they read for gist and specific information before discussing how they feel about these jobs. The text provides examples of *-ing* and *-ed* adjectives, and students study and practise the differences in meaning between these adjectives. The text also provides examples of how to state future intentions. The grammar section looks at planned actions, ambitions and dreams. Students study and practise the three structures *going to*, *hoping to* and *'d like to*. In the final speaking activity, students make plans with partners and then tell others about their future intentions.

Objectives

By the end of the lesson, students should have:

- learned more about jobs that require work at night
- read for gist and for specific information
- studied, understood the difference between and practised *-ing* and *-ed* adjectives
- learned and practised ways of expressing future intentions, using *going to*, *hoping to* and *'d like to*
- completed writing and speaking activities that involve making plans

Timings

Exercise 1b can be omitted if there is not enough time as it is similar to 3c. The written part of exercise 6 could be done for homework.

Possible lesson break: after exercise 4d.

READING

1a Refer students to the title of the lesson. Ask them what *night shift* means. Elicit what we would say for people who work during the day (day shift). Point students to the jobs listed in exercise 1a. Check that they understand all of them. Then ask them in pairs to decide which jobs they think require people to work at night. Discuss each one in class, asking whether they have to always be at night or sometimes by day and sometimes by night.

> **Suggested answers:** astronomer, baker, call-centre worker, cleaner, lorry driver, nurse, police officer, security guard

1b You can also include advantages for this activity. Divide students into groups and let them brainstorm for a couple of minutes. Then all the groups report back to the whole class. Make a list on the board of those that the class as a whole agrees with.

> students' own answers

2 Students do activity as per Coursebook. Give students no more than a minute to read this short paragraph. Do feedback as a class.

3a Do activity as per Coursebook.

> **Peter Moore:** limited social life; **John Millar:** job is boring because it's quiet; **Tony Baggio:** job is tiring, and his wife is pregnant; **Indira Patel:** depressing, as she misses friends and family

3b Students do activity as per Coursebook. Students can check in pairs before doing the feedback.

> **1** John Millar; **2** Peter Moore, Indira Patel; **3** John Millar, Tony Baggio, Indira Patel; **4** Tony Baggio; **5** Indira Patel; **6** Tony Baggio, Indira Patel; **7** Peter Moore, Indira Patel; **8** Peter Moore, John Millar

As practice to deduce meaning from context, ask students to find out the words or phrases in the text that mean the following:

extremely interested (fascinated)

very surprising or very good (amazing)

when you follow a college course, but you study from home (distance learning)

the attitudes and atmosphere in a group of people who work or play together (team spirit)

making you feel sad or unhappy (depressing)

3c Students discuss the questions in pairs and then report back about their partners.

This could become a writing activity, for homework or in class.

VOCABULARY: -ing/-ed adjectives

This is an important topic. Students often confuse -ing and -ed adjectives and it is very common to hear a student say *I am boring* when he or she means *bored*.

4a Ask students to look at the two sentences. Ask them to identify the two adjectives in each sentence which are related. What endings do they have? Elicit from students why they think they have different endings and what the difference in meaning is. Then ask students to answer the two questions.

> tiring, tired; bored, boring
> **1** tired, bored; **2** tiring, boring

4b Students do activity as per Coursebook. Ask students to tell you why they chose the adjectives. When you have checked this, ask students what type of word we make these adjectives from (a verb).

> **1** frightened, frightening; **2** interesting, interested

4c Students do activity as per Coursebook in pairs and then check with another pair before class checking.

> limited (limit), closed (close), fascinated (fascinate), amazing (amaze), boring (bore), tiring (tire), interesting (interest), depressing (depress)

4d Students fill in the gaps individually and then ask each other in pairs. Then do class feedback. When you find out the answers, ask the partner how they felt or what they thought about so that they are forced to use the other form of the adjective.

> **1** interesting; **2** exciting; **3** tired; **4** fascinated; **5** amazing; **6** embarrassing; **7** surprised; **8** frightened

E Students can now do exercise 6 from the Extra practice activities on page 141 either in class or for homework.

GRAMMAR: future intentions

5a Students start by doing the activity as per Coursebook. Then ask students to look more closely at the sentences. Ask them how many verb forms in bold there are. Are they about the present, past or future? Ask them to guess the difference in meaning between the three verb forms being used.

> **1** Peter Moore; **2** Peter Moore; **3** John Millar; **4** Indira Patel

5b Students look for more examples in the text.

> **Peter Moore:** I'm never going to change my job.
> **John Millar:** I'm going to read my course books during the long quiet nights! / I'd like to be a teacher. / I'm going to apply for a teacher-training course when I finish my degree.
> **Tony Baggio:** I'm going to leave this job soon. / I'm hoping to be a builder.
> **Indira Patel:** I don't know what I'm going to do really.

5c Using the examples from the text, ask students to answer the three questions.

The negative forms of these three structures are different. Make sure that students understand this and practise it. Elicit examples of sentences in the negative for all three forms to show they have understood. Refer students to the Language reference on page 140 to check what they have learned or if they are having problems.

E Students can now do exercises 2 and 3 from the Extra practice activities on page 141 either in class or for homework.

> **1** sentences 1 and 3; **2** sentences 2 and 4;
> **3** negatives: I'm not going to / I'm hoping not to / I wouldn't like to;
> questions: Are you going to … ? / Are you hoping to … ? / Would you like to … ?

WRITING

6 Students do the activity either in class or for homework. Encourage students to be particularly creative with this activity so that they don't all end up having the same sentences. If students are having trouble coming up with ideas, you might brainstorm possible topic areas such as work and study / free time and leisure / family and relationships / holidays and travel / this weekend / next week / later this year / next year / in ten years' time.

• Students share their sentences with partners. Partners should comment on the content and on the form, i.e. point out any mistakes in the writing. Finally, do a class feedback of the most interesting plans that students have.

SPEAKING

7a Tell students that they are going to make plans to solve problems. Remind them that when people want to suggest solutions to problems, they use certain phrases. Elicit *Why don't we … ?*, *I think we should …*

• Then model a problem, e.g.:

We can't use this classroom tomorrow as it is being painted. What shall we do?

Elicit suggestions using the two phrases for suggestions. Finally, put students in pairs. They should read the problems and then suggest and agree on plans to solve them.

7b Split up the pairs and make new pairs. The new partners should now share their plans with each other. Finally, have a classroom discussion and decide as a class what plans you have to solve the problems.

E You can now do photocopiable activity 8A to revise and practise future patterns (*going to, hoping, 'd like to*).

HOMEWORK OPTIONS

Students do the exercises on pages 48–49 of the Workbook.

8.3 SCENARIO: A NIGHT OUT

IN THIS LESSON

Lesson topic and staging

The topic of this lesson is going out to events, particularly at the Edinburgh Festival, and planning a night out. Students start by discussing the things they like to do when going for a night out. They then discover about the Edinburgh Festival. Students scan a list of events for specific information and then hear a recording in which they listen for gist and specific information as tourists choose which events from the programme they would like to attend – the context for introducing the language of expressing preferences. Students practise this and they also study the different intonations in *wh-* questions. For the final task, they work with a different programme for the festival and plan together the events they are going to attend, using the key language and the information in the 'Other Useful Phrases' box.

Objectives

By the end of the lesson, students should have:

• talked about going out to events, particularly those at the Edinburgh Festival
• read for specific information
• listened for gist and specific information
• learned and practised language for expressing preferences
• studied and practised intonation in *wh-* questions
• completed a speaking task using language for expressing preferences

Common European Framework

Students can use language effectively to express preferences and plan an event/occasion.

Timings

If there is not enough time, you could omit exercise 6.

Possible lesson break: after exercise 4b.

PREPARATION

1 Ask students to look at the title of the lesson. Elicit from them what *a night out* means.

• Point students to the list of activities and get them to ask and answer the questions in pairs. Then conduct a class feedback session and take note of any other activities that students do.

SITUATION

Read through the introduction to the Edinburgh Festival with the students. You can ask the following questions:

When is the festival? (August every year)

Where is it? (Edinburgh, Scotland)

How many different types of event are there? (nine)

Ask students if they know anything about the Edinburgh Festival.

2a Students do this activity quickly, choosing from the four events listed. Give them no more than two minutes.

(!) When students are looking for information quickly in a text, they can be put off by blanks for missing information. Assure students that all the information that they need from the text is already there.

> **1** Movies in the park; **2** Mini-theatre;
> **3** Castle classics, World beats; **4** Castle classics, Mini-theatre; **5** Movies in the park, World beats

(i) The Edinburgh Festival is, in fact, not one festival but a group of festivals that all take place every year in August in Edinburgh, Scotland. The original Edinburgh International Festival, a festival of classical and modern dance, music, theatre and opera first took place in 1947. It is now particularly famous for the Fringe Festival, a collection of smaller festivals that take place around the International Festival. The Edinburgh Festival is famous because of the variety of different shows and events. In 2006 alone, over 1.5 million tickets were sold just for the Fringe Festival.

2b Students do activity as per Coursebook, individually and then checking in pairs. When they have finished, ask students which events they'd like to go to and why.

> **1** location; **2** famous; **3** world; **4** popcorn; **5** songs;
> **6** plays; **7** actor; **8** father; **9** around; **10** forget

2.11

3a Students do activity as per Coursebook.

> Castle classics and World beats

3b As students have already listened once, ask them to work in pairs and predict the answers to the eight questions before listening. In this way students can see how much they pick up from just one listening.

(☼) As an introduction to the next section, ask students to tell you the phrases that showed them the answers to the questions. This will make exercise 4a more of a check activity.

> **1** E; **2** C; **3** P; **4** E; **5** P; **6** C; **7** C; **8** P

Tracks 2.11 and 2.12

Paul, Emma, Christine

P: OK then, so what shall we do after dinner? What's on at about eight o'clock, Emma?

E: Well, there's a classical music concert in the castle or else an open-air movie. <u>What would you prefer to do, Christine?</u>

C: I'm not sure, what kind of film is it?

E: It's an Indian film, a Bollywood film, you know, with loads of songs and dancing. This one's a romantic comedy.

C: Hmm, <u>I don't fancy that.</u> <u>I'd prefer to go to the classical concert.</u> What about you, Paul?

P: I think <u>I'd rather see the film.</u> <u>I'm not that keen on the concert.</u> I don't really like classical music. What about you Emma, <u>what would you rather do?</u>

E: <u>Well, to be honest, I don't mind.</u> I like all music. The movie sounds good because I've never seen a Bollywood film before, and they're good fun, the dancing's brilliant, so I've been told. But, the concert sounds good because it's in the castle, and I think that'll be lovely, a really good atmosphere for the music.

P: It's in the castle?

C: Yes, in the main hall. Are you more interested now?

P: Yes, I am. We haven't been to the castle yet, and I'd like to see it at night.

C: Great! Let's go to the concert then. What shall we do after that?

E: After that?

C: Oh yes, Emma, no one goes to bed before midnight during the festival. You have to see as much as you can.

E: OK, fair enough. Well, <u>I'm more interested in the Japanese drummers than the one-man theatre show.</u>

C: Yeah, the drummers do sound interesting, but perhaps we shouldn't go to a second music event.

E: Hmm, maybe. Paul, which would you prefer to go to?

P: Oh, <u>I'd love to see the drummers.</u> They sound amazing. And it's a great chance to see something different and unusual. <u>I'd rather see that than a play about Shakespeare.</u>

C: But it says that the play's really funny. And how interesting is two hours of drumming going to be?

E: Oh Christine, I'm sure the Taiko drumming will be really interesting. I've seen some of it on TV, and I'd love to see it live.

C: OK then, let's go and see the drummers. But tomorrow, no music, OK?

P, E: OK.

KEY LANGUAGE: expressing preferences

2.12

4a Before doing this activity, elicit from students what *expressing preferences* means. Ask students if they remember any examples from the listening that showed people expressing preferences. Elicit any examples of language for expressing preferences that your students know.

Then students individually predict the missing words from the examples. They can check in pairs first and then listen and check. When they've finished the activity, you can listen and repeat the phrases (note that they will have more opportunity to pronounce *wh-* questions in the next section).

Focus students on questions 3, 4, 9 and 10. Ask students what *'d* stands for. Elicit why we use *would* and not just use the present tense (using the present tense would mean it's a general feeling, not specific to one event or one time).

> **1** prefer; **2** fancy; **3** prefer; **4** rather; **5** keen;
> **6** would; **7** mind; **8** than; **9** love; **10** rather

> **Track 2.12**
> See audioscript for Track 2.11.

4b Students do activity as per Coursebook.

> **a** 1, 6; **b** 3, 4, 8, 10; **c** 2, 5; **d** 9; **e** 7

For stronger students, put the following two sentences on the board:

I'd rather not go to the classical concert.

I fancy going to the Japanese drummers.

Elicit the structures (*would/'d rather not* + infinitive; *fancy* + *-ing*) and then get students to identify where they would go in exercise 4b (*c* and *d*).

You might like to do exercise 6 before going to the next section.

E Students can do exercise 4 from the Extra practice activities on page 141 either in class or for homework.

pronunciation

2.13

5 Check that students remember the meaning of *intonation* before the activity. Students do activity as per Coursebook. When the activity is finished, elicit from students the difference between the intonation of *wh-* questions and *yes/no* questions (*wh-* questions have a falling intonation, *yes/no* questions a rising intonation). When you have finished doing listen and repeat, you can mix in some *yes/no* questions of your own so students practise the different intonation patterns.

falling intonation

> **Track 2.13**
> **1** What would you like to do?
> **2** Where would you like to go?
> **3** What would you prefer to do?
> **4** What would you rather do?
> **5** What do you fancy doing?

6 Students do the activity individually and then in pairs. Encourage students to ask each other questions using the intonation patterns from exercise 5 and reply using the key language from 4a.

TASK: planning a night out

Before starting the task, ask students to look at the OTHER USEFUL PHRASES box. Go through the phrases in the box, checking understanding. Then get students to practise this language in pairs by planning a night out together, using the suggested outings in exercise 1. Model the role-play with a student in front of the class first.

7a Ask students to look at the programme of events on page 119. Students spend some time reading and deciding what they will say about each event.

7b Students do activity as per Coursebook. Make sure they use the correct language and intonation patterns for *wh-* questions. Check each group has agreed on three events before moving onto exercise 7c.

7c Students do activity as per Coursebook. Alternatively, create new groups with only one student in each from the old groups. This will mean students repeating the activity to get agreement with a completely new set of people. Finish with a class feedback, telling them that they are now planning a whole-class trip to the festival.

Either in class or for homework, ask students to write about their preferences for a night out in their home town.

E You can now do photocopiable activity 8B to revise the language for showing preferences.

HOMEWORK OPTIONS

Students can do exercise 7 from the Extra practice activities on page 141.

Students do the exercises on page 50 of the Workbook.

8.4 STUDY AND WRITING SKILLS

Lesson topic and staging

This lesson focuses on a study skill, improving memory, and a writing skill, telling a story. At the start of the first section, students test their memory. They extract information from a graph and then look at a text on memory strategies, reading it for gist and for specific information. Finally they discuss the strategies and evaluate their usefulness.

In the second half of the lesson, students begin by talking about legends and stories from their country. They then read a story for gist and study the structure of stories. The text introduces the time expressions which are used when telling a story. Students practise these time expressions and then study the use of adjectives in a story. To conclude, they write a story using the structure they studied, as well as time expressions and adjectives that add interest.

Objectives

By the end of the lesson, students should have:

- discussed and learned more about memory
- extracted information from a graph
- read for gist and specific information
- discussed and evaluated different memory strategies
- studied the structure of stories
- learned and practised the use of time expressions
- studied how adjectives make stories more interesting
- written a story, paying attention to structure, time expressions and adjectives that add interest

Timings

Exercise 3b can be omitted if there is not enough time. Exercise 10 can be given for homework.

Possible lesson break: after exercise 4b.

STUDY SKILLS: improving your memory

Before beginning the tasks, ask students the following questions:

Do you think you have a good memory?

What is your earliest memory? Can you remember your first day at school?

What things are you good at remembering? What things are you bad at remembering?

- Alternatively you can write these on the board and get students to ask each other. When you have done this, ask students what they think the topic of the lesson is.

1 This can be done as a mini-test. Make sure students have a piece of paper and a pen and ask them to write down their answers. Then tell students to compare their answers with a partner. How well have they remembered? Did they think their memory was better than it really is or worse?

2 Ask students to look at the graph on the page. Let them study it for a minute and then elicit from them the information they can get from the graph. Students then do activity as per Coursebook.

(!) Explain that the blue section shows what you remember if you don't review and the purple one what you remember if you review. The horizontal line at the top shows that regular reviews ensure 100% recall.

When students have finished this activity, ask them if they agree with the graph's figures. Why / Why not?

1 about 50%, about 10%; 2 after the first day; 3 review what you learned

3a Ask students to think individually about the methods they use to try and remember things. Encourage them to think about what they use to remember words in the classroom, but also shopping lists, names and addresses, birthdays, etc. Students then share their ideas with partners. As feedback, ask students if they heard any new ideas for remembering things.

3b Students do activity as per Coursebook. Give students no more than 30 seconds.

two – organisation and association

3c Before starting this activity, you may like to elicit the meaning of the following words:

association (n) – memory or feeling that is connected to a particular thing or place

connection (n) – relationship between things

detail (n) – information that helps you to complete what you know about something

- How you do this activity will largely depend on the size and the make-up of your class. If the class is quite small and trustworthy, you can ask the students to work in their pairs through the three activities and then feed back the results as a class.

- However, if you are concerned that the tasks won't be done properly, then divide the text into three parts. Firstly ask students to read down to the end of the yellow box. Then give students a minute to remember the words, cover the box and then another minute to write down as many as they can remember. Students can then compare their answers in pairs. Then ask students to read until the bottom of the blue box. Ask students to classify the words in groups. They then revise for one minute, cover the box and write the words out. They check in their pairs. Can they see any improvement? Finally, students read the section on association. Check that students understand what they are doing and then give them about four minutes to plan their 'scene'. Students then relate it to their partner.

4a Do this activity as a class feedback. Take a vote on which strategy was the most effective for the class. Ask the class if they have any other strategies which you can try out in class.

4b To make this really effective, do this activity at the end of the lesson. Students individually do this activity and can then compare the strategies to see which one worked best for them.

⚠ To make sure students take advantage of these strategies, mention them whenever students need to learn vocabulary, otherwise they will quickly forget them.

WRITING SKILLS: a story

5 Ask the questions to the class as a whole and to individual students. You may like to get some students to tell the stories they know.

6 You may like to pre-teach the following words:

full (adj) – (to refer to the moon) when the moon looks completely round

octopus (n) – a sea creature with a soft body and eight tentacles or arms

gathered (v) – put together in the same place by someone or something

canoe (n) – a long narrow boat that is pointed at both ends

container (n) – what you keep things in, e.g. a box or a bowl

• Give students time to read the text (about four minutes) and then in pairs let them predict the end of the story. Find out their predicted endings in class feedback but do not tell them the ending.

💡 To check they have understood the story so far, you can ask students to tell you the story as a summary which you write up on the board, e.g.:

Who? – Kupe, a great fisherman and chief

Where? – Tahiti

What did they do? – fish

What happened? – octopus eating all fish

What to do? – find and kill octopus

How? – built enormous canoe, loaded with food and water and prepared for a long sea journey

How many people? – 72

How long? – many days and many nights

Why was it failing? – octopus faster than canoe

Kupe's wife? – saw a long island like a cloud, Aotearoa

What then? – landed canoe on east side; chased octopus and fought him

Students then read the end of the story on page 119. Ask them if they were correct in their predictions.

7 Ask students to look at the sections of a story. Check students understand the meaning of *events*. Ask students to work in pairs and assign the headings to the paragraphs. (Tell them that one of the headings will have two paragraphs.) When students have completed this activity and checked, point out that they now have a template to tell their story. Elicit the order from the students and put it on the board:

Background information

First events

Later events

Final events

Result / Conclusion

> **a** 5; **b** 3, 4; **c** 2; **d** 1; **e** 6

8a Students do activity as per Coursebook. Ask students to check with their partners. Elicit from students why we use time expressions (to make the story clearer and more logical). Write up all the time expressions on the board.

> **Answers to 8a and 9a**
> *(time expressions in bold, adjectives underlined)*
> Kupe was a great fisherman and chief who lived on the island of Hawaiiki (Tahiti). **When the moon was full**, Kupe and the other fishermen went out to sea and caught fish. **Usually**, they caught lots of fish, of all colours and sizes.
>
> **One night**, the fishermen did not catch a single fish. They realised that a large octopus was eating all the fish. Kupe gathered his people and told them his plan. 'Without fish we cannot live here. We're going to find this giant octopus and kill it, however long it takes!'
>
> The people built an enormous canoe. **When it was ready**, they loaded it with food and water, and prepared for a long sea journey. In all, there were 72 brave people on board, including Kupe's wife and children.
>
> They chased the sea monster across the endless Pacific Ocean **for many days and nights**, but the octopus was much faster than the canoe. The food and water were running out, and the people were suffering. **Finally, one morning,** Kupe's wife, Hine-te-Aparagi, saw a long cloud in the distance. Land was near! She named the land Aotearoa, land of the long white cloud. Everyone in the boat was amazed by this beautiful new country.
>
> *continued…*

Before long, they landed the canoe on the east coast and collected <u>fresh</u> food and water. **Then**, with <u>fresh</u> energy, they chased the octopus down the east coast. **After some time**, Kupe and his friends entered a <u>dangerous</u> area of water between the north and south islands of Aotearoa and **at last** they caught the octopus. A <u>fierce</u> sea battle began. The octopus smashed its <u>strong</u> arms into the canoe and made a hole in the side of it. **Then** the octopus held the canoe very tightly. It seemed that the end was near for Kupe.

Suddenly, Kupe had an idea. He threw some <u>big</u> water containers into the sea. The octopus thought that the containers were people. It released the canoe and attacked the containers. **At that moment,** Kupe jumped onto the back of the octopus. He raised his <u>sharp</u> knife high into the air. He struck the octopus hard on the head and killed it.

Finally, after a <u>difficult</u> journey of thousands of miles and the defeat of the <u>giant</u> octopus, Kupe's people could settle on this <u>new</u> and <u>wonderful</u> land of two islands, Aotearoa.

8b Students first do the activity individually and then in pairs. Elicit from students why the answer is correct and why the other options are wrong.

E Students can do exercise 8 from the Extra practice activities on page 141 either in class or for homework.

1 Suddenly (this happens quickly, whereas the other expressions refer to things that happen after time has passed);
2 Before long (the answer means 'a short while later', whereas the other options could be a long time later);
3 Soon (the answer means 'after some time', whereas the other answers mean it happens quickly);
4 Finally (the answer means 'after a long time', whereas the other options suggest a short time)

9a Students do activity as per Coursebook.

Answers: see answers for exercise 8a.

9b Elicit from students the meaning of the adjectives in the box before starting the activity. Then students do activity as per Coursebook.

Suggested answers:
1 I saw a giant fish, about three metres long.
2 The brave king fought the fierce dragon.
3 There was a fierce/giant dog at the gate.
4 Twenty brave men and women made the dangerous/difficult journey.
5 We looked for a bridge to cross the dangerous river.

This only touches the issue of using adjectives to make a story interesting. If you have time, build a story on the board without adjectives and then get students to pepper the story with adjectives. The following can be a template for your story:

One day _____
went to _____
and saw _____
He / She / It _____
so _____
At the end _____
and _____
They all lived happily ever after.

10 Students do activity as per Coursebook, either in class or for homework. Whether you or the students check the writing, the important thing is to focus on the structure of the story (exercise 7), time expressions and the use of adjectives.

When the texts have been checked, circulate the stories around the class and have an appreciation session on the stories. Which do students like the best and why?

HOMEWORK OPTIONS

Students do the exercises on page 51 of the Workbook.

Work and industry

9.1 EMPLOYMENT

Lesson topic and staging

At the start of this unit on work and industry, this lesson looks at changes in working conditions and job satisfaction. Students begin by discussing what they look for in a job. They then read for gist and for specific information an email announcing a survey on job satisfaction. Students listen to two of the interviews, listening for gist and for specific information. They finish this section by discussing their opinions about the company and about working in their own country.

Both the listening and the reading provide examples for vocabulary and grammar work. Students study vocabulary connected with work and then revise the use of *used to*. There follows both structural and pronunciation practice of *used to* in all its forms. Students finish by doing a class survey and then a written activity, both using the target structure.

Objectives

By the end of the lesson, students should have:

- talked about important factors in a job
- read for gist and specific information
- listened for gist and specific information
- discussed how they feel about working in a company and in their country
- studied vocabulary connected with work
- revised and practised *used to*
- completed speaking and writing activities using the target structure

Timings

If you feel your students have no pronunciation problems with *use to* and *used to*, you can omit exercises 7a and 7b. Exercise 9 can be given for homework if there is not enough time.

Possible lesson break: after exercise 4.

SPEAKING

Ask students to look at the picture. What job is the man doing? Ask students if they'd like to do this job. Why / Why not?

1 Divide students into small groups. Check they understand the meaning of the following words:

pleasant (adj) – enjoyable, nice and friendly

colleagues (n pl) – people you work with

Students do the activity in groups and then report back. You can summarise the class's opinions on the board. Ask students if there are any other issues that they think are important when looking for a job. Put those on the board too.

READING

2a The reading activity sets the scene for the following listening activity. Students do activity as per Coursebook.

> They want to know how staff think the company has changed in recent years; an external organisation will conduct the research, which will include interviews with the employees.

2b Students do activity as per Coursebook. Check they understand the following words after the activity is completed:

views (n pl) – opinions about something

range (n) – a group of things that are different but generally of the same type

maintain (v) – to make something continue in the same way or at the same standard

> 1, 2 and 3 have misunderstood the email.

LISTENING

2.14–2.15

3a Tell students they are now going to listen to two of the interviews between the management consultants and the Maxicomp employees. Play the recording only once. Students do activity as per Coursebook.

> 1 Rory; 2 Shami

3b Read with the students through the questions. Students work individually to try and answer the questions before listening again. Then, when they have listened, let them check in pairs before doing class feedback.

> 1b; 2a; 3c; 4c

Track 2.14

Consultant, Shami

C: Come in. Hello. It's Shami, isn't it?

S: That's right.

C: OK, let me just have a look at the information here … you work in the Marketing <u>Department</u>?

S: Yeah.

C: And … you've been with the company for six years.

S: That's right.

C: Alright, first of all let's talk about your general feelings about your job. Do you feel the same way now as you did six years ago?

S: Well, no, not really. I mean, I think *I used to be* more enthusiastic. Maybe it's because I'm older now.

C: Well, you're still only 28. That's not exactly old!

S: No, I suppose not.

C: What else has changed?

S: I work longer hours now. When I started, **I didn't use to finish** work so late. Now, I go home after seven nearly every day, but I don't think I really achieve any more.

C: I see. What about the company? Is it helping you to develop new skills?

S: Yes, up to a point. I've done one or two management <u>training course</u>s in the last couple of years. I think I'm ready for <u>promotion</u> now.

C: What about other aspects of the job? Do you get the opportunity to travel much?

S: No, not much. But I don't really mind that. You see, I have to look after my mother and …

Track 2.15

Rory, Consultant

R: Good morning! I'm Rory Carroll.

C: Hello Rory. Have a seat. Well, you seem to have the <u>long</u>est <u>service</u> record – seventeen years!

R: That's right.

C: Well, you're obviously happy here!

R: I am, yes, although *it used to be* more fun.

C: Why's that?

R: Well, it was more sociable. **I used to go out** more with my colleagues, after work and for lunch. When I first started here, we had very long <u>lunch break</u>s, sometimes for two hours. Now it's more like thirty minutes. And we all used the gym together. That doesn't happen much now.

C: **Did you use to <u>work</u>** more <u>as a team</u>?

R: Yes, I suppose we did. It's interesting you mention that. We're more on our own now. **I also used to travel** a lot more too. They've cut down on that.

C: Has anything changed for the better?

R: Yes, there are more opportunities to learn new skills and develop your career. It's more professional now. Also, **they didn't use to pay** you properly. The money's much better now! That's probably why I'm still here!

C: What about yourself? Have you changed at the same time as the company?

R: No, I don't think so. I think I'm pretty much the same person I was all those years ago.

3c Divide students into small groups and ask them to discuss the three questions, then report back for whole-class feedback.

VOCABULARY: work

4 Firstly, ask students to find the words and phrases in the email and the audioscript on page 159 and underline them. Then in pairs, students look at the context and guess their meaning. While they are doing this, write the following sentences on the board:

Everyone in the office hates each other. We don't __ _____. (work as a team)

I'm so hungry. I can't wait for the _____. (lunch break)

Peter is a very valuable member of our _____. (staff)

Before I start work, I have to go on a _____. (training course)

She works in the Sales _____. (Department)

The company bought her a watch for her _____. She joined the company in 1980. (long service)

Steve won the _____ of the Year award. (Employee)

With a 60% market share, the company is the _____. (market leader)

If I work hard, I will get a _____. (promotion)

Ask students to fill in the gaps with the words from the box. When students have completed this, they can write their own sentences to remember the words and phrases.

> **email:** staff, employee, market leader
> For the other words and phrases, see audioscript for Tracks 2.14 and 2.15.

GRAMMAR: *used to*

Students read the description of *used to* and look at the example sentences.

⚠ Students may not understand the difference between past habits and past states. Ask the following questions to help clarify the difference:

In sentence a), did Rory travel a lot? (yes)

Did Rory travel every day? (We don't know but probably not.)

In sentence b), was it fun a lot? (yes)

Was it fun all the time? (yes)

5a Students do activity as per Coursebook. Make sure they note the difference between *used to* and *used*. *Used* is the past simple of *use*, e.g.:

I used to go to a lot of meetings, but I don't anymore.

Michael used my computer yesterday, now it doesn't work properly.

- Students read the grammar note about usage of *used to*. Elicit from students their own examples of *used to* in sentences about themselves.

  Answers: see audioscript for Tracks 2.14 and 2.15 (past habits in bold and past states in italics).

5b Students do activity as per Coursebook. Then write up on the board one of the sentences they produced as part of exercise 5a. Ask them to turn it into a negative sentence, then into a question. Make sure students notice that we drop the *d* from *use<u>d</u> to* as the past tense is shown with the use of the auxiliary verb *did*.

- When you have done this, get students to check they understand with the Language reference on page 142.

  I didn't use to / Did you use to?

E Students can do exercises 1 and 2 from the Extra practice activities on page 143 either in class or for homework.

5c Students do activity as per Coursebook.

  1 didn't use to; **2** use to; **3** used to; **4** use to; **5** used to; **6** didn't use to

6 Students first do this activity individually and then in pairs.

Students use at least three of the verbs to write about themselves. Then students share information and take notes on partners. Finally, students report back to the class what they found out about other students without saying who said it, e.g. *She used to listen to Britney Spears*. Students have to guess who it is from the sentence. Students sometimes forget, in the heat of the activity, that *used to* means they don't do it any more. Remind them of this.

pronunciation

2.16

7a Students do activity as per Coursebook. Make sure students have heard the differences clearly before moving onto the next activity.

  1 /juːst/; **2** /juːs/; **3** /juːs/; **4** /juːz/; **5** /juːzd/; **6** /juːz/

7b Students do the activity first as a class and then individually. You might like students to make their own sentences to show the difference too.

  Track 2.16
  1 She used to work late.
  2 Did you use to go out more with colleagues?
  3 He didn't use to listen to me.
  4 She didn't use the gym every day.
  5 They used their opportunities well.
  6 Did the company use the results of the survey?

SPEAKING

8 Tell students that they are going to do a class survey. Put students into pairs. Student As turn to page 119, Student Bs to page 124. Give students a few minutes to think about the questions they are going to ask. Remind them that they want to ask more than one question to keep the conversation going.

To really make this activity effective, tell students they have to keep the conversation going with a person until the teacher tells them to change partners. Give each conversation one minute before they change partners. If a student didn't use to do any of the things on the list, tell them to try something else.

- When students have done four or five conversations, put them back into their original pairs and they can discuss what they found out. This can finish with a class feedback session.

WRITING

9 This can be done in class or for homework. If done in class, students can write their sentences and not put a name on them. Then collect the sheets of paper and pass them round. Students should read the sheet they've been given and correct any mistakes, then write the name of the student they think it is at the bottom of the sheet.

HOMEWORK OPTIONS

Students do the exercises on pages 52–53 of the Workbook.

You can now do photocopiable activity 9A to practise the vocabulary of job conditions.

9.2 GOLD

IN THIS LESSON

Lesson topic and staging

This lesson focuses on gold and its uses. Students begin by doing a pre-reading activity, discussing what they know or feel about gold. They then read for specific information and also deduce meaning from context. This is followed by a vocabulary section where students discover compound nouns, through examples from the text. Students learn to recognise and create compound nouns. The present simple passive is also introduced through examples from the text. Students learn usage and form and have the opportunity to practise the structure in controlled activities before using it in free practice at the end of the lesson, when they talk about industry in their country.

Objectives

By the end of the lesson, students should have:

- talked about what gold is and how they feel about it
- read for specific information
- read to work out meaning from context
- learned about compound nouns and practised making and using them
- learned about the use and form of the present simple passive and practised the structure
- used the present simple passive to talk about industry in their own country

Timings

Exercise 4 can be given for homework if there is not enough time.

Possible lesson break: after exercise 2c.

READING

1a Students look at the questions in the exercise and discuss them in pairs. Then discuss as a class. You could also ask the following questions:

Is gold expensive?

Why is gold expensive?

1b Students do activity as per Coursebook, individually and then in pairs.

> **3** connectors; in electronics – computers, pocket calculators, washing machines, televisions, recordable CDs, cars, credit cards, spacecraft; teeth, jewellery; **4** gold leaf

1c Give students the opportunity to do the activity before reading again as they may have found some of the answers when reading for the first time. Students do the activity individually and then in pairs.

> **1**b, d, f, g; **2**b,c; **3**a, e; **4**c, f

1d Students do activity as per Coursebook. If students find this difficult, you can give them the paragraph where the word can be found. When they have finished this activity, ask students to create their own sentences using the words to show that they have understood the meaning.

> **1** conducts (paragraph 2); **2** connections (paragraph 2); **3** reliable (paragraph 2); **4** alloy (paragraph 4); **5** decorative (paragraph 5)

VOCABULARY: compound nouns

2a Make sure Coursebooks are closed. Write *compound noun* on the board and ask students if they know what it is. If they don't, tell them that *compound noun*, *bathroom* and *coursebook* are all compound nouns. Students should now be able to tell you what it is. Ask them to open the courseboooks and read the description. Explain that the two nouns in a compound noun can also be joined with a hyphen, e.g. *role-play*. Brainstorm with the class which compound nouns they already know. Try and fill the board with them. Students then do activity as per Coursebook.

> **1** newspaper; **2** video shop; **3** orange juice; **4** chatroom(s); **5** airline, suitcase

2b You can ask your students to add two extra questions using compound nouns before asking and answering the questions in pairs.

⚠ Some students will assume that whenever two nouns are together, they become compound nouns. This is not the case, e.g. *gold wires* or *gold leaf* are not compound nouns. There is no satisfactory answer to this. Compound nouns become so because of the amount of use they have.

⚠ Unfortunately, there is no rule to predict whether a compound noun is written as two words, as in *orange juice*, one word, as in *bedroom*, or hyphenated, as in *role-play*. The only solution is to look up the words in a dictionary such as *Longman Dictionary of Contemporary English*.

2c Students do activity as per Coursebook.

> pocket calculators, credit cards, spacecraft, space shuttle, bathrooms, perfume bottles, glass makers

GRAMMAR: present simple passive

3a This activity is better done with students. Write the three sentences on the board and do tasks 1 and 2 with the class. Ask the question, *Do you think the agent is important?* (no) Then ask students what structure they think this is.

- Students then open their books and read the description of the passive.

> **1** used, mixed, used; **2** no

3b Students do this exercise quickly in pairs then check as a whole class. Make sure they note that the two sentences have the same meaning. The difference is in what the writer wants to emphasise.

> **1**a; **2**b; **3** by

3c Elicit from students the structure for the present passive and write it on the board (subject + *is/are* + past participle [+ *by* + agent]). Ask them to give example sentences. Then do the same with the negative form. You can refer students to the first sentence in exercise 3a for this (subject + *is/are* + *not* + past participle [+ *by* + agent]). Finally do the same for questions and, as before, elicit examples.

> *Is/Are* + subject + past participle (+ *by* + agent)?
> e.g. *Is gold damaged by the environment?*

3d Students do activity as per Coursebook individually and then in pairs.

- Refer students to the Language reference on page 142 if they are having problems recognising and making the passive.

E Students can do exercises 3 and 4 from the Extra practice activities on page 143 either in class or for homework.

> Where is gold used … ? / Gold is used / Why is it used? / it is not damaged / they are used where safety is important. / How is it used? / It is used a wide variety of ways. / very fine gold wires are used to connect / Each piece of wire is made of very pure gold / pure gold is not used / It is mixed with other metals / It is found in bathrooms / it is produced by hand and is used by builders / It is applied to the roofs

4 Students first do the activity individually, and then in pairs.

Refer students to the two sentences in lines 7–12. Point out to students that they are having a process described to them. Ask your students what happens first (oil is found), then what happens (a rig is moved into position) and what happens next (oil from the ground or sea bed is separated into different types of oil). This ties in well with photocopiable activity 9B.

You can ask the following questions to check comprehension:

What is oil made of? (small plants and animals that died millions of years ago)

Where is most of the oil? (the Arab World)

What is moved to collect oil? (a rig)

Where is oil separated? (in a refinery)

How long does it take us to use 18,000 million litres of oil? (two days)

> **1** is made; **2** is found; **3** is moved; **4** is separated; **5** is used; **6** are used

SPEAKING

5 Give students some time to prepare their information before putting them in pairs. This activity will be more enjoyable if you have different nationalities. If your class are all from the same country, then ask them to prepare passive sentences about their country in general, not just about industry.

HOMEWORK OPTIONS

Students do the exercises on pages 54–55 of the Workbook.

You can now do photocopiable activity 9B to revise and practise the present passive.

9.3 SCENARIO: IMPORT-EXPORT

Lesson topic and staging

This lesson looks at import and export and builds up to a task in which students take part in a negotiation. The lesson begins with students discussing the issue of sales and selling. This is followed by a vocabulary activity on key words related to buying and selling. The situation is introduced through a reading activity and students read a short advert for specific information. They then listen to a business negotiation, again for specific information. The recording presents the type of questions asked in a negotiation and the key language for negotiating. Students practise the key language as well as the use of stress when making proposals. Finally, they use the vocabulary, key language and what they learned about stress to conduct a negotiation and make a deal.

Objectives

By the end of the lesson, students should have:

- discussed buying and selling
- learned vocabulary related to buying and selling
- read for gist and specific information
- listened for gist and specific information
- analysed types of sentences used in negotiation
- learned and practised the language of negotiation
- learned about and practised stress in making proposals
- completed a negotiation role-play

Common European Framework

Students can use language effectively to negotiate and make a deal.

Timings

If there is not enough time, exercise 6a can be done for homework providing the lesson finishes at this time.

Possible lesson break: after exercise 3c, 4b or 5.

PREPARATION

1a Make sure students understand the meaning of the following words:

sale (n) – (here) a time when a shop sells its goods at a cheaper price

discount (n) – a reduction in the usual price of something

bargain (n) – something you buy cheaply or for less than its usual price

bargain (v) – to discuss the conditions of a sale to try and get a lower price

- Students work in pairs and discuss the questions. Then do class feedback.

1b Students do activity as per Coursebook. When completed, ask students in pairs to prepare their own example sentences to show they have understood the meaning. This could be done on the board.

> 1 import; 2 exports; 3 manufacturers; 4 buyers; 5 retailers; 6 supply

SITUATION

The initial reading text sets the situation for the listening. Tell students that they will later listen to a negotiation. Before they do this, focus their attention on the introduction (at the top of the page) and the advert. Check they understand the following words:

purchasing (n) – a department in a company that buys things

delivery (n) – when something is taken to a place

2 Give students one minute to read the introduction and the advert and answer the questions.

- You may want to ask the following questions to confirm understanding of the introduction:

  What is being imported? (digital music players)

  Who makes them? (Guangdong Digital)

  Who sells them to shops? (Route One)

  Who are making the negotiation? (Richard Hallows and Lu Han)

  What are their positions in their companies? (Purchasing Manager and Sales Representative)

> 1c; 2 Ontario, Canada; from Asia

3a Students do the activity in pairs.

> 1 Price: B, B, S; 2 Delivery time: B, B, S; 3 Quantity and discounts: S, B, B

`2.17`

3b Students do activity as per Coursebook. They can also check their answers from exercise 3a. Students double-check in pairs and then do class feedback.

> 1
> How much are they per item?
> How much would you like to pay?
> 2
> What's your normal delivery time?
> We need delivery in two weeks. Can you do that?
> 3
> How many would you like to order?
> What discount can you offer?

3c Students read through the information and try and circle the correct details before listening again. There is a good possibility that some of the students are able to answer after one listening and giving them the opportunity to do so will increase their confidence in their listening. You may want to check that students understand the meaning of *quantity*.

- Students then listen and check. They double-check in pairs and discuss the final question together. Then do a class feedback. Ask students for their opinions as to who got the best deal and make sure they give their reasons.

> **1** $100; **2** 5%; **3** 15%; **4** 800; **5** $87; **6** 30 days

---

Track 2.17

Lu Han, Richard

L: So, which of our products are you interested in?

R: OK, well, we're interested in buying some digital music players, the IP4 model. How much are they per item?

L: Let's see. … Yes, they're $100 each.

R: $100? That seems rather high.

L: Really? I see. How much would you like to pay?

R: About 85.

L: I see. Well, I'm not sure that we can go that low, but we can offer you a discount. It depends on the quantity. How many would you like to order?

R: We'd like 500. What discount can you offer?

L: Well, I'm afraid we can only offer a 5 percent discount on 500, but if you order 1,000, we can offer 15 percent.

R: I see. That might be difficult. I'm not sure that we can sell 1,000. What about if we order 750?

L: Well, then we can give you a 10 percent discount.

R: Hmm, that's still a bit low. How about 12.5 percent?

L: 12.5 percent? I'm not sure we can offer that. Although, if you order 800, we can offer 12.5 percent.

R: Hmm, 800, well …

L: It's not very many more, and the discount is good.

R: Well, yes, OK then. We'll order 800.

L: Fine, and we'll give a 12.5 percent discount. So, the final price is $87.50 per item.

R: Shall we call it $87? Keep it a round number? I mean, we hope to buy more in the future …

L: That sounds fine. $87 per item it is, then.

R: Great. Now, what's your normal delivery time?

L: It's usually 30 days after your order.

R: OK, the standard time. Actually, we need delivery in two weeks. Can you do that?

L: Two weeks? No, I'm afraid we can't do that.

R: Really?

L: Really. I'm afraid they won't be ready for delivery by then. Thirty days is the best we can do, I'm afraid.

R: OK, that'll be fine. Perhaps we can change things next time.

L: OK then. So, you order 800 IP4 music players at $87 dollars per item, and we deliver in 30 days. Is that a deal?

R: That's a deal.

L: Excellent. Is there anything else you're interested in? We're offering a great deal on digital cameras at the moment.

R: Really? Oh, what's the deal? If it's a good bargain, I might be interested. Which model …

KEY LANGUAGE: negotiating

2.17

4a Before students listen again, ask them to try and fill in the information themselves. They may remember from previous listening or may already know the answers.

- Students listen again and fill in the missing information, then check in pairs.

> **1** seems; **2** sure; **3** can; **4** if; **5** bit; **6** How; **7** Shall; **8** sounds

4b Students do the activity first individually and then in pairs.

> **a** 3, 4, 6, 7; **b** 1, 2, 5, 8

E Students can do exercise 5 from the Extra practice activities on page 143 either in class or for homework.

💡 Write the following sentences on the board:

$500? That is very / seems rather expensive.

I'm not sure that we can / We can't deliver them by then.

Well, we can / I'm afraid we can only offer a 2.5% discount.

I see. That will / might be difficult.

I'm afraid there's a bit of a / a problem with that.

I think $50 is very / a little low.

Tell students to look at the proposals. Tell students that in English when we make a proposal, we generally use soft and less direct language. Ask them to individually choose the words that make the sentences softer or less direct. Elicit from students why we often use this language in negotiations.

> **1** seems rather; **2** I'm not sure that we can; **3** I'm afraid we can; **4** might; **5** a bit of a; **6** a little
> Softer language makes it less direct and more polite. It suggests that more negotiation can take place. If a direct proposal is made, it suggests there can be no negotiation on the proposal.

pronunciation

2.18

5 Tell students that stress can be very useful in proposals. Elicit from students why this is true (to make your proposals clear). Students work individually and then in pairs to guess which words are stressed. Students then do activity as per Coursebook.

> **1** 5 percent, 500; **2** 1,000, 15 percent; **3** 750

6a Students could do this for homework or in class. If in class, students work together to write the dialogue.

Students can do this in groups on the board if you have a small enough class. Let them write it up. Then identify any mistakes or errors and then give students the chance to correct.

6b Students do the activity in pairs.

TASK: making a deal

7a/b Identify all the Student As and Bs in the class. Then put Student As into groups, and Student Bs in separate groups. Student As turn to page 118, Student Bs turn to page 110. Give students a few minutes to read the text. Then, in their groups, get students to build their own 'Useful Phrases' boxes.

• Put students in pairs. (Note: There is a lot of pairwork in this lesson so you should try and keep changing the pairs to ensure variety.).Then students conduct their negotiation. Walk around listening to each negotiation, taking notes of errors or interesting uses of language, good examples of negotiating, etc. Make a note of the best negotiations. You may like these to be redone in front of the whole class.

• When the task is completed, give feedback and ask students to discuss how their negotiations went.

• Students can then swap roles and do the activity again.

For homework, students can prepare written proposals for their negotiations.

HOMEWORK OPTIONS

Students can do exercises 6 and 7 from the Extra practice activities on page 143.

Students do the exercises on page 56 of the Workbook.

9.4 STUDY AND WRITING SKILLS

IN THIS LESSON

Lesson topic and staging

The study skill practised in this lesson is the ability to give a short talk. The lesson begins with students looking at aspects to think about before giving a talk. They listen to the beginning of a short talk on the history of chocolate in order to identify those specific aspects. Students go on to listen to the main body of the talk, noting specific information as well as phrases used to show progress during the talk. Students find out about what to do when preparing a talk, and finally prepare and give a talk of their own.

In the second half of the lesson, students focus on the writing skill of describing a process. They begin by reading for specific information to identify stages in the process of making chocolate. Students then identify and brainstorm sequencing phrases for describing a process. They also connect their work on passive forms with writing about a process. Finally students prepare and write a description of the process of making tea.

Objectives

By the end of the lesson, students should have:
• identified aspects to think about before giving a talk
• listened for specific information
• identified sequencing phrases in a talk
• thought about what to do when preparing a talk
• prepared, given and evaluated a talk
• analysed the written description of a process
• identified and brainstormed sequencing phrases for writing
• connected simple passive with describing a process
• written a description of a process

Timings

Exercise 8 could be given for homework if there is not enough time.

Possible lesson break: after exercise 4b.

STUDY SKILLS: giving a short talk

Before starting this section, ask students to discuss the following in pairs:

Have you ever listened to a talk?

Where was it?

Who was giving the talk?

What was the topic?

Was it a good talk?

Why was it a good talk / bad talk?

If you had given the talk what would you have done differently?

- Then let students share their ideas in a quick classroom feedback session.

2.19

1 Read through the scene-setting introduction with the students. Read the questions carefully and elicit possible answers to each one. Students then listen to the beginning of the talk and check in pairs. Do a class feedback.

> **1** a tour of a chocolate factory (mainly the history of chocolate); **2** to inform visitors to the chocolate factory; **3** tourists, a mixture of foreigners and native speakers; **4** about ten minutes

> **Track 2.19**
>
> *Louise, Visitors*
>
> L: Good morning everyone. Welcome to Cadbury World. My name's Louise and I'm your guide this morning. OK, let's see where everybody comes from today. Put your hands up if you're from the UK. Uh-huh. Anyone from Birmingham?
>
> V1: Yes!
>
> L: Good to see one or two locals. Alright, so the rest of you are visitors from abroad? And where are you from?
>
> V2: From the US, Florida.
>
> V3: I'm French.
>
> V4: Spain.
>
> V5: Japan.
>
> V6: We're from Turkey.
>
> L: Oh, I had a lovely holiday there last year. Anyway, it looks like we've got quite a lot of foreign visitors today. Now, has anyone been here before? No, OK, so it's everybody's first time. Alright, your tour this morning will last about one hour. First of all, I'm going to tell you a few key things about the history of chocolate, then I'll say a little bit about the company and after that I'll say a few words about how chocolate is made. All that will take about ten minutes. Then we'll go round the factory. How does that sound?
>
> V7: Good. Will we taste any chocolate?
>
> L: Oh yes. Don't worry about that. There'll be a chance to taste some of our delicious products at the end!

2.20

2a Tell students that they are now going to listen to the main body of the talk. Read through the gapped text to begin with. Students can try and predict which answer will go in the gaps. Let them listen individually and then check with a partner.

> **1** 600; **2** drink; **3** Mexico City; **4** 1517; **5** 1528; **6** rich people; **7** 100 years; **8** secret; **9** houses; **10** cheaper

> **Track 2.20**
>
> *Louise, Visitors*
>
> L: OK. So, let's look at the history of chocolate. To start with, does anybody know where chocolate first came from?
>
> V8: From Latin America, I think.
>
> L: Yes, that's right. It was the Mayans (who lived in what's now Central America and Mexico) who first discovered the delights of chocolate in about 600AD. They found that they could make a delicious drink from roasted cocoa beans. Do all our foreign visitors know the meaning of roasted?
>
> V3: Cooked in an oven.
>
> L: Exactly. The Mayans called their chocolate drink chocolatl. It was a real luxury because cocoa beans were very valuable. In fact, people sometimes used to give them as presents, or even used them as money. Soon, chocolatl spread to the Aztec civilisation around modern Mexico City. In 1517, the Spaniard Hernán Cortés arrived in Mexico. He travelled to meet the Aztec emperor, Moctezuma, who introduced Cortés to his favourite drink – chocolatl. They served the drink to Cortés in a cup made of gold. If you look at the slide, you can see them drinking together.
>
> When Cortés returned to Spain in 1528, he loaded his ships with cocoa beans and equipment for making the chocolate drink. Soon chocolate became a popular drink with rich people in Spain. But it took nearly 100 years for the news of cocoa and chocolate to spread across Europe, as the Spanish kept it a secret. In the 17th century, chocolate houses – like coffee shops today – became popular in London and other European cities. But it wasn't until the 19th century that chocolate became cheaper and available to a large percentage of the population. Also in the 19th century, they found a way to make chocolate hard, solid – to make the eating chocolate we love today! So, that was a very brief history of chocolate. To sum up, it started as a drink in Central America, it came to Europe with the Spanish, it spread slowly across the continent and finally became something a lot of people could afford to eat.
>
> Now, I know you're all very keen to start the tour, but let's turn now to the company just for a minute …

2b Tell students that when someone is giving a talk, it helps listeners if the speaker uses phrases that show where they are in the talk. These are called 'sequencing phrases'. Ask students to look at the audioscript on page 160 and identify the sequencing phrases for the four steps in exercise 2b.

> **1** To start with; **2** So, that was a very brief history of chocolate; **3** To sum up; **4** let's turn now to

2c Students do activity as per Coursebook.

> **1** First, I'd like to talk about / Let me begin by *-ing* / I'd like to start by *-ing*
> **2** That's all I want to say about
> **3** To summarise, / In conclusion, / To conclude,
> **4** Turning now to

3   Students do activity as per Coursebook. They should then, in pairs, think about how useful each point is for preparing a talk and make suggestions of their own.

> **1** information; **2** order; **3** notes; **4** charts; **5** pronunciation; **6** Practise

4a Students should prepare their talk individually for about ten minutes. Walk round the class helping students as and when necessary.

(!) Students naturally think they should write the whole talk out on paper. This is inadvisable because a) it takes much longer and b) it will not sound natural when given. Encourage your students to only make notes when preparing the talk. You could offer them the following simple template:

INTRODUCTION:

   Topic sentence

   Supporting statement

   Key points (maximum 3)

BODY:

   Point 1:

   Point 2:

   Point 3:

CONCLUSION:

4b Put students in groups where they give their talks while the rest of the group evaluates according to the six criteria. Students give feedback after each talk and you can check further in class feedback.

(☼) Students can vote for the best talk in the group to be given to the whole class.

WRITING SKILLS: describing a process

Explain to students that describing a process in writing is similar to giving a spoken talk.

5   Students first predict by looking at the pictures and then check by reading. You may need to check they understand the following words:

pod (n) – the long green part of a plant which the seeds grow in

split (v) – tear or break into more than one piece

pile (n) – a lot of similar things put on top of each other

spread out (v) – to arrange a group of things so that they cover a flat surface

> **1**D; **2**A; **3**E; **4**B; **5**C

6a Explain that the sequencing phrases in writing are similar to those in speaking but not exactly the same. Elicit from students the sequencing phrases they used when giving a talk, then let them do the activity as per Coursebook.

6b Students work in groups to brainstorm any other sequencing phrases they know.

(E) Students can do exercise 8 from the Extra practice activities on page 143 either in class or for homework.

7   Students read the first sentence of the instructions. Quickly revise the passive with students so that they are all in tune before completing the activity.

> **Answers to 6a and 7**
> *(sequencing phrases underlined, passive forms in bold)*
> To begin with, cocoa pods **are cut** from cocoa trees with large knives, taking care not to damage nearby flowers. The women of the family collect the pods in large baskets, which they carry on their heads. Next, the pods **are split open** with a knife and the beans **are removed**. Following this, a pile of wet cocoa beans **is put** on banana leaves, which **are spread out** in a circle on the ground. More leaves **are put** on top to cover the pile. After five to six days, the wet mass of beans **is dried** in the sun. Lastly, the beans **are put** into sacks for transport all over the world.

8   This can be done either in class or for homework. Writing on the board in groups would work very well with this activity.

> **Suggested answer:**
> To begin with, tea plants are grown in special beds for about a year. After that, they are planted in the tea fields. After about four years, the tea plants are picked by hand. Following this, the leaves are dried for 10 to 20 hours. Lastly, the leaves are crushed in a machine.

HOMEWORK OPTIONS

Students do the exercises on page 57 of the Workbook.

Review

GRAMMAR

1

> 1b; 2c; 3a; 4b; 5a; 6c; 7b; 8a; 9c; 10c

2

> 1 used to; 2 couldn't; 3 had to; 4 didn't use to

VOCABULARY

3a

> 1 commit, solve; 2 evidence, fingerprints;
> 3 colleague, employee, staff; 4 doze, sleep in

3b

> They are all scientific subjects that people can
> study.

4

> 1 history of; 2 interested in; 3 relationship with;
> 4 happen to; 5 belong to; 6 successful in

KEY LANGUAGE

2.21

5

> Anna would like to do something active. Rob
> would rather go to a concert.

6

> 1c; 2h; 3l; 4b; 5j; 6e; 7a; 8g; 9k; 10f; 11m; 12d; 13i

Track 2.21
Anna, Rob
A: I'm bored. Let's go out this evening.
R: OK. I'd love to go to the theatre. I haven't been for ages.
A: I'm not sure about that. I'm not that keen on the theatre. What's on?
R: There's a play by David Mamet. The tickets are £20, £25 or £30.
A: Oh, that seems a bit high to me, for a play in our local theatre.
R: Well, what would you prefer to do?

continued…

A: Mmm, I'm more interested in something active. I think I'd rather go dancing.
R: I don't fancy dancing. I'd prefer to go to a concert.
A: A concert? OK, let's see what's on. But what about if we go dancing at the weekend?
R: I don't know. Look, why don't you go dancing with your friends at the weekend?
A: But I'd rather go with you.
R: If you go with your friends, I'll cook a really nice dinner for us on Sunday.
A: OK, that sounds fine!

LANGUAGE CHECK

7

> 1 You don't have **to** study medicine to be a psychologist.
> 2 The science building is separate **from** the main school.
> 3 We belong **to** a classical music group.
> 4 They had **to** solve the crime very quickly.
> 5 I usually **fall** asleep very quickly when I go to bed.
> 6 When are you going **to** start the course?
> 7 Would you prefer **to** see a film or a play?
> 8 We didn't use **to** take long lunch breaks.
> 9 Silver **is** used in a lot of jewellery.
> 10 The prices seem a bit high to me.

LOOK BACK

8 Students do the exercise in small pairs or groups.

- listen to an interview with a forensic scientist: 7.1, exercise 4;
- learn the names of some scientific subjects: 7.2, exercise 1;
- describe a chart about UK examinations: 7.4, exercise 10;
- listen to a talk about sleep: 8.1, exercise 3;
- plan a night out: 8.3, exercise 7;
- write a short story: 8.4, exercise 10;
- talk about what classmates used to do: 9.1, exercise 8;
- read about the uses of gold: 9.2, exercise 1;
- give a short talk: 9.4, exercise 4

10 Global affairs

10.1 UNITED NATIONS

IN THIS LESSON

Lesson topic and staging

The unit is about global affairs and this lesson looks at the work of the United Nations and in particular that of the Secretary General of the UN. Students begin by discussing what they already know about the organisation, then check by listening for specific information. This is a followed by an entry from an encyclopaedia, focussing more narrowly on the Secretary General, which students read for gist and for specific information. Students hear another recording, listening again for specific information. The listening section is followed by vocabulary work on organisations and positions in organisations, and then by the grammar presentation. Examples from the recording are used to revise the present continuous for future arrangements. Students practise with an information gap activity. To conclude, they do a speaking and writing activity about what others in the class plan for the following week, using the target structure.

Objectives

By the end of the lesson, students should have:

- discussed and learned more about the United Nations
- listened for specific information
- read for gist and specific information
- studied words to describe organisations and positions in organisations
- revised and practised the present continuous for future arrangements
- completed speaking and writing activities using the present continuous

Timings

Exercise 7b can be done for homework if there is not enough time.

Possible lesson break: after exercise 3b.

SPEAKING

1a Ask the students the first question before they open their book. Write up the information on the board. Then turn to page 84 and let students work in pairs to answer the questions.

`2.22`

1b Students do activity as per Coursebook. Play the recording once and then students can check in pairs before you do class feedback.

> **1** 24 October 1945; **2** 191; **3** New York; **4** the incumbent at the time of writing is from South Korea; **5** religious education and entertainment

> **Track 2.22**
> Fifty countries founded the United Nations after the Second World War, on the 24th of October 1945, to be exact. After such a terrible war, they founded the UN in order to maintain world peace and security, to develop friendly relations between countries and to improve living conditions and human rights across the world. There are now 191 countries in the UN, that's nearly every country in the world, and representatives from these countries meet at the UN headquarters in New York.
> For most people, the Secretary General of the UN is the face of this massive organisation. The Secretary General is the person that we usually see on the television news when the UN does something important. Over the years, the Secretary General has come from many different countries, such as Egypt, Peru and Sweden. The current Secretary General is from South Korea.
> The UN works in a wide range of areas, with a general aim to improve the lives of ordinary people and to keep peace in the world. For example, the UN helps refugees, helps the economic development of poorer countries and runs the court of International Justice. Two areas that the UN is not involved in are entertainment and religious education.

READING

2a Tell students they are now going to find out some more information about the United Nations. Give students no more than 30 seconds to get the gist of the text and answer the question.

> **3** the Secretary General and his/her department

2b Allow students to predict the answers before doing the activity. Otherwise do activity as per Coursebook.

> **1** does not say; **2** true; **3** does not say; **4** true; **5** false; **6** true; **7** false

i Under the Charter, the Secretary General is appointed by the General Assembly upon the recommendation of the Security Council. The Secretary General at the time of writing is Ban Ki-moon (South Korea). His recent predecessors include Kofi Annan (Ghana – January 1996 to December 2006); Boutros Boutros-Ghali (Egypt, January 1992 – December 1996); Javier Pérez de Cuéllar (Peru – January 1982 to December 1991).

LISTENING

Read the introductory sentence with the students. Ask students the following questions:

How busy do you think the Secretary General is?

What activities do you think a Secretary General does in a typical week?

`2.23`

3a Students do activity as per Coursebook. Play the recording only once. If you have strong students, you can also ask them who the meetings are with.

> four: the Syrian foreign minister, the Ambassador from the Congo, the President of the Security Council and the Brazilian President

3b Let students look through the questions and predict the answers as they have already listened once. Then they do the activity as per Coursebook.

> **1** Monday 11.15 a.m.; **2** Ambassador from the Congo; **3** Development Committee; **4** President of the Security Council; **5** Empire State Building, to hold a press conference with the Messengers of Peace; **6** Brazilian President

Track 2.23

Beth, Vihn

B: Hi there, Vihn. How are you?

V: Hi Beth. I'm fine thanks. You alright?

B: Yeah, fine. Are you ready to update the website? I've got the Secretary General's schedule for next week here.

V: Sure. Fire away. What's he doing on Monday?

B: Well, actually, he isn't doing anything early in the morning, but at 11.15 a.m. he's meeting the Syrian foreign minister.

V: Sorry, which minister? My computer wasn't quite ready.

B: Or you weren't listening! The foreign minister. Of Syria.

V: Fine. Got that now. Anything after that?

B: Yep. At four o'clock he's meeting the Ambassador from the Congo. And that's it for Monday. Ready for Tuesday? Or are you still waiting for the computer to catch up?

V: Sure, I'm ready. You can go as fast as you want now.

B: OK, so, at ten he's giving a statement to the Development Committee, about the UN's plans for next year. Then, after lunch, he's seeing the President of the Security Council. The meeting is at three, and it'll probably be a long one, so he's not meeting anyone else that day.

V: Sure thing. Wednesday?

B: Yes, Wednesday, well, we've organised the morning, but we're not sure about the afternoon.

V: Fine, tell me about the morning now and we'll do the rest later.

continued…

B: Well, in the morning he's going to the Empire State Building where he's holding a press conference with the Messengers of Peace.

V: What time exactly? I can't really just say 'in the morning'!

B: Oh sorry, I thought I said. That's at 10.30.

V: Uh-huh. Fine. The press conference sounds a good idea. It'll get some publicity.

B: We hope so. Anyway, after that, at midday he's meeting the Brazilian President to discuss the rain forest protection plan.

V: Fine. Got that. What's next?

B: Well, that's what we're not sure about because on Thursday he's travelling to Europe. Before that, he might meet his assistants who are travelling with him, or he might phone the British Prime Minister. He's going to decide tomorrow. So, I'll update you then.

V: OK. Well, I'll put up the information that you've already given me, and then add that extra information tomorrow. How long is he staying in Europe?

B: Two weeks, and you won't need to put up the daily schedule while he's away.

V: Fine, I've got plenty of stuff to do anyway. Erm, may I ask, what are you doing tonight?

B: Oh, I'm going out for dinner with my husband, there's a new restaurant that's opened near us.

V: Oh, your husband …

B: Yes. Why did you ask?

V: Oh, no reason. Have a nice evening.

B: Thank you, you too. Are you doing anything?

V: No, no, a quiet night in for me.

B: OK then, well, talk to you again when the SG returns.

V: Sure, bye.

B: Bye.

VOCABULARY: people and organisations

4a Tell students to look at the words in the box. Explain that they describe organisations and people/positions in organisations. Students do the activity as per Coursebook, individually and then in pairs.

> **A** ambassador, assistant, civil servant, head of a department, minister, president, spokesperson
> **B** committee, department, staff

4b Students do activity as per Coursebook for the first part. For the second part, students work in pairs to make definitions, then nominate students to write definitions on the board. Give other students the opportunity to correct or improve the definitions on the board.

> **1** committee; **2** minister; **3** department;
> **4** spokesperson; **5** assistant
>
> **Possible definitions:**
> *ambassador*: someone who represents his/her country abroad
> *civil servant*: someone who works for the government
> *head of a department*: someone who is the boss of part of a company or organisation
> *president*: the most important person in a company or organisation
> *staff*: the people who work for a company or organisation

GRAMMAR: present continuous for future arrangements

(!) This should be merely revision for most students.

5   Ask students to keep their books closed. Write sentences a), b) and c) on the board and put questions 1 and 2 to them. Try and elicit the information in the grammar tip, which they should already know. They can then open their books and check by reading the description.

•   If students have trouble understanding the use of present continuous for future arrangements, they can look up the Language reference on page 144.

(E) Students can do exercises 1 and 2 from the Extra practice activities on page 145 either in class or for homework.

> **1** future; **2c**

6   Read the instructions together with the class. Before putting students into pairs, brainstorm as a class the sort of questions that students could ask, e.g. *What's Jane doing Wednesday? Who is Jane meeting on Monday?*, etc.

Then put students in pairs and allocate Student As and Bs. Student As turn to page 120, Bs to page 123. Give students two minutes' preparation time before they begin.

SPEAKING AND WRITING

7a To do this activity begin by putting students in pairs. Then after a minute change the pairs. Keep doing this until most of the students have met each other. Then check the information with the class as a whole.

7b This activity could be done in class or for homework. If in class, students would need about 15 minutes' writing time. Then pass the sheets of paper around for other students to correct and give feedback.

HOMEWORK OPTIONS

Students can do exercise 6 from the Extra practice activities on page 145.

Students do the exercises on pages 58–59 of the Workbook.

10.2 BIG BUSINESS

IN THIS LESSON

Lesson topic and staging

The focus of this lesson is 'Big Business'. Students begin by talking about large companies. They then read a text about the history of Microsoft, identifying gist and specific information, and deducing the meaning of new words from context. The text provides the examples for the introduction of the past passive, which students learn and practise. They listen to a recording, identifying specific information as well as the past passive structure. Finally students have another opportunity to discuss issues related to big business.

Objectives

By the end of the lesson, students should have:

- discussed big companies
- read for gist and specific information
- guessed the meaning of unknown words from context
- learned and practised the past passive
- listened for specific information
- discussed the role of big companies

Timings

You may wish to omit exercise 8 if there is not enough time or replace it with the option. Exercise 7 could be done for homework.

Possible lesson break: after exercise 5b.

SPEAKING

1 Students do activity as per Coursebook.

> BP (British Petroleum) – oil, natural gas and petrol – UK
> Coca-Cola – soft drinks – USA
> Fiat – cars – Italy
> Google – search engine – USA
> Honda – cars – Japan
> IBM – computers – USA
> McDonald's – fast food – USA
> Nestlé – food (milk, chocolate, coffee) – Switzerland
> Nintendo – games – Japan
> Nokia – mobile phones – Finland
> Philips – TVs, phones, coffee makers, lights – the Netherlands
> Samsung – electronic products – Korea
> Shell – oil, natural gas and petrol – the Netherlands and UK
> Sony – electronic goods, games, media – Japan

READING

2a Students do activity as per Coursebook. Give the students no more than two minutes to do this otherwise they'll read too intensively.

> In 1975, Microsoft concentrated on selling computers and software to businesses but then changed its focus from business to the consumer.

2b Before beginning this exercise, make sure students understand the meaning of *noughties* (2000–2009). Then students do activity as per Coursebook.

> 1970s: 5; 1980s: 2; 1990s: 1, 3, 6; 2000s: 4, 7

3 Before starting this exercise, remind students that to find a meaning from context, they should first identify the type of word they are looking for. Students do activity as per Coursebook and then check their answers in pairs before doing class feedback. Then ask students to construct their own example sentences to show they have understood the meaning.

🔧 Students may find this type of activity too difficult. If so, you could give them the paragraph where the word can be found, e.g. the answers to 1–4 are all in the first paragraph. Don't just give the answers jumbled up, as this would be too easy.

> 1 belief; 2 software; 3 concentrated; 4 campus; 5 slogan; 6 launched/released

4 Have a short class discussion on this question. Ask students if they think such a strong company in an industry is a good thing. Then ask if anyone knows what Bill Gates does with all his money. (He sets up charities and gives away large amounts of money to projects to help people.) Ask students if they think this justifies one person having so much power.

ⓘ How Bill Gates spends his money: In 2000 he founded the Bill & Melinda Gates Foundation. This charitable organisation has funded school scholarships for under-represented minorities (including a 210 million dollar donation to the University of Cambridge). The fund has also donated over seven billion dollars to various causes.

GRAMMAR: past simple passive

Before starting this section, make sure students' Coursebooks are closed. Then write up the three example sentences from page 86 on the board. Ask students for each sentence *What happened?*, *Who did it?* Elicit from students the structure (past simple passive) and ask them which of the two questions we asked for each sentence is more important (*What happened?*). Then open the books at page 86 and go through the introduction.

5a Students do activity as per Coursebook individually and then check in pairs.

> Microsoft was set up in Albuquerque / The two men were guided by a belief / the company was criticised / Microsoft Encarta was launched / the first encyclopaedia that was designed to run on a computer / The company slogan was also changed / Windows 95 was released / more than a million copies were sold in the first four days / MSN, the Microsoft Network online service, was also launched / Microsoft was named the company / Gates's book *Business @ the Speed of Thought* was published / Windows XP was released worldwide / Plans were announced to develop the campus in Redmond / Microsoft Windows Vista was launched

5b Once students have read the instructions, take two of the example sentences and write them on the board. Ask students to change them into negatives and questions, then elicit the form for both.

(E) Students can do exercises 3 and 4 from the Extra practice activities on page 145 either in class or for homework.

> **Negative:** subject + *wasn't/weren't* + past participle
> **Question:** *Was/Were* + subject + past participle + *?*

6a This follows on directly from building the question in the previous exercise. Students do activity as per Coursebook individually. Do not check their answers.

`2.24`

6b Students do activity as per Coursebook and then double-check in pairs. Do not play the recording more than once.

> **Answers:** see audioscript for Track 2.25 (the questions are underlined).

`2.25`

6c Students do activity as per Coursebook. Then ask students the following questions:
Is there anything you find surprising in this story?
What else do you know about Fiat?

(i) Six more facts about Fiat:
- One of the founders of Fiat was Giovanni Agnelli. The Agnellis still control much of the company.
- Fiat also used to build planes.
- Fiat have won 'Car of the Year' 11 times.
- The famous Italian moped, Vespa, is made by Fiat.
- Fiat is based in Turin.
- Fiat owns Ferrari and has a strong connection with Juventus football club.

> **1** 1899, in Turin, in Italy; **2** on the roof of the factory; **3** in the mid 1920s; **4** *La Stampa*; **5** a lot of services for employees, e.g. health care, schools, sports clubs and holiday camps for children; **6** France, Spain and Poland

> **Tracks 2.24 and 2.25**
> Q: When was Fiat set up?
> A: It was set up in 1899, in Turin, in Italy. The first factory was opened in 1900. One hundred and fifty workers were employed there and they produced 24 cars. At the time, Italy had a population of 32 million people and most of them worked in farming. This was an exciting period in history: cinema and radio were invented around this time too.
> Q: Where were cars tested in the early years?
> A: On the roof of the factory! The Fiat factory at Lingotto was completed in 1922. It was the largest in Europe and had five floors. On the roof there was a track where cars were tested.
> Q: When were car adverts aimed at women for the first time?
> A: In the mid 1920s. Standards of living were rising and changes in society were occurring.
> Q: Which newspaper was bought by Fiat in 1926, *Corriere della Sera* or *La Stampa*?
> A: *La Stampa*. It means 'The Press' in Italian. It's a newspaper from Turin, but people read it in other parts of Italy, too.
> Q: What was set up in the late 1920s?
> A: A lot of services for employees, for example, health care, schools, sports clubs and holiday camps for children. Other companies soon copied these ideas. Some of the services are still active today.
> Q: Where were Fiat cars constructed in the early 1930s?
> A: Fiat increased its activities abroad at this time and cars were constructed in France, Spain and Poland. The company also opened a bank in Berlin.

7 This activity could be done in class or for homework. If in class, students do activity as per Coursebook, individually and then in pairs.

> **1** was set up; **2** sold; **3** grew; **4** moved;
> **5** were created; **6** developed; **7** was produced;
> **8** were exported; **9** put; **10** were introduced;
> **11** died; **12** became

SPEAKING

8 Students discuss these questions and then give feedback to the whole class.

☀ You could turn exercise 8 into a debate. Turn one of the questions into a sentence, e.g. *Big companies have too much power*. Divide your class into two groups (you may need to run two debates and therefore four groups if you have a big class). One group will support the motion and the other group will be against it. Tell students they will work to the following format:

Stage 1: Each group states its position (agree or disagree and introduce the three arguments it will use).

Stage 2: The 'For' group and the 'Against' group present one argument and answer questions.

Stage 3: The groups present their second argument and answer questions.

Stage 4: The groups present their third argument and answer questions.

Stage 5: Each group presents its conclusions.

Assign at least one student to each stage and give students 15–20 minutes to prepare. Then run the debate and afterwards have a free class vote to decide on the winner.

E You can now do photocopiable activity 10A to practise the past passive.

HOMEWORK OPTIONS

Students do the exercises on pages 60–61 of the Workbook.

10.3 SCENARIO: AN OLYMPIC BID

IN THIS LESSON

Lesson topic and staging

In this lesson, students look at the Olympic Games, specifically preparing an Olympic bid. Students begin the lesson by discussing Summer Olympics in general. This is followed by a listening task on the London bid to host the Olympics. Students listen to the recording for gist and for specific information and then identify how adverbs and adjectives are used to provide emphasis. They also look at the use of pausing and stress for emphasis. Finally, students put this knowledge in practice in the concluding task, preparing and giving a presentation for an Olympic bid.

Objectives

By the end of the lesson, students should have:

- talked about the Summer Olympics
- listened for gist and for specific information
- learned about and practised the use of *just* and *only* for emphasis
- learned about and practised the use of adjectives for emphasis
- learned about and practised the use of pause and stress for emphasis
- completed a presentation, using emphasising language and techniques

Common European Framework

Students can use language effectively to give a clear prepared presentation on a familiar topic.

Timings

Exercises 1b, 5c and/or 8 can be omitted if there is not enough time.

Possible lesson break: after exercise 4 or 5c.

SITUATION

1a Discuss with your students as a group. You can also ask them about famous athletes from their country who have taken part in the Olympics.

1b Before starting, check that students understand the meaning of the verb *to host*. Students work individually and then in pairs before checking. Are they surprised? Ask students which city from their own country (but not in the list) they would recommend for the Olympics and why.

i Cities which have hosted the Summer Olympics: Athens 1896, Paris 1900, St Louis 1904, London 1908, Stockholm 1912, Antwerp 1920, Paris 1924, Amsterdam 1928, Los Angeles 1932, Berlin 1936, London 1948, Helsinki 1952, Melbourne 1956, Rome 1960, Tokyo 1964, Mexico City 1968, Munich 1972, Montreal 1976, Moscow 1980, Los Angeles 1984, Seoul 1988, Barcelona 1992, Atlanta 1996, Sydney 2000, Athens 2004, Beijing 2008, London 2012

The three cities are Madrid, New York and Osaka.

`2.26`

2a Before starting the activity, ask the following questions:

How does a city get chosen for the Olympics?

What resources does a city need to host Olympic Games?

- Then students do activity as per Coursebook. Play the recording only once.

1d; 2b; 3c; 4a

2b Before starting this activity, you can check understanding of the following words:

inspire (v) – to encourage someone by making them feel confident to do something

memorable (adj) – very good, enjoyable or unusual and worth remembering

venue (n) – place where a meeting, concert, etc. takes place

existing (adj) – present or being used now

aquatic (adj) – involving or happening in water

spacious (adj) – large, with plenty of space

comprehensive (adj) – including all necessary facts, details or facilities

(!) It is important to pre-teach the adjectives as students will spend more time on these later.

- Let students initially try and answer from the one listening they already have done for exercise 2a. Then do activity as per Coursebook. Let students check answers in pairs before doing class feedback.

1 true; 2 false; 3 true; 4 false; 5 false; 6 false; 7 true; 8 true

Tracks 2.26 and 2.27

1
First, we want to deliver a magical experience, an electrifying atmosphere for competitors and spectators. Our aim is to inspire young people in Britain and across the world to play sport. We will do whatever we can to inspire children to choose sport, wherever they live, whatever they do, whatever they believe. These will be a memorable Games. A Games that will inspire young people to believe in the Olympic ideal.

2
And that magic begins with the venues. We'll use existing world-class venues, spectacular city centre locations, and most importantly, we'll create an Olympic Park which is just seven minutes from the centre of London. In the Olympic Park there'll be a magnificent 80,000-seat Olympic stadium and a fantastic aquatic centre for the swimming events. Half of the venues will be only five minutes from the athletes' accommodation and only ten per cent will be more than twenty minutes away.

3
The Olympic Park will contain the Olympic village; we'll put athletes at the heart of the games. There'll be 8,000 double rooms and this accommodation will be modern, spacious and comfortable. Athletes will be just a short walk from the main stadium. They'll be at the centre of the Olympic experience.

4
The Olympic Park will be only seven minutes from Central London by train via a new high-speed train service. Nine other railway and underground lines will form the basis of a comprehensive public transport system serving every venue. A special Olympic bus service will provide quick and easy journeys between venues. Finally, we'll give free public transport to all athletes, officials and spectators.

KEY LANGUAGE: adding emphasis

`2.27`

3a Give students a chance to try and remember the answers before doing the activity as per Coursebook. When completed, ask students to guess why these words are being used.

1 just; 2 only; 3 Only; 4 just; 5 only

Track 2.27
See audioscript for Track 2.26.

3b Read through the explanation with students and let them answer the question.

positive

4 Tell students that adjectives can also be used to show emphasis. Check first that they understand the meaning of all the adjectives in the activity. Do the recall activity together as a class. Then let them check the audioscript on pages 161–162 in pairs. Do class feedback, then let them find other adjectives in the text. Elicit from students why adjectives give emphasis (because an adjective provides more information about a noun, thus giving it more focus, e.g. a *bright red car* versus *a car*).

E Students can do exercise 5 from the Extra practice activities on page 145 either in class or for homework.

> **1** magical experience, memorable Games (electrifying); **2** world-class venues, magnificent 80,000 seat stadium (spectacular, fantastic); **3** modern and comfortable accommodation (spacious); **4** high-speed train service, comprehensive public transport system (special, quick, easy, free)

pronunciation
2.28

5a Read through the instructions. Make sure students understand what *pause* and *stress* are. Give them an example. Ask them whether pauses and stress are used in talks or presentations in their language (mostly, yes) and discuss occasions (e.g. political speeches, lectures, sales presentations). Elicit from students why particular words are stressed (because they give extra information, are key to persuading people or are emotionally loaded).

5b Drill as a whole class and individually.

> **Track 2.28**
> First, // we want to deliver // a magical experience, // an electrifying atmosphere // for competitors and spectators. // Our aim // is to inspire young people // in Britain // and across the world // to play sport.

5c Give students time to think about this and then put students in pairs to work with each other. Then do class feedback.

6 Students need time to prepare their thoughts before doing this activity. Give them about five minutes' preparation time on their own., then put them into pairs to practise together. Make sure they concentrate on how they say things rather than on how much they can say.

TASK: making a presentation

7a Read through the instructions together with the students. You may like to check understanding with the following questions:

What are the IOC choosing?
How many choices are there?
Who is going to prepare the presentation?

- Then look at the OTHER USEFUL PHRASES box with the students, making sure they understand how the language will be used (to mark the stages of the presentation). They can also use this language as prompts for their notes as they prepare. Brainstorm any other language structures they might need.

- Divide students into groups and then into pairs within the groups. Pair As then turn to page 122, Bs to page 125 and Cs to page 120. Give them about 10–15 minutes' preparation time. Remind them that they will be expected to use adverbs, adjectives, pausing and stress to show emphasis and failure to do so may affect their chances of success.

- As students are preparing, walk around, monitor and make sure they all take part. You may decide to allocate different speakers to sections of the presentation so both members of the pairs speak.

7b Make sure students understand that they will have to give feedback on other people's presentation under the headings shown. You can also tell them they will be expected to ask questions. Once all the presentations are finished, you can then have a feedback / question and answer session where students use their notes

7c Have a quick initial ideas session.

8 In their groups, students decide on the best city for the Olympics, based on the notes they have taken. Make sure they know they cannot vote for their own city. Each group then presents its decisions. Finally have a free class vote to see which city wins.

For homework, students can prepare a final report on why they chose a city.

E You can now do photocopiable activity 10B to practise Adding Emphasis phrases and the OTHER USEFUL PHRASES of this lesson. It also allows some practice of present continuous for future arrangements.

HOMEWORK OPTIONS

Students can do exercise 7 from the Extra practice activities on page 145.

Students do the exercises on page 62 of the Workbook.

10.4 STUDY AND WRITING SKILLS

IN THIS LESSON

Lesson topic and staging

The study skill practised in the first half of this lesson is how to improve listening ability. Students begin by looking at the difference between listening for the general idea (gist) and listening for detail (specific information), as well as their own ability with the two micro skills. They practise improvement techniques such as activating existing knowledge and predicting content and vocabulary. Students then listen to a recording for gist and specific information and also identify phrases that speakers use to signal the importance of what they are saying or going to say. Finally, they discuss the subject of the recording, Interpol.

In the second half of the lesson, students focus on the skill of writing a 'for and against' essay. They discuss the topic of CCTV and read a 'for and against' essay, for gist as well as for specific information. They then identify stages and progression in the essay and analyse phrases that we can use to talk about advantages and disadvantages. They study the use of linkers in the essay and practise their usage. Finally, they put their work into practice by writing a 'for and against' essay of their own.

Objectives

By the end of the lesson, students should have:

- discussed the skill of listening
- discussed their ability with listening for gist and specific information
- practised activating their knowledge of a text before listening
- practised predicting the content and vocabulary before listening
- listened for gist and specific information
- identified importance markers in a listening text
- discussed the pros and cons of CCTV
- read a for and against essay on CCTV for gist and for specific information
- identified and analysed the constituent parts of a for and against essay
- identified and practised the types of phrases used in a for and against essay
- studied and practised the use of linkers
- written a for and against essay of their own

Timings

You can omit exercises 6 and/or 8b if there is not enough time.

Exercise 12b can be given for homework.

Possible lesson break: after exercise 6.

STUDY SKILLS: improving your listening

1 Ask your students to read the title to this section. Do they think listening is important? Why is listening a skill for learning a language? Is it natural or can they practise to get better? Students then read the instructions and do the activity as per Coursebook. Check that they have correctly identified the exercises.

2 Students read through the instructions (the paragraph in bold) and answer the questions first individually and then in groups of three. Then repeat the discussion as a whole class. Without students looking at their books, try and elicit the different things they can do before listening which will help comprehension.

3a Ask students to read the introduction to exercises 3a–3c, i.e. the six lines starting *There are a number of things we can do …*

- Tell students that they will soon listen to a talk about Interpol. Point out the picture which shows the Interpol emblem and let them discuss the questions in small groups, then report back as a class. When this is completed, explain that they have just shared knowledge about Interpol and are better prepared to listen to a talk about it.

> The Interpol (International police) emblem, in use since 1950, is made up of: a world globe to show that Interpol's activities are worldwide; olive branches either side of the globe to symbolise peace; the name *Interpol* below the globe in the centre of the olive branches; a vertical sword behind the globe, representing police action; the abbreviations *OIPC* (Organisation Internationale de Police Criminelle) and *ICPO* (International Criminal Police Organisation) above the globe either side of the sword and the scales below the olive branches to symbolise justice.

3b Students do activity as per Coursebook individually and then compare work in pairs.

☀ To make the listening more focussed, discuss the questions you have prepared and as a class decide on ten questions to look up and answer. Then make sure all students answer these questions in exercise 4a.

3c Students do this activity individually and then share in pairs, explaining why they chose the words they did. Finally do a class feedback.

2.29

4a Before starting the listening, ask students what they have done. Can they identify all the pre-listening activities that help prepare for what they are going to hear? Then do activity as per Coursebook.

4b Students do activity as per Coursebook individually and then check in pairs.

Track 2.29

Good evening. Thank you for inviting me here this evening to talk about Interpol, the world's largest police organisation. Now, what do you think of when you think of Interpol? A lot of people get their image of Interpol from books or films. Perhaps they think of a French policeman from the 1960s, wearing a long pale coat. Or perhaps they think of something like a James Bond film, or *Mission Impossible*, with beautiful secret agents. Actually, Interpol is rather different to this and tonight I'm going to give you an idea about the real Interpol. First of all, I'll say a little about Interpol's history. Then I'll talk about Interpol today; I'll tell you how it's organised and, finally, what it does. There'll be some time at the end for questions.

Although the idea for Interpol was born in 1914 at a conference in Monaco, the First World War interrupted its development. It was eventually created in 1923, in Vienna, Austria, although it had a different name at that time. In the beginning, there were fourteen member countries. The work of the organisation was interrupted by the Second World War. In 1946, Interpol reappeared with a new headquarters in Paris, and it has remained in France since then. In 1989 the headquarters was moved to Lyon, where it is today.

Now let's look at the modern Interpol. First of all, how is it organised? Interpol now has 184 member countries. And let me point out that it's those countries that pay for it! A hundred and eighty four countries – that makes it the second biggest international organisation after the United Nations. The headquarters in Lyon operates 24 hours a day, 365 days a year. Staff from more than 80 countries work side-by-side, using the organisation's four official languages: Arabic, English, French and Spanish. There are also six regional offices around the world. In all, we have about 450 staff. Yes, that's right – perhaps 450 doesn't sound a lot to you. But that figure is just for the staff in Lyon and the regional offices. Each member country also has its own Interpol office. The staff there come from the national police force. Don't forget that most Interpol officers stay in their own country, and don't spend their time travelling the world fighting crime, as they do in the books and films! In the final part of my talk, I'm going to say something about what Interpol does. Basically, we help police forces catch criminals. But, and I must draw your attention to this, we never break the law in any country.

One of our priorities is problems connected with drugs. Another important area is trafficking in human beings – people trafficking – especially women and children from developing countries. We also take a great interest in public safety and terrorism.

Another key priority is financial crime. Why? Because criminals are using new technology to get information such as passwords or credit card details through the Internet.

continued…

So how can we catch these criminals? Well, the most important thing we do is to run a global police communication system, so police around the world can share information about crime and criminals. The system allows police in one country to check the databases of police in another country. Interpol itself manages several databases, including names and photos of criminals, fingerprints, etc. Another important thing we do is to provide training courses for national police forces, and organise international conferences on crime. In 2001, about 1,400 criminals were found thanks to the efforts of Interpol.

So there we are. To conclude, we can say that Interpol is over 80 years old, and has grown a lot from the organisation that was set up in Vienna in 1923. Today, our headquarters is in Lyon, France, and 184 countries are members. We fight international crime using modern technology. We do everything we can to make the world a safer place for you and your families. Thank you for listening. Are there any questions?

Q: Yes, do you think organisations like Interpol have too much information about us – the public? For example, everywhere we go there are cameras taking photographs of us. There's no private space anymore. What's your opinion about this?

A: Mmm, now that's a very interesting and important question. Er, let me see if I can give you a short answer …

5 Read through the instructions with the students. Ask them first to predict what goes in the blanks, and then to check with the audioscript.

This work on importance markers ties in with the work on emphasis in Lesson 10.3. Ask students to recreate sentences from their talk in Lesson 10.3 using the importance markers from Lesson 10.4. Make sure they understand that the use of importance markers is another way to emphasise important information to a listener.

1 point; **2** forget; **3** draw; **4** priorities; **5** area; **6** key; **7** most; **8** Another

6 Do this as a quick class discussion.

WRITING SKILLS: a for and against essay

7 Make sure students understand what CCTV is (closed circuit television – this is a camera system that videos people on the road, in the street, in offices, etc.). Students first discuss this in groups and then as a whole class. In the feedback, you can actually make a list of advantages and disadvantages to compare with the article the students are going to read.

8a Students do activity as per Coursebook

8b Have a very quick class discussion on this. Make sure students say why / why not.

9a Tell the students that there are normally three sections to an essay. Elicit the sections (introduction, main body, conclusion). Tell students that with a for and against essay, the main body is divided into two parts. Elicit the parts (advantages and disadvantages). Students then do activity as per Coursebook.

> **a** paragraph 3 (advantages); **b** paragraph 4 (conclusion); **c** paragraph 1 (introduction); **d** paragraph 2 (disadvantages)
> Paragraphs 2 and 3 form the main body of the essay.

9b Students do activity as per Coursebook, individually and then in pairs. When this is completed, tell students that all the information they have from exercises 9a and 9b provides a template for writing most essays, which they should use when planning their compositions.

> **1** C; **2** I; **3** MB; **4** I; **5** C

10a Students do activity as per Coursebook. Ask them to build those phrases into example sentences to show they understand.

(!) Students may not easily understand what structure comes next. It is quite common to hear a student say, e.g., *Another advantage is that cure for illness*. Make it clear that with the exception of *One serious disadvantage of ...* , which is followed by a noun and then *is that ...* , all those phrases must be followed by a main clause. This is why you need to let them make their own example sentences.

> One serious disadvantage of / Another problem with them is that
> A major advantage is that / Another advantage is that

10b Students do activity as per Coursebook.

> **Possible answers:**
> The main advantage of CCTV cameras is that they help to catch criminals.
> The main disadvantage of CCTV cameras is that people are watching us all the time.
> One of the good points about CCTV cameras is that ordinary people feel safer.
> One of the bad points about CCTV cameras is that the government has spent a lot of money on them.

11 Ask students to identify the examples of *although*, *on the other hand* and *therefore* and circle them in the text. Ask them which of the three is used in a two-clause sentence (*although*), and then which one links two sentences which offer different opinions (*on the other hand*). Finally, elicit the use of *therefore* (to show the effect of something). Students then do activity as per Coursebook.

> **1** Although; **2** On the other hand; **3** Therefore; **4** On the other hand; **5** Although

Ⓔ Students can do exercise 8 from the Extra practice activities on page 145 either in class or for homework.

12a Students discuss each of the issues in their pairs and make a list of advantages and disadvantages in preparation for their essay. During this time, you should walk around monitoring. Make sure you have seen and approved the final list before students can go on to exercise 12b.

In their pairs, students choose the topic(s) they are going to write about. They present their list of advantages and disadvantages to the whole class, who give their comments.

12b Students can do this activity either in class or for homework. If in class, get the pairs to first write individual texts, then check and correct each other's and finally prepare the final text. This emphasises to students the importance of peer correction.

If you have a strong class, with talkative students holding strong views, let them choose their own contemporary topics to write about. These can become mini-projects. However, be careful of sensitive issues coming into your class.

HOMEWORK OPTIONS

Students do the exercises on page 63 of the Workbook.

The environment

11

11.1 GLOBAL WARMING

IN THIS LESSON

Lesson topic and staging

This unit focuses on issues connected with the environment and this lesson deals specifically with global warming. Students begin by discussing some aspects of global warming and activating vocabulary associated with the topic. They look at a text explaining global warming and read it for specific information. The listening section continues with the same theme. Students hear a documentary and listen for gist and for specific information. They also revise how to look at a chart, and then discuss what they have heard. The listening provides examples of the present perfect continuous, which is analysed in comparison with the present perfect simple. Students extensively practise this structure in controlled and freer activities. They conclude the lesson by discussing issues connected with global warming.

Objectives

By the end of the lesson, students should have:

- discussed causes and effects of global warming
- activated vocabulary on the topic
- read for specific information
- listened for gist and specific information
- learned and practised the present perfect continuous in comparison with the present perfect simple
- discussed their opinions about global warming

Timings

If there is not enough time, you could omit exercise 3c. Exercise 5 could be given for homework.

Possible lesson break: after exercise 3c.

SPEAKING AND VOCABULARY: global warming

1 Point students to the picture. Ask the following questions:

What can you see in the picture? (ice/iceberg)

Is there a lot of ice? Why/Why not?

What causes this? (global warming)

Then put students into pairs and discuss question 1. Before starting question 2, check that they understand the meaning of all the words in the box (they all have been previously taught). Do question 3 with the whole class.

READING

2a Tell students they are now going to read a description of global warming. They then do activity as per Coursebook.

2b Students do activity as per Coursebook.

> **1** natural climate change due to changing amount of energy from the sun; global warming caused by increasing levels of CO_2 in the atmosphere; **2** plants use CO_2 to make energy and oxygen; CO_2 not used by plants forms a blanket in the atmosphere and keeps the planet warm; **3** due to burning of fossil fuels; **4** the planet will get too hot

LISTENING

`2.30`

3a The reading gave students background information for the listening. Explain that they are now going to find out more about global warming by listening to a documentary. They then do activity as per Coursebook, individually, and then checking in pairs. Play the recording only once.

> **1**a; **2**d; **3**f; **4**b; **5**e; **6**c

3b Before students listen again, let them try to answer the questions from the first listening. Then do activity as per Coursebook and finally check in pairs.

> **1** 40 years; **2** 20 years; **3** that we are changing the world's climate; **4** the Arctic; **5** the sea ice is melting earlier every year and they can't find food; **6** sea levels are rising; **7** less rain resulting in droughts; **8** the sea is getting warmer; **9** blue: temperature change due to natural processes; red: temperature change when including burning of fossil fuels

Track 2.30

Presenter, John, Bruce

P: I've been a scientist for over 40 years, and I've been making nature documentaries for the last 20 years and, to be honest, 15 years ago I didn't believe that we were changing the world's climate. However, for the last ten years I've been travelling around the world to find out if, in fact, we are changing the world's climate. I've met many scientists and I've visited some of the world's most special environments. And, now, I've definitely changed my mind.

We can see the early effects of global warming in the polar regions – the Arctic and the Antarctic. John Watts is a polar scientist in the Arctic.

J: 'I've been working here since 1980, and, recently, things have been changing very quickly. The sea ice is melting earlier every year and this means that life for the polar bears is getting harder and harder, because they can only find food when the ocean is covered with ice. There are now 25 percent fewer polar bears compared to when I first came here.'

Sea levels are rising because the polar ice and mountain glaciers are melting. This means that islands in the Pacific Ocean are disappearing under the sea. As well as this, the seas are also getting hotter. This is causing problems for both the rainforests and the coral reefs.

The warmer seas mean there's less rain in the rainforests. In the Amazon rainforest, the larger trees are dying and there are serious droughts. As well as this, the warmer sea water is killing coral reefs in many parts of the world. Coral reefs are very sensitive to temperature changes and we're now losing some of the richest environments in the world.

But, are we causing these changes or is it just a natural process? Bruce Sindall has a computer model that seems to answer this question.

B: 'With this programme, I can show how the temperature of the planet has been changing for the last 100 years and I can show what effect the burning of fossil fuels has on the temperature changes. The first line on the graph – the blue line – shows you the temperature changes because of natural processes, such as volcanoes and the energy from the sun. As you can see, the temperature goes up and down without a strong trend.

The second line shows you what happens when we include the CO_2 that is produced by the use of fossil fuels. As you can see, the average temperature has been increasing very quickly since 1950, and this will continue. The increase in CO_2 in the atmosphere has been increasing the planet's temperature.'

So, is this the end of the world? Well, not yet. We have the power to slow, and possibly to stop, the rise in temperature. We have to produce less CO_2, and to do that we have to change the way we live our lives.

3c Do this pairwork discussion quickly and then do classroom feedback. Make sure students consider not only what countries can do, but also what they as individuals can do (e.g. Avril Lavigne, the singer, stopped using deodorant for a time so she didn't affect global warming).

GRAMMAR: present perfect continuous

4 Look through the four sentences with your students. Ask them to identify the sentence which uses the present perfect (a). Quickly revise the present perfect: draw a timeline on the board, marking *past* at one end, *now* in the middle and *future* at the other end. Ask students to draw a line on the timeline to show the present perfect (a straight line starting in the past leading to *now*, the same as that shown on page 33).

- Students answer questions 1–3, first individually and then with the class. Make sure they remember the difference between state and non-state verbs. Elicit examples of state verbs (e.g. *be, have, become, know*, etc.).

- Elicit from students how to draw the timeline for the present perfect continuous (a wiggly line in the past that extends to *now*, wiggly to show that it represents repeated or continuous actions rather than a constant state). Students confirm the rule by reading the paragraph after question 3.

- Finally, elicit the negative form and the interrogative form.

- Students that are having problems understanding can refer to the Language reference on page 146.

E Students can do exercises 1–4 from the Extra practice activities on page 147 either in class or for homework.

> **1** unfinished; **2** sentences b, c and d; **3** sentence a

5 Students do activity as per Coursebook. Check in pairs and then do as a class.

> **1** have been rising; **2** have known (state);
> **3** have been using; **4** have … been (state);
> **5** has … been making

6 This is a continuation of the previous activity. Students do the exercise and then put the questions to their partner. You could also make this into a survey, with students going round the class asking the questions. Either way, make sure that students feed back their results to the class as this will give further practice of the form.

> **1** have … been learning; **2** have … known;
> **3** have … been coming; **4** have … had;
> **5** have … been reading; **6** have … had

SPEAKING

7 Read through the activity together with your students. You may have to check they understand the following words:

reduce (v) – to make smaller or less in size or amount

eco-tax (n) – a tax which helps to protect the environment

wind farms (n pl) – places where wind is collected to be used as power

- Students first read through the statements. Give them a few minutes to prepare their arguments. You might like to brainstorm the language they will need on the board. Students discuss in pairs and come to an agreement. Then do this in groups and finally have a class discussion.

💡 Students take the statement they most agree with and write a composition, using writing skills they have learned throughout the course (particularly in Lessons 5.4 and 10.4).

HOMEWORK OPTIONS

Students can do exercise 8 from the Extra practice activities on page 147.

Students do the exercises on pages 64–65 of the Workbook.

11.2 WASTE NOT, WANT NOT

IN THIS LESSON

Lesson topic and staging

The theme of this lesson is how to protect the environment by cutting down on waste. The lesson starts with students learning the vocabulary for containers and materials. They then look at an email discussion on wasteful packaging, reading it for gist and for specific information and practising reference questions. The text also provides the examples for the introduction (or revision for some students) of phrasal verbs. Students practise using phrasal verbs and then finally discuss and find out more about cutting down on waste.

Objectives

By the end of the lesson, students should have:

- learned or revised the vocabulary for containers and materials
- read for gist, specific information and reference
- learned about (or revised) and practised phrasal verbs
- discussed and found out more about cutting down on waste

Timings

Exercise 4 could be given for homework if there is not enough time.

Possible lesson break: after exercise 2c.

VOCABULARY: containers and materials

Before beginning the lesson in the Coursebook, write *waste not, want not* on the board. Elicit from students the meaning of *waste* and then the whole meaning of the idiom (if you don't waste things, you won't need anything else). The idiom uses the verb form of *waste*. Elicit the noun form (*waste*, although you might also hear *wastefulness*). Elicit the meaning of the noun (things we throw away). Ask the students to discuss the following questions in groups and then as a class:

What things do we throw away / count as waste?

Is waste good for the environment? Why / Why not?

1a Students do activity as per Coursebook. Ask them if they were surprised by the answer. Do they think their own country would have more waste or less waste? Why?

> Students check their answer on page 110. The photo shows one month's packaging waste for a British family = 20kg.

1b There are two tasks in this section. Make sure students finish the first and check it before moving onto the next section.

⟨☼⟩ Ask students to identify products that use the containers, e.g. oil in a glasss bottle.

> 1 packet; 2 can/tin; 3 tube; 4 box; 5 pot; 6 jar; 7 bottle; 8 carton
> aluminium can, cardboard box, glass jar, metal can/tin, paper packet, plastic bottle/carton/pot/tube

1c Do this quickly as classwork. You can follow up with the following questions:

What happens to the containers when we throw them away?

What could we do with them instead?

• Keep the discussion short as students will spend more time on this at the end of the lesson.

READING

2a Tell students that they are going to read an email discussion on waste. Read the instructions with the students and then let them do the activity as per Coursebook. Give them no more than a minute to read, otherwise they will start reading for specific information.

> 2

2b Ask students to do this activity first without reading the text again, as they may be able to remember. Then students check against the text, individually and then in pairs. You may want to check they have understood the following words:

coconut (n) – large brown seed of a tropical tree, which has a hard shell and inside is white with a milky liquid you can drink

noodle (n) – a long thin piece of food made from a mixture of flour, water and eggs

biodegradable (adj) – materials or chemicals are biodegradable when they can be changed naturally by bacteria into substances that do not damage the environment

vapour (n) – a mass of small drops of liquid which float in the air, for example because the liquid has been heated

convenience food (n) – food that is partly or completely prepared and that is sold frozen or in cans, packages, etc. so that it can be prepared quickly and easily

> sentences 2 and 3

2c Students do activity as per Coursebook.

⟨!⟩ Students have done reference questions before, but not often, and they may have forgotten. You might like to model one for them before they do this exercise.

> 1 the wrapping of the coconut in this way;
> 2 packaging; 3 biodegradable materials;
> 4 the amount of packaging waste recovered;
> 5 the rubbish bag still existing hundreds of years from now; 6 people who are living alone

GRAMMAR: phrasal verbs

Phrasal verbs should be revision for most students in the class. Start off by putting a phrasal verb sentence on the board, e.g. *I grew up in France*. Elicit from the students the verb in the sentence (*grew up*). Elicit how many parts the verb has (two), what we normally call the second part of this verb (preposition), whether it works like a preposition (no) and how it works (it changes the meaning of the verb). Then read through the introduction with the students.

3 Students do the activity with you as per Coursebook. Make sure they notice and understand that in 1a, the preposition works as a preposition and does not affect the meaning of the verb but in 1b, the preposition acts as a particle and the meaning of *go* has therefore changed.

• Refer students to the Language reference on page 146.

⟨E⟩ Students can do exercises 5 and 6 from the Extra practice activities on page 147 either in class or for homework.

> **1a** 's going; **1b** is going up; **2a** cut; **2b** cuts down
> 1b (is going up) and 2b (cuts down) are phrasal verbs.
> *is going up* means 'is increasing'; *cuts down* means 'reduces'

4 Students do activity as per Coursebook.

⟨☼⟩ Elicit from the students all the main verbs that they have used in phrasal verbs so far in this unit. Get them to brainstorm or find out in the dictionary any other phrasal verbs that use the same main verbs. Then ask them to create example sentences to show the meaning. You could also do this with the particles but it would generate a much larger list.

> 1 up; 2 out; 3 out; 4 up; 5 down; 6 away; 7 back; 8 down

SPEAKING

5a Note that in this activity, students are talking about what individuals can do to cut down on waste. Students work in small groups. Then re-group them so that no two students from one group are together in the second round, and ask them to compare ideas. Finally, build a class list before going on to exercise 5b.

5b Before doing the activity, you might like students to read the box on page 124 and find the answers to the following questions:

Why are e-cards better? (because they are not made of paper or card)

How do you remember to reuse plastic bags? (put them in your pocket or bag)

If you print, what should you do? (print on both sides)

Which is better, showers or baths? (showers because they use less water)

• Students do activity as per Coursebook. Then do class feedback.

P Ask students to prepare a report or presentation on their own country's attempts to deal with waste. They should think about the following:

What is your country already doing? (examples)

What are the effects of this? Is it effective?

What more could your country do?

How effective would it be?

As a small quiz, ask your students the following questions. See if they can guess the answers.

How long does it take for trash to biodegrade?

Plastic soda bottles	forever
Glass bottles	one million years
Batteries	100 years
Aluminium/Tin cans	50 to 100 years
Plastic bags	ten to 20 years
Orange peel	six months
Paper	two to five months

E You can now do photocopiable activity 11A to practise phrasal verbs.

HOMEWORK OPTIONS

Students can do exercise 9 from the Extra practice activities on page 147.

Students do the exercises on pages 66–67 of the Workbook.

11.3 SCENARIO: LOCAL REGENERATION

IN THIS LESSON

Lesson topic and staging

This lesson focuses on the issue of local regeneration, e.g. turning urban wasteland into parks. Students start by talking about the quality of their own environment, at the same time learning the key vocabulary for the topic. The situation, discussing an urban regeneration project, is introduced through a reading activity and students scan a short text for specific information. Then they hear the funding committee discuss the project and listen both for gist and for specific information. This recording provides the examples for the revision and extension of question tags. Students analyse and practise question tags, including intonation patterns. Finally, they put all the vocabulary and key language from the lesson into practice by working on the task, discussing the allocation of funds to a project.

Objectives

By the end of the lesson, students should have:

• talked about their own environment while learning and practising vocabulary related to local regeneration

• read for specific information

• listened for gist and specific information

• analysed and practised question tags

• learned and practised intonation for question tags

• completed a speaking task which involves discussing how to allocate funds

Common European Framework

Students can use language effectively to argue for and against a case and encourage agreement.

Timings

Exercise 4c could be given for homework if there is not enough time.

Possible lesson break: after exercise 3b.

PREPARATION

Before starting the activity, make sure students read the title of the lesson, *Local regeneration*. Ask them what they think it means.

1 Read through the instructions and the sentences. You may need to pre-teach the following words:

canals (n pl) – long passages dug into the ground and filled with water, either for boats to use or to take water to a place *derelict* (adj) – a building or land that is in very bad condition because it has not been used for a long time

scruffy (adj) – dirty and untidy

wasteland (n) – an unattractive area, often with old ruined buildings, factories, etc. on it

well-kept (adj) – very well cared for, looking neat and clean

run-down (adj) – a building or area that is run-down is in very bad condition

dump (v) – to get rid of something you do not want

woods (n pl) – a small forest

- Ask students to match some of the sentences to the pictures displayed on pages 96–97, to check they have understood the meanings.

- Students do this activity individually to begin with and then compare their responses in pairs. Then discuss as a whole class. You can also ask your students the following questions:

  What other problems does your local urban environment have?

  How would you like to improve your local area?

  > **Possible answer:**
  > There isn't much street lighting in my area, so it feels dangerous at night.
  > I'd like to have more places for young people to meet and play.

▌SITUATION▐

Read the introduction with the students and make sure they understand what *local community groups* are. Ask them if they have any in their home community.

☼ If quite a few students don't know of any local community groups in their home town, you can set a homework activity to find out about one and bring it to the next class. Usually the best place to go is their own local council websites on the Internet.

2a Tell students they are now going to look at the project of a local community group in detail. Students then do activity as per Coursebook. You might like to spend a little time discussing why students chose their answers to question 2.

> **1** to regenerate an area of wasteland into an urban wildlife park; **2** students' own answers; **3** £5,000

2b Read through the instructions together and make sure all students understand them, before they do the activity as per Coursebook.

> guidelines 1, 2, 3 and 6

2.31

3a Tell students they are now going to listen to a meeting discussing the proposal. Students do activity as per Coursebook, individually and then in pairs.

> guidelines discussed (in this order): 6, 1, 2, 3, 4
> They generally agree with each other.

3b Allow students to predict the answers before listening and checking as they may remember them from the previous listening.

> **1** true; **2** false; **3** true; **4** false; **5** true

> **Tracks 2.31 and 2.32**
> *Poppy, Rick*
> P: Right then, so, the next project is Wild City. What do you think of this one?
> R: Well, the best thing is that it's definitely a green project. I mean, you can't get much greener than a wildlife park, can you?
> P: Indeed, you can't. And it certainly makes the local area a better place to live, doesn't it?
> R: Mm-hm. Urban wasteland areas really ruin any local area, they make the whole place feel run-down and scruffy.
> P: Exactly. So, what about the other points on the guidelines? The project solves a problem, doesn't it? Getting rid of the wasteland. And of course, it involves local people working together.
> R: Sure. But there are a couple of points that it doesn't meet, aren't there?
> P: Well yes, but that's quite normal, isn't it?
> R: Sure, but this project needs £5,000 a year. And we can't really give them that much money.
> P: No, that's true. What do you think they need that money for?
> R: Well, I reckon it's to pay for the local people who'll look after the park.
> P: Hmm. I guess so. Well, they could do it unpaid, couldn't they?
> R: Hmm, perhaps, but we've seen that fail before, haven't we? If no one gets any money at all, then things like parks soon get run-down. You know, there's more litter, you start getting graffiti, that kind of thing.
> P: Mmm yes, that's all true. Why don't we offer £2,000 a year?
> R: Yes, that's fine. Right, well, there's one more point that the project doesn't meet.
> P: Is there? Which one?

▌KEY LANGUAGE: question tags▐

2.32

4a Students have done question tags before so this should be revision and students should be able to fill in the blanks without listening. Let them try it and check their answers. If they have got it right, it is probably not worth playing them the recording right now.

- Read through the description of question tags at the top of page 97. Elicit from students the verbs we use with question tags (*be, do, have, can, must, shall,* etc.) Ask students which of these verbs we use with action verbs (*do*).

> **1** can; **2** doesn't; **3** couldn't; **4** haven't

> **Track 2.32**
> See audioscript for Track 2.31.

4b Students do activity as per Coursebook.

> And it certainly makes the local area a better place to live, doesn't it? / there are a couple of points that it doesn't meet, aren't there? / that's quite normal, isn't it?

Write the following sentences on the board and ask students to fill in the blanks:

If the statement …

has an auxiliary verb, we use the same _____ *in the question tag.* (auxiliary verb)

has be, we use the correct form of _____ . (be)

doesn't have an auxiliary verb or be, we use the correct form of _____ .(do)

*is affirmative, the question tag is*_____. (negative)

is negative, the question tag is _____. (affirmative)

If they have problems, list the answers, jumbled up.

Once they have completed the sentences, you can ask students to provide example question tags for each one.

4c Students do activity as per Coursebook.

E Students can do exercise 7 from the Extra practice activities on page 147 either in class or for homework.

> **1** doesn't it; **2** can we; **3** have they; **4** isn't it; **5** couldn't they

pronunciation

2.32

5a Before listening, revise intonation patterns in *yes/no* questions and *wh-* questions. Write examples on the board and show the intonation pattern using arrows. Then ask students which pattern they think is correct for question tags. Let them listen and check, and then read through the description. Ask students which intonation pattern we would use if we are not sure the listener will agree with us (rising).

> intonation goes down

5b Students do activity as per Coursebook.

TASK: allocating funds

6a Divide students into groups of at least four students. Read through the instructions with the students. Divide groups into two. Each half of the group reads one of the new projects on page 122, discusses the questions on page 97 for that project and then presents its results to the rest of the group. This will save time. As a group, they should then compare the two projects with the project they have already studied in the lesson.

6b Students read the instructions and then decide on the projects. Make sure they take note of the fact that they can make changes to projects to bring down costs.

6c Do as a class and discuss.

Each group can prepare a presentation of their decision, to give to the rest of the class. To conclude the task, your class can discuss their final decision.

Alternatively, students prepare a project of their own and write up the project proposal.

E You can now do photocopiable activity 11B to practise question tags.

HOMEWORK OPTIONS

Students can do exercise 8 from the Extra practice activities on page 147.

Students do the exercises on page 68 of the Workbook.

11.4 STUDY AND WRITING SKILLS

IN THIS LESSON

Lesson topic and staging

This lesson focuses on the study skill of exploring reading texts to enhance understanding, as well as the skill of writing a report, in the context of the planned building of an airport in an area of natural beauty.

Students begin the first part of the lesson by looking at some basic questions that they should ask themselves when approaching a text for the first time. Students try this approach out on a newsletter promoting a protest group against the building of an airport. They are then given more searching questions concerning the objectivity of a text, such as quality of information, reasons, missing information and language use (including revision of the use of words for emphasis), and they answer those questions by reading for specific information. Students end this section by evaluating the potential success of the newsletter.

In the second half of the lesson, students discuss when and why people write reports. They have to analyse a report on people's reaction to the proposed airport, which involves reading for gist and for specific information. Students look at both the organisation of the report and useful words and phrases. They apply the reading skills learned in the first half of the lesson and they also revise the language of reporting. Finally students are expected to write a report on a similar issue.

Objectives

By the end of the lesson, students should have:

- analysed and used questions to ask themselves when they first approach a new text
- analysed and practised questions in order to assess the objectivity of a text, e.g. quality of information, reasons, missing information and language use
- revised using words for emphasis
- discussed when and why people write reports
- read for gist and specific information
- analysed how reports are organised
- explored useful words and phrases that can be used in reports
- revised the language of reporting
- written a report

Timings

Exercise 8 could be omitted if there is not enough time.

Exercise 10 can be done for homework.

Possible lesson break: after exercise 3b.

STUDY SKILLS: exploring reading texts

1 Look with the students at the questions in exercise 1. Elicit why these questions might be useful.

2 Students do activity as per Coursebook, individually and then in pairs.

> **1** in a newsletter sent (or hand delivered) to residents of the village of Finchfield; **2** Barclay Smethurst (Acting President, Finchfield Action Group); the residents of Finchfield; **3** possibly in April; **4** plans to build an airport near the village; **5** to coordinate local opposition to the airport plans

3a This is quite a large activity and needs to be broken down into stages. Firstly, ask students to read and answer questions 1 and 2 individually and then in pairs. Then discuss as a class. Ask students why they thought some information was opinion and not fact.

- Then read through question 3 and ask students to answer the points individually and then in pairs. Note with students that it is necessary to give more than one reason when giving an argument. Referring back to the first two questions, ask students which of the reasons are based on fact and which are based on opinion (the first one is certainly opinion; we don't know for the second and third ones as no facts are supplied).

- Students now look at questions 4 and 5 and answer them individually and then in pairs. When you have checked, ask students if they think the missing information is relevant (yes). Then ask, if it is relevant, why the writer has not included it in his newsletter (because it would weaken his argument). Ask students what this tells us (when we are developing an argument with the intention to persuade, we often leave out information which does not support our argument).

- Finally, look at questions 6, 7 and 8, the language questions. Students answer them individually and then in pairs. When you have finished checking, ask students why the author has used the language in this way (to give emphasis). Ask how this is done. (*Attractive* is an emotive word and adding an emotive adjective to something makes us notice it more. The use of *very* suggests longer than shorter and makes us think. *Majority* means anything between 50 and 100% and is usually used when the number is nearer 50% but we want people to think it is more.) Tell students that these are all ways of giving emphasis to an argument and of persuading people.

💡 Write the following small passage on the board and ask students to rewrite it to emphasise what we want, without telling lies:

JOIN US IN OUR FIGHT AGAINST THE COUNCIL.

We have asked the council to clean our park. They have refused. If the park is not cleaned, our children will have to play somewhere else in the next village. 51% of families in this village have children. Help us change the council's mind.

Alternatively, this activity could be done after exercise 3b.

> **1 fact:** the government wants to build four or five new airports in this country in the next 20 years; one possible location is in our area; **opinion:** attractive village of Finchfield; we do not believe this is a good location;
> **2** impossible to say but assume yes, or close to the truth;
> **3** three (quiet and beautiful area, would disrupt the lives of people who have lived here for generations, majority of local people are against the plans);
> **4** only against;
> **5** because 5,000 is not many people and it would weaken his argument about the number of people opposed to the airport;
> **6** It makes you less willing to want to spoil it by building an airport.
> **7** impossible to say; suggests 20 or 200, but may only be five;
> **8** anything over 50%; suggests 75% but may only be 51%

3b Students discuss in pairs and then in groups before doing a class discussion. You can ask students what information they would like to hear at the meeting to help them decide whether to support the group or not.

> students' own answers

WRITING SKILLS: a report

4 Students discuss these questions in pairs and then as a class. They can also discuss the following questions:

What were the reports about?

Did they include facts and figures? If so, why were they there?

How did you know it was a report and not an essay?

5 Students do activity as per Coursebook. Give students no more than one minute to do this otherwise it will become an intensive reading exercise.

> **2** (Reactions to plans for a new airport in Finchfield)

6 Students may be able to do this activity without reading again. Give them the chance to do this before they start reading intensively and do the activity as per Coursebook. Make sure that they identify the difference between headings and sub-headings. Tell students that they can use this as a template when they come to write their own reports.

> **1** F; **2** C; **3** A; **4** E; **5** D; **6** B

7a Students look back at the questions in exercise 1 and do the activity first individually and then in pairs.

> **1** a report sent to the Finchfield Action Group;
> **2** PSG Research, the Finchfield Action Group;
> **3** some time after 17 September 2007; **4** survey of local people's attitudes to plans to build a new airport; **5** PSG Research were asked to carry out this survey by the Finchfield Action Group

7b Students look back at the questions in exercise 3a. Ask them to write at least one question under each of the four headings in that exercise. When students have written the questions, they should pass them to a partner who will then read the text and answer the questions. Then go through a class check of questions asked and information found.

To conclude this point, ask students what the major differences are between the newsletter and the report.

(Newsletter – no headings, mixes facts and opinions, omits any information that does not support the argument, does not offer advantages, uses emotive language to influence the reader.

Report – all stages have headings and are separate from each other, contains only facts until the conclusion which has opinion, contains reasons for as well as against the project, uses specific figures rather than general figures, reports people's opinions and does not use emotive language.)

Explain to students that the differences are the same as between a normal essay and a report. You can do this activity instead of exercise 8.

8 Students do activity as per Coursebook.

> A report has headings and subheadings.

9a Students first do activity as per Coursebook individually and then in pairs. After doing class feedback, explain to students that they should use these phrases in a report. To check they've understood the meaning, elicit possible endings to each of the phrases.

> **1** c; **2** e; **3** a; **4** f; **5** b; **6** d

9b Students do activity as per Coursebook. Point out to students that using different verbs to report ensures variety in their report.

> said, mentioned, felt, thought

10 This activity can be done either in class or for homework. Before starting to write, brainstorm as a class what language they will need (headings, phrases from exercise 9a and verbs from 9b.) As the final texts should be very similar, get students to correct each other's papers. You can also build a model text on the board as a whole-class exercise before students correct each other's papers.

HOMEWORK OPTIONS

Students do the exercises on page 69 of the Workbook.

12 Sports

12.1 MINORITY SPORTS

Lesson topic and staging

This lesson focuses on minority sports, particularly the way they are promoted and funded. Students begin by discussing sports and revising relevant vocabulary. They identify minority sports and revise the correct use of *do*, *go* and *play* with names of sports. The next step is to read for gist and for specific information a letter of complaint about the lack of support for minority sports. The recording is a current affairs programme which students listen to for gist and for specific information. The reading and listening texts both provide examples for the introduction of the second conditional. Students study and practise this structure and then finish by doing a freer speaking activity practising the second conditional.

Objectives

By the end of the lesson, students should have:

* talked about sports in their country and minority sports
* used *do*, *play* and *go* with the names of sports
* read for gist and specific information
* listened for gist and specific information
* learned and practised the second conditional
* completed an open-ended speaking activity requiring the use of the second conditional

Timings

The quiz in exercise 1c can be omitted if there is not enough time. Exercise 5 could be given for homework.

Possible lesson break: after exercise 3c.

VOCABULARY AND SPEAKING: sports

1a Tell students to look at pages 100 and 101. Ask them what they see. What are the photos examples of? (sports) Ask them if they know the names of the sports (judo and archery). Brainstorm with students the names of sports that they know. Make sure that they know what the sports they mention are. Also check that they understand the meaning of the sports vocabulary listed in the box for question 2, as well as the meaning of *minority* (the opposite of *majority*, which they saw in Lesson 11.4). Ask them what they think makes a sport a 'minority sport'.

1b Students do this activity in pairs and then check as a class. They may ask you why we use different verbs with different sports. There is no right answer to this question.

> **do:** gymnastics, archery, fencing, judo
> **go:** cycling, dragon boat racing, sailing
> **play:** badminton, table tennis, hockey, football

1c Students work together in pairs to guess the right answers for the questions. They can then check the answers or ask you during the feedback session.

☼ Cut up all the questions and all the answers. Students first try and answer the questions and then match the questions with the answers.

READING

2a Ask students to imagine they took part in a minority sport. How would they feel? Then ask them to do activity as per Coursebook.

> to persuade the government to invest more in minority sports

2b Students do activity as per Coursebook individually and then check in pairs. Then ask students the following questions:

Do you agree with the writer? Why / Why not?

What do you think the government could do about it?

What do you think they will do about it?

> **1** fencing, judo, archery; **2** to develop young people's interest in these sports; **3** poor facilities and funding; **4** enthusiastic and dedicated; **5** for the last few weeks she's been travelling around the country talking to young people about minority sports; **6** We need proper government investment in facilities and training.

LISTENING

2.33

3a Tell students they are going to listen to a programme where the Minister of Sport, a journalist and an actress are going to respond to questions related to minority sports. Ask them to tell you what they expect each of the guests on the programme to say about minority sports. Students then do activity as per Coursebook.

> **1** morning; **2** two; **3** agree

3b Let students try to answer the questions before listening a second time. They then listen and check in pairs. When they have finished this activity, ask them if the minister, the journalist and the actress behaved as they expected.

> The ideas mentioned are 1, 2, 4 and 7.

Track 2.33

Darren, Nikki, Lesley, Peter, Keri

D: Welcome back. I'm Darren Bright and as usual at this time we're looking at today's papers. With me in the studio this morning are Lesley Diggot-Blake, the Minister for Sport, the journalist and commentator Peter Jones, and the actress Keri Miller. Remember – this show is interactive, so if you want to comment on anything, or ask a question, just send your emails to *brightinthemorning* – that's all one word – *@sixtv. com*. The address is on your screen now, and Nikki over there will receive all your emails. Morning, Nikki.

N: Hi Darren.

D: Our first topic this morning is sport and in particular this letter in a newspaper from Michaela Scrivin about minority sports. Michaela wants more investment in minority sports and more stories about them in the media. Then, she says, we would be more successful in international competitions. Lesley Diggot-Blake, what do you think? Would we be better at minority sports if we spent more money on them?

L: To be honest, I was a little surprised when I saw this letter, because we've actually been investing a lot of money in minority sports over the last few years – last year, for example, £60 million was spent on new facilities around the country. Also, we're building a lot of facilities for the 2012 London Olympics and people doing minority sports will use them. There was something else that surprised me. Michaela suggests that our sportsmen and women haven't been very successful in minority sports in recent years. Think about our gymnasts a few years ago. Beth Tweddle was a gold medal winner. Can I say, though, that success isn't just about money …

D: Alright, sorry to interrupt, we'll come back to you later, but we've got our first email. It's from Rod, in Brighton. Rod says: 'What can you read about judo in the newspapers? Almost nothing. Can you see badminton on TV? Fat chance! The media is only interested in football. If the media showed more interest in other sports, kids would want to try them.' Peter Jones, you're a journalist, what's your view?

continued…

P: Well, I couldn't agree more. I think it's a great pity some sports, like football, get so much media attention while others like badminton or table tennis are often ignored. And this problem isn't going away any time soon, either. The BBC has recently decided to stop *Grandstand* – its famous sports programme. I used to watch Grandstand on Saturday afternoons when I was a kid and it introduced me to all kinds of different sports. Without that kind of programme, kids won't have the chance to watch those minority sports. However, the 2012 Olympics offer some hope. Because the UK is the host nation, we can enter more teams than usual. Hopefully, people will see more different sports on their TVs.

D: Alright, we've got another email here. It's from Heather in Plymouth. Heather says: 'I think kids should do a lot more sport at school. I've heard that in Sweden kids have ten hours of sport a week. If I was the Minister for Sport, I'd give every schoolchild the opportunity to do a much wider range of sports. What about hockey or judo for all? If they had more opportunities, they wouldn't be so unhealthy.' Keri, hockey and judo at every school?

K: Absolutely. It's really important that kids get the chance to experience different sports from an early age. I was really lucky because I went to a school where we did hockey, and fencing and archery, but nowadays, most kids aren't so lucky. Most schools just concentrate on the same one or two, you know, football, basketball …

D: OK, here's another email from Gareth in Cardiff. He says: 'In Britain, we think …'

3c Allow students to answer these questions in pairs and then do class feedback. In a multinational class you will get an insight into how different countries perceive sports. In a one-nationality class, although some students may just agree on each answer, you may get quite a discussion going. Students won't necessarily agree on their answers.

■ GRAMMAR: second conditional

4 The second conditional should be a completely new structure for all students in the class. Ask them to read sentences a), b) and c). Ask what the first word in each sentence is (*if*). Ask what that tells us (we are looking at a conditional). At this point, you might like to quickly revise the first conditional and how we use it.

● Ask students to answer question 1 and to explain what is meant by 'unreal' (the situation hasn't happened and is unlikely to happen under present conditions). Explain that this is when we use the second conditional. Students should then answer questions 2 and 3, which relate to form. Once they have answered the questions, elicit the affirmative form (*if* + subject + past simple, subject + *would* + infinitive), and then the negative and question forms.

- Tell students they can find out more about the second conditional in the Language reference on page 148.

E Students can do exercises 1 and 2 from the Extra practice activities on page 149 either in class or for homework.

> **1** unreal; **2** past simple, no; **3** infinitive

5 Students do activity as per Coursebook individually and then in pairs.

> **1** If I knew the answer, I **would tell** you. **2** Would she **increase** taxes if she was the Prime Minister? **3** If you **had** the power to change one thing in the world, what would it be? **4** They **wouldn't go** sailing if they didn't like it. **5** I wouldn't lend him any money if I **didn't** trust him.

- When you have finished this activity, refer students to the grammar tip and then write the following two sentences on the board:

a) *If I had more time, I'd play more sport.*

b) *If I had more time, I might play more sport.*

Ask students the following questions:

Which sentence would definitely result in sport being played? (a)

In sentence b), why do we use might? (because 'I' might do something else instead) *What else could 'I' do?* (e.g. go to the cinema, etc.)

Ask students to generate their own sentences using *might*.

6 Students work in pairs to begin with, and then carry on the discussion in groups. Then as a class, nominate the most interesting answers for the questions.

> **1** won; **2** met; **3** stopped, asked; **4** needed; **5** heard

E You can now do photocopiable activity 12A to practise the second conditional.

HOMEWORK OPTIONS

Students can do exercise 5 from the Extra practice activities on page 149.

Students do the exercises on pages 70–71 of the Workbook.

12.2 BIG SPORT, BIG BUSINESS

IN THIS LESSON

Lesson topic and staging

This lesson focuses on the connection between business and sport, particularly the way businesses advertise during the Football World Cup. The lesson begins by students sharing what they know about the World Cup. Next, they look at an article about how women were targeted by advertisers during the World Cup, reading it for gist and for specific information. Students also use the text to practise working out the meaning of unknown words from context, and then discuss some of the issues raised. The reading text provides examples for the grammar presentation, *too* and *enough*. Students study and practise them in controlled activities, then use them in a freer discussion on their own country, which finally leads to a writing activity.

Objectives

By the end of the lesson, students should have:

- talked about the World Cup
- read for gist and specific information
- worked out the meaning of words from context
- learned and practised the use of *too* and *enough*
- completed a speaking and writing activity that involves using *too* and *enough* as well as the second conditional from Lesson 12.1

Timings

Exercises 5 and/or 7 could be given for homework if there is not enough time.

Possible lesson break: after exercise 3.

SPEAKING

1 Students answer the questions in pairs and then in small groups. Then do class feedback.

Write the names of the following companies on the board:

Coca-Cola McDonald's Budweiser Continental Adidas Toshiba Gillette Hyundai

Elicit from students what each company sells. Ask if they think these companies are suitable sponsors for a World Cup. Why / Why not? Ask them what companies would be suitable sponsors.

World Cup	Winner	Loser	Host
1930	Uruguay	Argentina	Montevideo, Uruguay
1934	Italy	Czechoslovakia	Rome, Italy
1938	Italy	Hungary	Paris, France
1950	Uruguay	Brazil	Rio, Brazil
1954	West Germany	Hungary	Bern, Switzerland
1958	Brazil	Sweden	Stockholm, Sweden
1962	Brazil	Czechoslovakia	Santiago, Chile
1966	England	West Germany	London, England
1970	Brazil	Italy	Mexico City, Mexico
1974	West Germany	Netherlands	Munich, Germany
1978	Argentina	Netherlands	Buenos Aires, Argentina
1982	Italy	West Germany	Madrid, Spain
1986	Argentina	West Germany	Mexico City, Mexico
1990	West Germany	Argentina	Rome, Italy
1994	Brazil	Italy	Pasadena, California
1998	France	Brazil	Saint-Denis, France
2002	Brazil	Germany	Korea/Japan
2006	Italy	France	Germany

1 A Germany; B South Korea; C Sweden; D Brazil
2 see information above

READING

2a Tell students that they are now going to read about a topic connected with the World Cup. Ask them to look at the pictures and guess what it is about. Then students do activity as per Coursebook. Give them no more than one and a half minute to read so that they do not read intensively.

3 (Advertisers forget female fans)

2b Students do activity as per Coursebook. If you have a strong class, ask them to tell you why the false sentences are incorrect.

1 false; 2 true; 3 false; 4 true; 5 false; 6 false; 7 true; 8 true

2c Students do activity as per Coursebook. Then ask them to generate their own sentences to check that they have understood the meaning.

1 stadiums; 2 majority; 3 opportunity; 4 worldwide; 5 tend to

3 Students discuss the questions in pairs and then as a whole group. You can also ask the following questions:

Did you know there is a Women's World Cup?

What do you know about it?

Do you think businesses should only think of women for the Women's World Cup? Why / Why not?

The Women's World Cup has been played five times:

Year	Host	Winner	Runner-up	3rd Place
1991	China	United States	Norway	Sweden
1995	Sweden	Norway	Germany	United States
1999	United States	United States	China	Brazil
2003	United States	Germany	Sweden	United States
2007	China	Germany	Brazil	United States

For the 1999 World Cup, more than 1.1 million people attended.

GRAMMAR: *too* and *enough*

4a Students do activity as per Coursebook, individually and then in pairs.

1, 2 and 4

4b Students do activity as per Coursebook, individually and then in pairs.

1 enough; 2 not enough; 3 too many; 4 too much

4c Students do activity as per Coursebook. Ask them to come up with two or three sentences each which use *too* and *enough* with adjectives.

not clever enough, too interested

4d Students do activity as per Coursebook. Elicit examples for each answer. Tell students to refer to the Language reference on page 148 for more information about *too* and *enough*.

E Students can do exercise 3 from the Extra practice activities on page 149 either in class or for homework.

Too comes **before** nouns and **before** adjectives.
Enough comes **before** nouns and **after** adjectives.

5 Students do activity as per Coursebook, individually and then in pairs.

> 1 have enough free time; 2 have too much homework; 3 don't earn enough money; 4 buses and trains are too crowded (trains and buses are too crowded); 5 tickets are too expensive; 6 aren't enough sports facilities; 7 national football team is good enough; 8 is too much sport

SPEAKING

6a Students need to have some time on their own to think about the issues. Give them about five minutes to plan what they are going to say and then put them into pairs for a discussion. If students are from the same country, they should come to some agreement on the statements. If they are from different countries, they should make notes. Then split the pairs up to form new pairs. If students are from the same country, they should try and come to an agreement. If they are from different countries, they should tell their new partner about their former partner's country.

6b Students return to their original pairs and now also discuss how things could be better. Model this on the board beforehand by revising the second conditional. Finish with a class discussion.

WRITING

7 The writing activity could be done in class or for homework. If in class, this could be done as a group activity with each group writing their paragraphs on the board and the class working together to correct and improve.

HOMEWORK OPTIONS

Students do the exercises on pages 72–73 of the Workbook.

12.3 SCENARIO: SPORTS PSYCHOLOGY

IN THIS LESSON

Lesson topic and staging

This lesson focuses on sports psychology and, in particular, personality types and how they are associated to certain sports. Students start by thinking about the sports they have played and enjoyed. They then practise the vocabulary for personality types and match sports to personality. Next, they read about counsellors specialising in the psychology of sport, and look for specific information in their leaflet. They hear such a sports psychologist interviewing a client and they listen for gist and for specific information. The recording provides examples of conversation fillers that students learn and practise in this lesson. They also learn and practise the intonation patterns used when we list things. Finally, students turn to the task: they construct and conduct their own questionnaires on people's personalities in class, using the vocabulary for personality, conversation fillers and the right intonation for listing.

Objectives

By the end of the lesson, students should have:

- talked about sports they have played and enjoyed
- learned and practised vocabulary for describing personality
- read for specific information
- listened for gist and for specific information
- learned and practised conversation fillers
- learned and practised the intonation used when listing things
- constructed and conducted a questionnaire on personality

Common European Framework

Students can use language effectively to conduct or take part in a survey, either by asking questions or by responding.

Timings

Exercise 3b can be omitted if there is not enough time.

Possible lesson break: after exercise 3b.

PREPARATION

1a It would be better to do the two activities in exercise 1a separately. First students make a list of all the sports they have played in their life. Maybe have a quick class feedback to see that everyone has got a reasonable list before moving onto the next stage of the activity. Then, ask students to put them in order of enjoyment and finally to share the information in pairs.

(!) Some people have played more sports than others. You might like to consider increasing the scope of sports to things like playing chess, etc. if some students have very small lists. Also, some people enjoy sports more than others. In this case, when ordering the items on their list, they should note how they feel about each sport, e.g. they might say *very enjoyable* against their number 1 choice, whereas some people might have number 1 only as *quite enjoyable*. This will also heighten awareness of what they will do in exercise 3b and when making their own questionnaires.

1b Students do activity as per Coursebook. As a follow-up, elicit examples of other situations that exemplify the personality type. Students might also like to discuss which people they know who exemplify these personality types.

> **1** sociable; **2** competitive; **3** self-sufficient (individualistic); **4** risk-seeking; **5** non-competitive; **6** cautious/careful

1c Students do this activity in pairs. Each pair looks at the lists of sports they made in exercise 1a, particularly those sports that they identified as enjoyable. Students work together to guess which personality type goes with which sport. Then let the pairs share their conclusions with the rest of the class and see if other pairs have come to similar conclusions.

SITUATION

2a Students do activity as per Coursebook. They discuss question 3 in pairs and then feed back to the class. You can check they understand the following words:

train (v) – to prepare for a sport by practising and exercising or help someone else to do this

fit (adj) – healthy and strong, especially because you exercise regularly

suit (v) – to be acceptable, right or suitable for someone

> **1** psychologists help sportspeople to improve their performance and choice of sport; **2** professional sportspeople, coaches, sports lovers; **3** students' own answers

`2.34`

2b Students listen to the interview just once, then check as a class.

> **1**d; **2**b; **3**c (They don't discuss situation a.)

2c Students may already know the answers to these questions from one listening, so give them a chance to answer first before listening again and checking.

> **1** Q1: B; Q2: A; Q3: A; **2** rugby, white-water rafting

3a Students should not need a third listening for this task so either do this with exercise 2c or do it without listening again.

> 1b; 2c; 3a

Tracks 2.34, 2.35 and 2.36
Dr Mannit, Alex

Dr M: Well, Alex, thanks again for agreeing to take part in this research. The interview starts with a short questionnaire, and then we'll talk more about your personal experience.

A: OK.

Dr M: Right, well, here's the first question: If you had to do an exam next week, would you …
  A) work with friends in a study group and prepare with them?
  B) work with friends and study on your own?
  C) only study on your own?

A: Well … that's a difficult one … I have studied on my own for exams before, but for my last ones I worked in a study group, you know, with my friends, and I liked that.

Dr M: So, which would you do? A, B or C?

A: Right … erm, let me see … I think I'd do B, a bit of both.

Dr M: OK, and the next question: If you had a tennis game with a friend, would you …
  A) train hard before in order to win the match?
  B) practise a little and do your best?
  C) let your friend win?

A: Well, I don't play tennis.

Dr M: I understand, but if you did, what would you do?

A: OK, then I'd do A – I hate losing.

Dr M: Fine. And finally: If you could buy any car you wanted, would you buy …
  A) a fast sports car, like a Ferrari?
  B) a classic car, like a Rolls Royce?
  C) a reliable car, like a Honda?

A: Hmm, let me think … well, to be honest, I'd buy a Ferrari. I'd love to have such a fast car.

Dr M: OK, well, thank you for that, and for answering honestly. Would you like to know what your answers mean?

A: Yes, I would. Can you tell me now?

Dr M: Sure, let's see. You chose B for the first question, so you're quite sociable. You chose A for the second one, so you're very competitive. Finally, you would buy the Ferrari. This shows you are happy to take risks. From these answers, I think you would like team sports, and, as competition and risk are very important for you, I think you should try rugby, or perhaps white-water rafting.

A: Really? Well, the only sport I play is football, and I love that.

Dr M: Well, that's a competitive team sport, isn't it?

A: That's true.

Dr M: And have you ever tried adventure sports?

A: No, I haven't, but I think I'd like to try white-water rafting. It looks fun.

Dr M: Well, as I said, I think it would suit your personality.

3b Before doing this activity, tell students that all these personality type adjectives can be graded. Point out the example between brackets in the instructions. Elicit all the other possible examples for the adjectives in the box in exercise 1b.

> **Q1** A) very sociable; B) quite sociable; C) self-sufficient (individualistic); **Q2** A) very competitive B) quite competitive C) non-competitive; **Q3** A) very risk-seeking B) quite risk-seeking C) cautious/careful

KEY LANGUAGE: conversation fillers

`2.35`

4a Before listening, introduce the issue of conversation fillers. Tell students that sometimes when we are asked questions, we need a few seconds to arrange our thoughts. There are phrases we can use to do this. For example, write *That's a good question*. Tell students if they can think of circumstances when they would say this in their mother tongue (e.g. at an interview when someone asks you an important question like *Why are you the best person for this job?*). Elicit from students if they remember similar instances from the recording. Write any they recall on the board and then do this activity as per Coursebook. Students can then check if they remembered correctly.

Let students brainstorm and try and come up with other possible conversation fillers.

> **1** difficult; **2** see; **3** think, honest

> **Track 2.35**
> See audioscript for Track 2.34.

4b Students do activity as per Coursebook. Make sure they understand that if they say *Let me think …* or *Give me a moment …* , in reality they only have about one second before they need to continue speaking otherwise it is not a conversation filler, it is a conversation stopper!

Students can do exercise 4 from the Extra practice activities on page 149 either in class or for homework.

pronunciation

`2.36`

5a Tell students that there is a specific intonation pattern that we use when we are listing things. Show them the example in the exercise and the choice of intonations. Practise with them what the three options would sound like before they listen and choose the right one. Then students do activity as per Coursebook.

> **3** (rise, rise, fall)

5b Students do activity as per Coursebook.

Tell students to prepare a shopping list for a shopping trip they are going to do at the weekend. Then in pairs, they tell each other what's on their shopping lists using the right intonation.

> **Track 2.36**
> See audioscript for Track 2.34.

TASK: doing a survey

6a Tell students that their task in this lesson is to do a class survey to find out about the dominant personality types in their classroom. Read through the instructions stage by stage with the students and then do one model question as a class to show them how to do this. Then put students into pairs and walk around the class monitoring and making sure the three options are properly graded and make sense. Students, in their pairs, should make sure they both have a clean copy of the questionnaire they are going to use before the end of this activity.

6b Split up the pairs into Student As and Bs. Tell Student As they are going to interview each other. Student Bs are also going to interview each other. Explain that when they do the interviews, they should remember to do the following:

- make a note of each interviewee's answers;
- tell the interviewees about the results of the psychological analysis (i.e. their personality types) and make a note of it.

When they have finished interviewing their part of the class, the pairs come back together and tell each other about their interviews (i.e. Student As will talk about their interviews with other As and Bs will do the same). Make sure they answer the following questions in their discussion:

Who did you interview?

What answers did they choose?

What sports would be good for them?

What personality types are there in the class?

For homework, students prepare a class profile which they can present in chart form or written form in the next lesson, e.g.

For question 1, eight out of ten people chose a), and two people chose d). etc.

The class is sociable and competitive, … etc.

HOMEWORK OPTIONS

Students can do exercise 6 from the Extra practice activities on page 149.

Students do the exercises on page 74 of the Workbook.

12.4 STUDY AND WRITING SKILLS

Lesson topic and staging

This lesson focuses on the study skill of doing an exam and on the skill of writing a formal email.

In the first half of the lesson, students begin by thinking about their best and worst experiences of exams and how they felt. They then listen to a teacher giving exam tips, listening for gist and for specific information. Students think of other tips that could help and then do a quiz to find out more about looking after their health before an exam. Finally, they listen to students talking about how their exams went, the things they did wrong and the solutions. To conclude this part, students discuss what they have heard in this lesson and what they plan to do for future exams.

In the second half of the lesson, students think about going to study in an English-speaking country and prepare a list of questions that they would like to ask to find out about a school before going there. Students then read a model formal email asking for information about a language school. They read for specific information, analyse the organisation of the text and compare it to an informal email. Students also look at how commas are used in certain sentences. Finally, they use the template and the results of their analysis to write their own formal email to a school.

Objectives

By the end of the lesson, students should have:

- discussed experiences of exams
- listened for gist and specific information
- considered the connection between health and taking exams
- listened to things that go wrong in exams and how they can be avoided
- considered and planned what they will do in future for exams
- thought about studying in an English-speaking country
- prepared questions they would like to ask a language school
- read for specific information
- analysed a formal email for organisation
- practised using commas
- written a formal email to a language school

Timings

Exercise 10 could be omitted if there is not enough time.

The writing part of exercise 11a can be done for homework.

Possible lesson break: after exercise 5.

STUDY SKILLS: doing exams

1 Students do this in small groups and then as a class. If you hear of any particular things that students did that are relevant to the rest of this lesson, then make a note of them so you can refer to them later. Personalisation always brings a lesson to life. Be careful with timing on this activity as students can probably talk for ever on this subject.

2.37

2a Students do activity as per Coursebook. Let them check in pairs before doing class feedback.

> 2, 3 and 7

2b Make sure students understand that you want them to listen to all the eight points from exercise 2a that were mentioned and identify the advice given for them. Allow students to remember what they can before playing the recording again, although it is unlikely their notes will be detailed enough after one listening. Let pairs of students pool their answers together before doing class feedback.

> 1 False – after a while you don't learn anything new. Better to spend time improving general level of English and doing grammar self-study.
> 2 True – Don't go to a party the night before, and don't stay up until three in the morning revising. You need to be fresh so that you can think quickly.
> 3 True – Last year a student was two minutes late and he wasn't allowed into the exam room.
> 4 True, but the most important thing is to do exactly what the exam asks you to do.
> 5 False – If you don't know which answer is correct, make a guess. You might be right. Don't leave any gaps. Answer every question.
> 6 False – It's a waste of time. Spend time thinking of good ideas, or planning your work.
> 7 True – If you can't answer a question, go on to the next one, and come back to it later, if you have time.
> 8 False – Students waste a lot of time looking up words that they don't really need to look up. Just check one or two key words.

Track 2.37

Lecturer, Students

L: OK everyone. That's it for this year. I hope you've enjoyed the course and feel that you've learned a lot. Here's a little handout with some tips on how to prepare for the exam. Before we look at that, can I also mention a few general points about doing exams? First of all, when you're revising, don't do lots and lots of practice tests. Of course, it's good to do some practice tests but, after a certain point, you don't learn anything new. It's better to spend the time improving your general level of English by reading books and newspapers, by watching a film in English, or by just doing some grammar self-study.

continued…

Secondly, make sure you're not tired on the day of the exam. Don't go to a party the night before, and don't stay up until three in the morning revising. You need to be fresh so that you can think quickly in the exam. Thirdly, don't be late for the exam. It seems obvious, doesn't it? But last year one student was two minutes late and he wasn't allowed into the exam room. They sent him away … Right, now, once you're in the exam, what's the most important thing?

s1: Use correct English?

L: Well, clearly, that's important, but the most important thing is … do exactly what the exam asks you to do. Follow the instructions on the exam paper. Make sure you understand what the questions are asking you to do. Read the questions two or three times before you start.
Some of the questions are multiple-choice questions, and you have to choose one answer from a, b, c or d. First of all, decide which ones you think are definitely wrong, and cross them out. Then choose from the others. If you don't know which answer is correct, make a guess. You might be right. Don't leave any gaps. Answer every question.
There are also questions that ask you to write something. Now, let me ask you a question. Let's imagine you're doing a piece of writing in an exam. Is it a good idea to do a draft, that's a first copy, and then make a final copy?

ss: Yes, I think so.

L: Well, actually, no. I think this is a waste of time. In my experience, there's almost no difference between the draft and the final piece of writing. And it usually takes ten minutes or more to rewrite. It's much better to spend that time thinking of good ideas, or planning your work.

s2: But sometimes we make mistakes and we need to change something, or cross something out.

L: Yes, that's OK. After all, it's an exam. You're not expected to write a beautiful-looking piece of writing. The important thing is that it's clear. One final thing concerns timing. Don't spend too long on one question. If you can't answer a question, go on to the next one, and come back to it later, if you have time. OK, would you like to ask anything?

s3: Yes, can we use dictionaries?

L: No, you can't. And, actually, that's good. Research shows that students who can use dictionaries in exams waste a lot of time looking up words that they don't really need to look up. If any time you can use a dictionary in an exam, try not to use it too much. Just check one or two key words. Right, well, good luck. I hope to see some of you again next year …

2c Students work together in groups to do this. Ask them to think about the advice they have already heard and anything else that might help. In feedback, discuss with the class the suitability of any advice suggested.

3a Before doing the quiz, ask students what they know about health and exams, e.g. always go to sleep early the night before an exam. Students work in pairs to do the quiz.

3b Students check their answers with the key on page 111. Ask them if they were surprised by any of the information. Again, ask them to come up with any other health advice for tests and discuss the suitability of each piece of advice.

2.38

4a Tell students they are going to listen to other students talking about the exams they have just completed and the mistakes they made. Before listening, elicit from students the most common mistakes that they make in exams.

> 1d; 2c; 3a; 4b

4b Students do activity as per Coursebook individually and then check in pairs.

> **1** do more revision and make a revision timetable;
> **2** write down some notes; **3** make a writing plan;
> **4** give lots of examples

Track 2.38
Interviewer, Jenny, Bethany, Alan, Bill

I: Hi, I'm from the university radio. Can I ask you what you thought about that exam?

J: Oh, I thought it was pretty hard, actually, but I suppose I've only got myself to blame. I didn't do enough revision – I started it too late. I couldn't remember much, so I couldn't do many of the questions. Next time, I'm going to do more revision, and make a revision timetable.

I: Hi, we're making a programme for the university radio. What did you think of that exam?

B: Well, it was OK, but I didn't have enough time to finish the last question – but at least I wrote down some notes about my ideas for that question. I might still get a few marks for that.

I: Excuse me, how do you think you did in that exam?

A: Oh, I think I'll pass it, but I really messed up one question. It was an essay about women and sport, and, well, I thought I had a lot of ideas so I just started writing – I didn't bother to make a plan. And that was a big mistake. Half way through, I didn't know what to say. I got confused and, well, I tried to start again, but it was too late. Next time I'll make sure I make a plan, even if I think I've got lots of ideas.

I: Hello, can I just ask whether the exam was OK?

B: Yeah sure. It was fine really. One question was a bit difficult – it was about different personality types and I didn't have very many ideas. But, I remembered my lecturer's advice, and made sure that I gave a lot of examples for each idea. So, in the end, my answer wasn't too short. And the other questions were pretty easy, so yeah, I reckon I've done well.

4c Students discuss this quickly as a whole group. If students come up with different problems that were not mentioned in the recording, ask them to suggest solutions to avoid their mistakes.

5 Students discuss the questions first in pairs and then as a whole class. Make sure that each of your students has thought about the subject and has made a commitment to doing something to improve their performance in exams.

WRITING SKILLS: a formal email

6 Find out which students in your class have been to an English-speaking country and attended a course. If you have some, ask them to share their experiences with the rest of the class. You can ask them the following questions:

What was the school like?

Where did you stay?

Was it what you expected? Why / Why not?

If there are no students who have done this, ask them only the final question in the activity.

- If you are teaching in an English-speaking country already, your students can talk about their present experience.

7 Students do activity as per Coursebook individually. Then ask them to compare their questions with a partner. Finally get some examples of good questions from the pairs.

Before doing this activity, you might like to brainstorm with the class the sort of things you would want to find out before going to the school or even choosing a school.

8 You want students to read this quickly and find the questions only, so don't give them more than a minute. A good tip to teach them beforehand is that when they are looking for questions in a text, they should scan it for question marks.

9 This exercise focuses on the difference between formal and informal letters. It also makes the point that, although it is widely assumed that Internet communication is informal, there is also a need for a formal style since a growing range of types of communication is now done through the Net.

To begin with, ask students the following questions:

Do you ever need to be formal when writing an email? (yes)

When? (writing emails to your bank, to complain, etc.)

What would a formal email look like in comparison to a formal letter? (Don't give an answer to this as they will know by the end of this exercise.)

Students then do activity as per Coursebook, in pairs and then as a class.

Tell students to imagine the email is a formal letter that they are sending by post. Where would they put their address, the school's address, the date, etc.? How would they finish the letter?

> **1** I would like / Would you mind / Could you tell me if / As I mentioned / Would I be able to / I look forward to hearing from you
> **2** paragraph 1: course she wants to do; paragraph 2: the English part of the course (number of teachers, exams, certificate); paragraph 3: sports; paragraph 4: accommodation
> **3** use of full forms in formal email, contractions in informal email; use of formal phrases; different ways to begin and end; different use of vocabulary, e.g. *dead, popped out*; use of questions like *Guess what?*; use of exclamation marks

10 Students do activity as per Coursebook. You can elicit from the students why commas are placed where they are (because the first phrase foregrounds the main clause), but do not spend too much time on this as rules for commas are notoriously unreliable.

> **1** Would you mind sending me some information about the accommodation, please?
> **2** If I came earlier in the summer, would the course be cheaper?
> **3** Concerning the evening activities, will our teachers come with us?
> **4** As I mentioned in my last email, my level of English is quite good.
> **5** However, I still have problems understanding native speakers.

11a This can be done for homework or in class. If in class, do activity as per Coursebook.

11b In class, students swap emails. Ask students to respond to what they see in the email. If there is anything they don't understand, they should ask a question or ask for clarification in their reply. When students have completed this and returned their replies, ask pairs to read out their emails and replies and the class discusses any problems with relevance, grammar, content, etc.

If you have a smart class, you could do this for real, via email.

E You can now do photocopiable activity 12B to practise the vocabulary studied in Unit 12.

HOMEWORK OPTIONS

Students do the exercises on page 75 of the Workbook.

Review

UNITS 10–12

GRAMMAR

1

> a type of boat racing from south-east Asia, with colourful boats and lots of people in them

2

> **1** is taking place; **2** are competing; **3** have been racing; **4** were made; **5** were rowed; **6** was set up; **7** has been increasing; **8** has been going up; **9** were held; **10** have been taking place

`2.39`

3a

> The man is definitely going; the woman isn't sure.

Track 2.39

Ben, Penny

B: Talking of holidays, are you going to the dragon boat festival again this year?

P: I don't know. It's too far for a weekend and James is really busy at work. How about you?

B: Yes, we booked last week. We enjoyed it so much last year. We're leaving early and stopping off to see my parents on the way.

P: Oh, that's a good idea. Where are you staying in Vancouver?

B: We've booked a hotel near the festival. It looks quite good.

P: Mmm, I don't think we can afford a hotel this year. We haven't got enough spare money at the moment. What's the entertainment going to be like? I mean, do you know anything about the bands?

B: Yeah, but only that several bands are coming from south-east Asia.

P: Oh, that sounds good. I love Asian music. I don't know, ... if we went this year, we'd have to be very careful with money.

B: Have you thought about camping? Your kids would love it.

P: You know, that's a really good idea. Yes, if we camped, then we could take our own food, too, so it would be a lot cheaper.

B: Look, why don't I find out about some campsites in the area?

P: That's really nice of you, but have you got enough time for that?

B: Yeah, no problem. I want to check out some other things on the Internet anyway ...

3b

> 1d; 2f ; 3a; 4h; 5c; 6g; 7e; 8b

4

> **2, 6, 7** correct
> **1** The ambassador is **arriving** at ten tomorrow morning.
> **3** Elizabeth Kostova's first book **was** published last year.
> **4** This supermarket has **been** using paper bags for years.
> **5** We need to cut **down** the rubbish we produce.
> **8** The sports centre would be more popular if it **taught** gymnastics.
> **9** There are too **many** adverts for junk food on TV.
> **10** My son isn't **good enough** for the school football team.

VOCABULARY

5

> **1** glass; **2** jars; **3** plastic; **4** pots; **5** cardboard; **6** cartons; **7** packets; **8** boxes; **9** aluminium; **10** cans

6

> **across:** committee, staff, assistant
> **down:** ambassador, minister, department
> **up:** president
> **diagonally right to left:** spokesperson
> **diagonally left to right:** civil servant

C	O	M	M	I	T	T	E	E	X	O	S
F	I	N	I	J	K	N	S	Q	U	P	T
L	A	V	N	E	B	E	R	D	O	L	D
O	M	A	I	B	H	D	M	K	P	S	E
E	B	W	S	L	V	I	E	I	A	G	P
R	A	Z	T	E	S	S	T	A	F	F	A
J	S	D	E	C	P	E	S	Y	H	O	R
P	S	F	R	E	I	R	R	T	G	H	T
H	A	X	R	S	B	P	N	V	L	M	M
S	D	S	Z	H	J	V	P	I	A	D	E
I	O	Q	O	C	G	U	Z	K	R	N	N
N	R	Y	A	S	S	I	S	T	A	N	T

KEY LANGUAGE

2.40

7a

They agree to meet at 3.00 on Thursday afternoon.

7b

1b; 2e; 3a; 4h; 5f; 6d; 7g; 8c

Track 2.40

Tutor, Student

T: You wanted a meeting next week about your project, didn't you?

S: That's right.

T: OK, let's try to arrange one. Let me see ... I can do Tuesday at 11.00.

S: Erm, I'm in lectures all day Tuesday, I'm afraid. What about Wednesday at 9.00?

T: No, I'm not planning to come in till 11.00 on Wednesday. You couldn't do straight after lunch, could you, say 2.00?

S: Well, I could, but only for half an hour. I'm going to the dentist at 2.30.

T: I think we'll need more than half an hour, about an hour, I'd say. I'm free all day Friday.

S: Mmm, I'm taking the 10.30 train home on Friday, for the weekend. Nine isn't too early, is it?

T: Well, to tell the truth, yes. It takes me over an hour to get here. You aren't busy on Thursday afternoon, are you?

S: No, well, not until 4.00.

T: Well, what about 3.00 on Thursday then?

S: Yes, that's fine, thanks.

8 Students do activity as per Coursebook. Give them a minute or two beforehand to prepare what they are going to say. Then do a class feedback to check they have completed the activity.

(!) You can mark students either on how close they keep to the template given in exercise 7b, or on their fluency. Alternatively, you can mark for both.

LANGUAGE CHECK

9

1 My uncle is a **civil servant** in the public transport department.

2 Plans **were announced** to set up a new government department.

3 The new stadium is **only two** minutes from the underground.

4 He has **been writing** soap operas for the last ten years.

5 You can recycle those books. Don't throw **them away**.

6 They didn't listen very carefully, **did they**?

7 If **they had** the money, they'd send him to a sports academy.

8 We've spent **too much** money on your birthday.

9 She isn't **talented enough** to be an actor.

10 That's a **difficult one**. I really don't know the answer.

LOOK BACK

10 Students do the exercise in small pairs or groups.

- talk about the United Nations: 10.1, exercise 1;
- read about the development of Microsoft: 10.2, exercise 2;
- work on predicting vocabulary when listening: 10.4, exercise 3c;
- learn words for containers and materials: 11.2, exercise 1;
- listen to a funding committee discussing a project: 11.3, exercise 3;
- write a report about a building proposal: 11.4, exercise 10;
- learn how to talk about unreal situations: 12.1, exercises 4 and 5;
- read about big business in sport: 12.2, exercise 2;
- carry out a survey about personality: 12.3, exercise 6

Extra practice key

Unit 1

1 1 I often go snowboarding in winter. 2 It is not very cold in the UK. 3 When do people go skiing in your country? 4 There are a lot of droughts in Africa. 5 Do you like mountain biking? 6 Is the weather changeable in your country? 7 Where do you go swimming? 8 It never snows in the jungle.

2 1 is changing; 2 are getting; 3 have; 4 causes; 5 are dying

3 1 Do you live in the city or the countryside? 2 Are you interested in sports? 3 Are you working hard at the moment? 4 When do you usually relax? 5 Is the weather good in summer in your country? 6 Is it raining at the moment?

5 1d; 2c; 3e; 4b; 5a

6 2 humid; 3 foggy; 4 cloudy; 5 drought; 6 hurricane; 7 blizzard

7 1 sea kayaking, snorkelling, white-water rafting; 2 horse riding, wildlife watching; 3 skiing, snowboarding; 4 horse riding, mountain biking, skiing, snowboarding, trekking, wildlife watching

Unit 2

1 1 My mother left school when she was fourteen. 2 Did she start a new job last year? 3 When were you born? 4 Last weekend my brother married his girlfriend. 5 We did not have a lot of money last year. 6 'Did they have a good holiday?' 'Yes, they did.' 7 We ate a lot of pasta last night. 8 She went to university in 2006.

2 2 Were you sleeping at 11.00 last night? 3 What were you doing at 8.00 yesterday evening? 4 Were you studying English this time last year? 5 What else were you studying then? 6 Where were you living ten years ago?

3 1 was having, rang; 2 did, were coming; 3 was running, fell, broke; 4 met, was skiing; 5 wrote, was recovering

4 2 Maria was working at the supermarket when she received her exam results. 3 Sam was eating some nuts when his tooth broke. 4 Angela was waiting at the station when she found $100.

5 1c, f, h; 2a, e, g; 3b, d, i

6 2 creative; 3 friendly; 4 hard-working; 5 helpful; 6 inspirational; 7 lovely; 8 miserable; 9 sociable; 10 talented

7 1 hard-working; 2 miserable; 3 talented; 4 sociable; 5 helpful; 6 inspirational

8 1 at the moment; 2 at first; 3 until; 4 then; 5 Afterwards

Unit 3

1 1 Ø; 2 a; 3 an, The, an; 4 the; 5 a; 6 Ø, The; 7 Ø, the; 8 a, the

2 1a; 2a; 3b; 4b

3 2d who/that; 3e which/that; 4a which/that; 5c who/that; 6b which/that

4 1 That's the woman ~~which~~ bought my car. *who/that;* 2 Richard Branson is the person who ~~he~~ started Virgin. 3 It's a word ~~who~~ means 'powerful'. *which/that;* 4 I bought a newspaper that ~~it~~ had the whole story. 5 It was on the programme ~~what~~ follows the news. *that/which*

5 1 have a pizza; 2 try the vegetarian pizza; 3 go on Monday; 4 go to the Leisure Centre; 5 going swimming; 6 join this month; 7 do aerobics

6 1 station; 2 articles; 3 celebrities; 4 dramas; 5 presenter; 6 nature

7 1 scientist; 2 Psychology; 3 politician; 4 Photography; 5 artist; 6 Journalism

Unit 4

1 1 have been; 2 have trained; 3 have gone; 4 have employed; 5 have started; 6 haven't finished; 7 haven't visited; 8 have saved; 9 has been; 10 has taught

2 1 have visited; 2 went; 3 has built; 4 Have you ever; 5 phoned; 6 didn't see; 7 didn't finish; 8 have written

3 2 I've had a cold for five days. 3 Alice has known her husband since 1981. 4 Mark has been married for two years. 5 We've had this house for four years. 6 I've had this toothache since I got up.

4 2 shouldn't, because; 3 shouldn't, because; 4 should, so that; 5 shouldn't, because; 6 should, (in order) to

6 1 surgeon; 2 malnutrition; 3 insomnia; 4 surgery (hospital, clinic); 5 dentist; 6 injury; 7 depression; 8 private hospital; 9 lack of motivation; 10 poor memory

Unit 5

1 1 the cleverest; 2 more romantic than; 3 more tropical than; 3 best; 4 worse than; 5 the most expensive

2 1a) Lewis is taller than Jason. b) Kevin is the tallest boy. 2a) Lake Ontario is deeper than Lake Erie. b) Lake Superior is the deepest lake.
3a) A Hyundai is more expensive than a Smart car. b) A Porsche is the most expensive car.

3 1 Oxford is less dangerous than Nottingham. 2 New York is less expensive than London. 3 This lake is the least impressive. 4 Stonehenge is less mysterious than Carnac. 5 The south of France is less flat than the north. 6 This island is the least popular. 7 The Atlantic is less calm than the Mediterranean. 8 Cricket is the least exciting sport.

4 Cross out: 1 Much; 2 don't have many; 3 few; 4 many; 5 few; 6 little

5 1 I can see mountains **in** the background. 2 In this photo, a man **is waiting** at a bus stop. 3 On **the** right of the picture there's a river. 4 The people **are all talking** about something. 5 In **the** second photograph, a woman is going into a shop. 6 On the left **of** the photo there's a sports car. 7 It looks very fast.

6 2 forest; 3 hill; 4 rock; 5 wave; 6 crab

7 1 causes; 2 hope; 3 plants; 4 damage/harm; 5 shop; 6 ship; 7 shop; 8 shipped

9 1 correct; 2 My sisters all have brown eyes. In contrast, my eyes are blue. 3 Red squirrels come from the UK, whereas grey squirrels come from North America. 4 correct

Unit 6

1 1 I think people might live longer in the future. 2 Doctors definitely won't find cures for a lot of diseases. 3 Will people retire later in twenty years' time? 4 People may not take holidays a long way from home. 5 We won't fly as much as now. 6 Families might (*or* will probably) get smaller. 7 I will definitely retire when I'm 60. 8 The number of students at university will increase.

2 1 We'll definitely find a better fuel than petrol. 2 We'll probably get our news only from the Internet. 3 Couples might divorce more. 4 Humans probably won't go back to the Moon. 5 We definitely won't have more leisure time!

3 1b; 2d; 3e; 4a; 5c

5 1b; 2d; 3a; 4f; 5e; 6c

6 1 retired; 2 teenager; 3 middle-aged; 4 adult; 5 child; 6 elderly; 7 adolescent

7 1 careless; 2 unkind; 3 unhappy; 4 unlucky; 5 unusual; 6 hopeless (or *useless*)

8 1 as; 2 suitable; 3 graduates; 4 so; 5 childcare; 6 so

Unit 7

1 2 mustn't; 3 have to; 4 have to; 5 mustn't; 6 don't have to

2 1 don't have to; 2 must; 3 mustn't; 4 must; 5 have to; 6 must; 7 have to; 8 don't have to

3 2 He couldn't walk after the accident. 3 Could you understand that lecture? 4 They couldn't collect all the evidence at the scene. 5 We didn't have to study Economics at school. 6 I could speak Russian when I was a child. 7 We had to study Latin at our school. 8 Did you have to spend all that money yesterday?

4 1 This has led; 2 so; 3 This means; 4 causes

5 1 Biology; 2 History; 3 Medicine; 4 Astronomy; 5 Physics; 6 Chemistry; 7 Mathematics; 8 Economics

6 1 commits; 2 Investigators; 3 fingerprints; 4 evidence; 5 analyse; 6 discover; 7 solve

7 1c; 2d; 3b; 4f; 5a; 6e

Unit 8

1 1 to dream; 2 studying; 3 to have; 4 being; 5 falling; 6 to get; 7 going; 8 doing; 9 to sleep; 10 going

2 2 I hope to; 3 I'm going to; 4 I'd like to; 5 I hope to; 6 I'd like to; 7 I'm going to; 8 I hope to

4 1 fancy; 2 prefer; 3 mind; 4 interested; 5 rather

5 1 sleep through; 2 sleepless; 3 doze; 4 fall asleep; 5 feel sleepy

6 2 tired; 3 boring; 4 embarrassing; 5 frightening; 6 bored; 7 frightened; 8 embarrassed

7 1 boat trip; 2 theatre; 3 dancing; 4 concert; 5 museum; 6 dinner

8 1 suddenly; 2 at that moment; 3 after some time; 4 Finally; 5 before long

Unit 9

1 1 used to; 2 didn't use to; 3 used to; 4 didn't use to; 5 didn't use to

2 1 correct; 2 The company used to pay very good money. 3 I didn't use to work very hard. 4 I went on a long business trip to Korea last year. 5 correct; 6 Did you use to travel a lot on business? 7 We used to have longer holidays than we do now. 8 'Did you use to work harder?' 'Yes, we did.'

3 1 imports, are imported; 2 sells, are made; 3 book, is done; 4 are cleaned, come

4 1a (active); 2b (passive); 3b (passive)

5 1 That seems a bit high; 2 If you order; 3 How about; 4 I'm not sure we can pay that much; 5 Shall we call it; 5 That sounds fine

6 1 manufacturer; 2 colleagues; 3 employee; 4 retailer; 5 buyer

7 **Across:** 3 chat; 4 long; 5 training **Down:** 1 video; 2 market; 4 lunch

8 1 To begin with; 2 Following this; 3 Next; 4 After; 5 Lastly

Unit 10

1 1 The minister is flying to Geneva tomorrow. 2 Are you staying at the Hilton Hotel this week? 3 I'm giving a talk on education this afternoon. 4 The situation is getting worse. 5 They aren't building a new stadium for next year's Olympics. 6 Is the president coming to the conference?

2 1 F; 2 P; 3 F; 4 P; 5 F; 6 F

3 1 was set up; 2 was started; 3 began; 4 moved; 5 left; 6 was almost killed; 7 recovered; 8 was sold

4 2 no: ~~by Microsoft~~; 3 yes: by Picasso; 4 no: ~~by the present Secretary General~~; 5 yes: by a popular newspaper; 6 no: ~~by builders~~

5 1 Tickets will cost only £30.00. 2 They have built six world-class hotels. 3 The new hotel is just a few minutes from the station. 4 It was a memorable experience. 5 The stadium is only a short walk from the station. 6 The new stadium will give a magnificent view of the events.

6 1f; 2c; 3d; 4a; 5b; 6e

7 1 comprehensive; 2 high-speed; 3 comfortable; 4 world-class; 5 spacious; 6 fantastic

8 1 although; 2 Therefore; 3 On the other hand; 4 Although

Unit 11

1 2 We have been recycling plastic since 1995. 3 Arctic ice has been melting quickly for the last few years. 4 I have been reusing plastic bags for a few years. 5 The car industry has been reducing fuel pollution since the 1980s. 6 Global warming has been harming the Earth for a long time.

2 1 had; 2 been hiring; 3 been; 4 been saving; 5 known; 6 been burning; 7 been using; 8 understood

5 2 are carrying out; 3 cut down; 4 set up; 5 find out; 6 threw away; 7 Pick ... up; 8 wrote down

6 1 Are those your socks on the floor? Pick them up! 2 The price of petrol has been going up recently. 3 Can you give me back that book on recycling? 4 The founders of IBM have set up a new business. 5 Do you throw away old things?

7 1h; 2a; 3f; 4c; 5e; 6g; 7d; 8b

8 1 glacier; 2 rubbish; 3 sea ice; 4 wasteland; 5 well-kept; 6 rainforest

9 1 aluminium cans; 2 jars, glass; 3 paper; 4 bottles, cartons; 5 boxes, cardboard; 6 tube

Unit 12

1 1a; 2e; 3c; 4b; 5f; 6d

2 1 would ... do; 2 didn't have; 3 had; 4 would get; 5 weren't; 6 would be; 7 didn't have to; 8 would have; 9 didn't have; 10 would have to; 11 did; 12 would get

3 1 We can't get enough funding for our club. 2 There are too many aspects to this problem. 3 correct; 4 Most of our players aren't competitive enough to win. 5 correct; 6 correct; 7 It costs too much money to do this sport. 8 correct

4 1 That's a difficult one. 2 Well, 3 Let me; 4 to be honest, 5 I think I'd

5 1 football; 2 dragon boat racing; 3 badminton; 4 judo; 5 sailing; 6 cycling

6 1 self-sufficient; 2 sociable; 3 competitive; 4 cautious

Teaching notes for photocopiable activities

1A World weather (use after Lesson 1.2) **
Aim: to practise grammar (present simple versus present continuous) and vocabulary (types of weather)
Grouping: whole class, then pairwork
Procedure:

- Write the word *weather* on the board. Students brainstorm the types of weather they know and have studied in Lessons 1.1 and 1.2. Encourage students to word-build, using the related noun, adjective and *-ing* form of the verb. The final list on the board should include the following:
sun, sunny; rain, rainy, raining; snow, snowy, snowing; cloud, cloudy; fog, foggy; wind, windy; hurricane; thunderstorm; blizzard; drought; cold

- Cut out the photocopies and hand out the strip at the top (with the weather icons).

- Ask students to look at the icons. Ask them to guess which icon corresponds with which type of weather. This can be done as whole-class activity or initially through pairwork.

- Ask students what the weather is usually like there (where your school is). Write possible answers on the board. Then ask students to tell you what the weather is like today. Elicit a present simple answer (with a state verb, e.g. *It is rainy today*, and/or a present continuous sentence, *It is raining today*) and write these on the board. Then ask students to tell you why we use the structures the way we do in these sentences. This is to remind students of present simple and present continuous usage.

- Divide students into Student As and Student Bs and hand out the rest of the photocopy. Ask students to look at their respective maps. For each student, one map shows what the weather is usually like in certain cities. The other map shows what the weather is like today in certain cities. Tell students that some information is missing on their maps. They should ask their partners to find out the missing information, using questions and answers with present simple and present continuous. Do remember to model this to avoid confusion. Give students a few minutes to check the information they have and then, in pairs, the students will complete the activity. At the end of the activity ask students to read out their combined information about each city in full sentences.

- Ask students to think about the usual weather and today's weather in the cities. Ask them what they think people in those cities usually do or are doing today. Give an example, e.g.
Usually, in Oslo, people wear warm clothes. Today, people in Oslo are using their umbrellas.

- Give students a few minutes to prepare their sentences and then get feedback as a full-class activity.

1B Dictionary crossword (use after Lesson 1.4) **
Aim: to give students more contact and familiarity with dictionary entries; to revise vocabulary from Unit 1
Grouping: whole class, then individual, pairwork and group work (depending on options)
Procedure:

- Write the word *definition* on the board and ask students what it means. Ask them where you can find definitions

(answer: dictionaries), and then what information they expect to find in a dictionary definition. Answers include:
- type of word
- meaning
- pronunciation
- example sentence
- (possibly) opposite
- (possibly) more than one meaning

- Give out the crossword. Point out to the students that the definitions in the crossword are for words they have studied in the unit. Ask which thing that we normally find in definitions is missing (answer: example sentences). Elicit from the students that the first thing they may do to make the crossword easier is identify the types of word. Give an example (*1 across is an adjective, so is* rain *possible, or* snowing? *No, because* rain *is a noun and* snowing *is an* -ing *form.*)

- Students now do the crossword on their own.

- Then group students up into pairs or threes to compare answers. Do feedback as a whole group.

- For each definition, ask students to write example sentences which show the meanings of the words.

- Ask students in groups to make a small crossword of up to ten words with dictionary-type definitions, which can then be passed round the class for other groups to do.

Options:

You may like to add some of the answers and mark them 'Student A' and 'Student B' to make the activity an information gap.

You may also like to write in the first letter of each word if you think it is too difficult.

You may add in all the answers to the crossword and blank out the definitions, then get students to write the definitions for the answers.

> **Across: 1** bright; **2** mild; **5** rafting; **7** hurricane;
> **9** thunderstorm; **10** chill; **12** flying; **13** changeable;
> **14** fog; **15** season; **16** dark
> **Down: 1** blizzard; **2** major; **3** drought; **4** countryside;
> **6** trekking; **8** cool; **11** extremely; **14** flood

2A Murder at Chester House (use after Lesson 2.2) **
Aim: to revise grammar (past simple and past continuous)
Grouping: whole class, followed by groups of three, then six
Procedure:

- Write *Last night* on the board. Ask students what they did last night. Elicit answers promoting the use of the past simple. Then write *8.30*. Ask students what they were doing at 8.30 last night. Elicit answers promoting the use of the past continuous. Elicit the rules for past simple and past continuous so students are reminded of the different uses.

- Tell students that last night there was a murder at Chester House. Mrs Blue (write name on board) was killed. Explain that last night there were six other people at Chester House. Explain that the people of the house know that one of them is a killer and want to find out who the murderer is before they call the police.

- Cut up the six role cards. Divide students into groups of six. Then divide these groups into smaller groups of three.

Teaching notes for photocopiable activities

- Tell students that they will take the role of one of the people in the house. Explain that one of them is the criminal and that the criminal will always tell lies. Hand out the role cards and give students time to read them, without showing them to each other.
- Tell students that they should ask questions to find out where people were and what they were doing, e.g. *Where were you at … ?* and *What were you doing at … ?*
- Students then ask each other questions to find out the information.
- Put the students together into their original group of six; they will now ask the remaining members of their group questions to find out where they were and what they were doing.
- Once students have finished, each group of six should write down the name of the person who they think is the murderer.
- Tell students that you have now heard news that Miss Blue was murdered at 9 p.m. Give students a minute or two to re-check their notes and see if they want to change their answer.
- Give students the answer (the murderer is Mrs Yellow) and discuss with the class how they worked it out (main evidence = Mrs Yellow didn't mention Mr Green playing pool at 9 p.m., or that she was playing cards with Miss Orange at 7 p.m.; she also got the time of eating dinner wrong).

Option: If you have less time then do the whole activity with groups of six rather than starting with groups of three.

2B The family company (use after Lesson 2.3) **

Aim: to practise personality adjectives, past continuous and functional language from Lesson 2.3

Grouping: individual, pair and groupwork

Procedure:

- Tell the students that they are going to choose the best people to work in the family company Smith and Smith. Tell them there are four free posts in the company. Write the words *Salesman / Saleswoman*, *Marketing Manager*, *Accountant* and *Receptionist* on the board. Check that the students understand the meaning of each job title.
- Group students in pairs and tell them to write down what they think would be the best characteristics for people working in each job. Encourage them to use the personality adjectives while doing the task. Give students a few minutes to do this, then get classroom feedback. There are no right or wrong answers for this task but students' choices of what is needed for each post will affect the choice of people for the posts.
- Put students into groups of three or four.
- Hand out a copy of the whole worksheet to each student. Explain that there are six members of the Smith family who would like to work in their family company. Students must decide who is the right person for the right job.
- Point out to the students the three sections in the information for each applicant. Explain that what people say about themselves may not be the same as what other people say about them.
- Initially students should work on their own to fill in the table on the worksheets, using personality adjectives in the second column.

- When students have filled in the table, tell them that they will now have a meeting in their group to agree on who should get which job. Encourage the students to use the functional language on page 19 of the Coursebook during their meeting.
- When the meetings have finished, join two groups together to make larger groups and ask the students to have another meeting to make the final decisions and prepare the presentation of their decisions.
- Each group will now give presentations on who they have chosen for each post and why. You may like to ask the presenters questions to challenge their decisions and make them think more carefully about their decision.

3A What's on (use after 3.2) **

Aim: to practise vocabulary related to media and relative pronouns

Grouping: whole class, then individual, pairwork and group work

Procedure:

- Explain to the students that they are going to choose the best programme to watch tonight. Before you start, however, remind them about the different types of programme you can see on TV. Brainstorm this with the whole class. The following types of programme should come up: *comedy, game show, documentary, drama, film / movie* (ask for different types of movie too), *reality TV show, series, soap opera*.
- Tell students that last night you watched a very interesting programme: *It was a documentary / programme that showed people in a city of boats.* Write the sentence on the board. Point out that you used a relative clause to talk about the TV programme. Then write *A science programme about new pills for headaches*. Elicit relative clause sentences, e.g.
  There is / It is a science programme that talks about new pills for headaches.
  There is / It is a science programme that presents new pills for headaches.
- Cut the photocopies in two. Group students in pairs and hand out the information sheets for Student A and Student B. Ask students to work first individually to look at the TV programmes on their list and prepare relative clause sentences for each programme, like the ones on the board.
- When students have finished this, explain that they will now work with their partner to find out all the TV programmes that are on tonight between 8 and 10 p.m. and when they have all the information they must decide what they are going to watch. Tell students that they will be expected to give feedback and explain why they chose the programmes.
- Give students about ten minutes for this activity.
- Put two pairs (= four students) together. Get them to explain their choices to each other and then as a group of four decide what to watch.
- Get feedback from the groups. Encourage students to explain their choices using the relative clauses they created.
- As a final stage, ask students to plan a list of programmes for you to watch at the weekend, describing the programmes and explaining why you should watch them.

Teaching notes for photocopiable activities

3B Front page (use after Lesson 3.3) **

Aim: to practise the language of media and functional language from Lesson 3.3

Grouping: whole class, then individual and group work

Procedure:

- Tell the students that this activity is connected with newspapers. Ask them to list the names of different newspapers they know. Then ask the students to tell you the differences between the different newspapers. Some of them will be local, some of them will be more serious and some will be mostly gossip and entertainment. If you like you may teach *tabloid* and *broadsheet* but as newspaper sizes are changing, the term *broadsheet* is disappearing.

- Ask students which type of newspaper they prefer and why. Ask them, *Do you think the role of newspapers is changing because of the Internet? If so, how is it changing?*

- Put students into groups of three. Cut up the photocopies, handing out one role card and one set of headlines to each student. Tell the students that each one works as an editor on a famous newspaper. They have been given the headlines to some news stories. They need to decide which headline will go on the front page, and then which six other stories will be included and in what order. Ask students to read the headlines and spend a few minutes on their own ordering the headlines according to their role.

- Ask students to now have their group meeting, using the language in exercise 5d and the 'Other useful phrases' box on page 27 of the Coursebook. Tell them they must agree on the order of headlines.

- Ask students to present their conclusions to the rest of the class. Encourage a class discussion to decide what the class as a whole thinks the order of the headlines should be.

- Put students into groups again and tell them they are now preparing a weekly newspaper for people from their country who are living abroad. They should decide on the main stories that they will include from the past week. (If you have a mixed nationality class you may do this on the country where the class is taking place).

- Have a class feedback to decide which headlines will finally make the weekly newspaper.

> **a** serious local news; **b** serious local news; **c** serious international news; **d** serious international news; **e** serious international news; **f** local social news/gossip; **g** local entertainment news; **h** international entertainment news; **i** local sport news; **j** entertainement (local or international); **k** local social news/gossip

4A History quiz (use after Lesson 4.2) **

Aim: to revise the present perfect

Grouping: whole class, then individual and pairwork

Procedure:

- Say to students, *I am a teacher. I started teaching in _____ . So how long have I been a teacher?*

- Elicit the answer and then elicit the full sentence. Then elicit the question that you used. Write both up on the board and then elicit the rule for present perfect.

- Write up another period (e.g. *for five years*, *since 1961*), related to your life, e.g. how long you have been

married. Encourage students to ask questions to find out what you have done/been.

- Ask individual students to come up to the board and do the same thing.

- Tell students they are now going to do a history quiz. Put students into pairs and hand out the quiz sheets for Student As and Student Bs.

- Explain that they have half the sentences and half the dates. They should first make questions to find out the dates. Students individually prepare their questions, for example:

  When did England last win the World Cup?

  How long have we known about AIDS?

- To begin with, Student As ask their questions. Student Bs will guess which date on their half-sheet is correct and then make the right response in the present perfect.

  England hasn't won the World Cup for XX years / since 1966.

  We've known about Aids for XX years / since 1981.

- If the date is correct, Student A can move on to the next question. Student B ticks the answer.

- When Student B has answered all the questions correctly, he/she will then ask his/her questions and Student A will attempt to answer.

- The pair that finishes first is the winner.

- Make sure you double-check the answers, using full sentences, with the whole class at the end.

4B The advice game (use after Lesson 4.3) **

Aim: to revise and practise language for giving advice and reasons

Grouping: whole class, then groupwork

Procedure:

- Start the lesson by complaining, *I have a sore throat today. What can I do about it?* Elicit pieces of advice. Write the good ones on the board. (Refer students to Lesson 4.3 to remember how to give advice). Point to the advice on the board and ask students why they gave those pieces of advice (again students may need to refer to Lesson 4.3. to remind themselves how to give reasons).

- Tell students they are now going to play the Advice Game. Divide students into groups of four.

- Hand out a game board to each group. Make sure students have something to use as a counter (a coin, for example) as they go round the board.

- Students should take it in turns to give advice for the problems described on each frame of the board. The rest of the group then vote as to whether the advice and reason was good, OK or not good.

- If the advice and reason are considered good, the player can move forward two steps.

- If the advice and reason are considered OK, the player can move forward one step.

- If the advice and reason are not good, the player stays where he/she is and must address the same problem again next turn.

- If there is no reason or the advice is not relevant, the player goes back one step.

- Tell students that they must all do the last step.

Teaching notes for photocopiable activities

- The player who gets to the end of the board first is the winner.
- When the students have finished, go through each step of the game with the whole class sharing the pieces of advice and reasons.

Option: Students can write a letter of advice about one of the problems in the game, listing some of the advice and reasons given in class.

5A The shipping line (use after Lesson 5.2) **

Aim: to revise and practise expressions of quantity

Grouping: whole class, then group work

Procedure:

- Write on the board, *Yes, we have no bananas. Lots of them*. Ask students what is wrong with this sentence (with *Yes*, we cannot use *no*). Ask students what we can replace *no* with. Elicit the answer and write it on the board.
- Ask students, *If we replace* Yes *at the beginning of the sentence with* No, *what can we use instead of the second* no? Elicit answers and write them on the board. This should allow you to check and revise expressions of quantity.
- Now replace *bananas* with *sugar* and go through the process again.
- Ask students, *What do we say if we have bananas/sugar but not many/much?* Elicit the use of *few* and *little*.
- Write the word *transport* on the board. Ask students the meaning in noun form and verb form.
- Write the word *trade* on the board. Check the meaning. Ask students what the connection is between trade and transport (trade uses transport to transport goods).
- Ask students how goods are transported (by lorry, by plane, by boat). Explain that a lot of food, liquids and spices are still transported by boat.
- Divide students into groups of five. Explain that they are working for a shipping company trading across five ports around the world.
- Cut up and hand out the Shipping Cards to students. Explain that they have in front of them the goods that their port has to sell (i.e. *You have a lot of them*) and those that the port needs to buy (i.e. *You don't have a lot of them*).
- Tell students that they should 'visit' other ports and ask one question at a time, asking if that port has something that they need (e.g. tomatoes). If they have, then the student has made a sale, and the 'seller' and the 'buyer' write *Sold* and *Bought* against the goods on their card.
- Before students begin, elicit the question forms that they will need to use (e.g. *Do you have any tomatoes to sell?*). Students must respond with a full sentence, e.g. *Yes, I have a lot of tomatoes* or *No, I only have a few tomatoes*, if the product is not on the list. Again, elicit possible answers.
- Students should keep asking questions until they have bought and sold everything they can.
- When students have finished the activity, go through the deals, making sure they are all completed.

5B Charities (use after Lesson 5.3) **

Aim: to practise grammar (comparatives and superlatives) and vocabulary (language related to the environment, animals and charities, giving opinions)

Grouping: whole class, then groups of five, but the activity can be tailored to smaller numbers (just do not use all of the charities)

Procedure:

- Write the word *charity* on the board. Ask students what it means, referring them to Lesson 5.3 if necessary. Students brainstorm the words they learned when talking about charities, which should include *accommodation, awful, captivity, donate, endangered, extinct/extinction, rescue, sanctuary, suffering, volunteer*.
- Cut up the photocopies into five cards and explain the task. Students are going to work in groups of up to five. Each group has a large amount of money to donate to a charity. Tell students to look at the different charities available. You will assign each student in the group one of the charities to represent. Students prepare an argument to convince people why their charity is more deserving than the others. Then the group as a whole must decide which charity will get the money.
- Give students a few minutes to read the descriptions and prepare their arguments (which need to include comparisons between their charity and the other charities).
- Remind students to use the vocabulary of giving opinions on page 11 of Lesson 1.3 and comparatives and superlatives.
- Students now give the rest of the group their mini-presentations and then discuss as a whole group which charity they will choose to give the money to.
- When the groups have finished the task, ask each of them which charity they have chosen and why.

6A How will it be? (use after Lesson 6.3) **

Aim: to revise and practise *will, might* and *may* for predictions, first conditional and the language of expressing opinions

Grouping: whole class, then group work

Procedure:

- Ask students what they think life will be like in 50 years. Elicit answers. Then write *There will be more violence on TV* on the board. Say to students, *I want to ask your opinion. How can I do this?* (Students may need to refer to Lesson 6.3 to find the answer.)
- Get students to look at the expressions from exercise 3a on page 53 of the Coursebook and to use them to respond to the sentences on the board.
- Explain to the students that when responding, they could replace *will* with *may* or *might* to show their opinion. Elicit examples.
- Explain also that they can use first conditional if they think something could possibly happen, e.g. *If the government doesn't change the law, there will be more violence on TV*. Elicit other examples.
- Divide students into four groups, A, B, C and D. Tell them they will now have a discussion in their group on what life will be like in 50 years' time.
- Cut up the photocopies and hand out the cards (A to Group A, B to Group B, etc.). Students should use the language of giving opinion, *will, may* or *might* and first conditional whenever possible.
- When all the groups have prepared their arguments, divide the students again so that there is one student

from Group A, one from B, one from C and one from D in each new group.

- Tell the students that they now must introduce their issues and try to convince the rest of the group to agree with them.

- Have a class feedback when the discussions are finished and get the opinion of the whole class on the issues.

Option: If you think there are too many issues for your students, use only one from each card and let the students decide which one to choose. You can always use the issues in another lesson if you wish.

6B Wordsearch (use after Lesson 6.4) **

Aim: to revise vocabulary from Unit 6

Grouping: whole class, then individual and pairwork

Procedure:

- Make sure students' Coursebooks are closed.

- Brainstorm with students the new vocabulary they learned in Unit 6. Ask them to say one or two words each. Write the words on the board. Do not add words students don't say or identify which are right or wrong.

- Get students to provide example sentences. (This can be done either as pairwork or whole-class work).

- Cut the photocopies in two and hand out wordsearches to students.

- Tell students that each of them has half the wordsearch. Individually they should identify the words from the gapped sentences they have and then find the word in the wordsearch.

- When they have completed their part of the wordsearch students should work in pairs and tell the clues to their partner, who has to guess the word and then find it in the wordsearch. They must not show each other their papers.

- When students have finished they can check together.

- Then check as whole class.

Option: As this is halfway through the course, get students to create their own wordsearch puzzles like this one using important vocabulary items from the first six units. These can then be passed around the class as revision before the class test.

M	I	N	I	S	T	E	R	I	U	A
D	E	Y	R	E	T	I	R	E	D	D
O	A	G	R	A	D	U	A	T	E	I
I	C	F	I	A	N	C	E	E	F	V
S	L	P	I	E	F	A	N	I	I	O
P	E	R	M	I	S	S	I	O	N	R
O	A	D	M	W	R	N	F	R	I	C
C	N	I	I	N	L	A	W	O	T	E
K	I	F	A	S	H	I	O	N	E	D
E	N	E	U	F	I	H	K	E	L	F
T	G	R	U	N	L	U	C	K	Y	I

1 graduate; **2** fashioned; **3** retired; **4** unlucky; **5** in law; **6** pocket; **7** cleaning; **8** permission; **9** fiancée; **10** definitely; **11** minister; **12** divorced

7A Scientific duties (use after Lesson 7.1) **

Aim: to revise vocabulary for science; to revise and practise *must* and *have to*

Grouping: whole class, then individual and group work

Procedure:

- Write *nurse* on the board. Elicit the meaning of the word. Ask students what they think the duties of a nurse are.

- Write the answers up on the board and then write *must* and *have to* to remind students to use them when talking about duties. Make sure to also ask what a nurse doesn't have to do.

- Elicit the rule for *must* and *have to*. Also elicit the rule for questions using *must* and *have to*.

- Make as many photocopies of the worksheet as there are students in the class, plus two or three. Cut up the photocopies down the middle, so that the questions and the job list are on separate pieces of paper.

- Hand out a job list to each student. Check that they understand the meanings of all eight jobs.

- Now cut the eight job titles out of the extra photocopies that you made and hand out one job to each student. Tell students that they must not show anyone which job they have.

- Individually, students should write down what they think the duties of their job are, e.g. *A surgeon must always be clean, uses a scalpel, but doesn't have to work alone.*

- Hand out the questions to the students. Explain they have to find out who has the other seven jobs in your class by asking the questions in the list using *have to*. Students should go round the class asking questions and finding the jobs. Remind students that they must not guess the job or say which job it is. They should just put a name beside the job on the job list and say nothing.

- When a student thinks he/she has found all the other jobs, he/she should tell you.

- Get class feedback.

Option: Students can choose a job and note down the duties and can repeat the exercise.

7B New for my town (use after Lesson 7.3) **

Aim: to revise language for developing an argument

Grouping: whole class, then group work

Procedure:

- Write on the board *What makes a town successful?* Elicit from students what a town needs to make it successful and popular. (You could integrate *must* and *have to* here). Write the best suggestions on the board.

- Ask students to look at the suggestions on the board. Elicit from the students why these things would contribute to the success/popularity of a town. Encourage the students to use language from 'Developing an argument' on page 62 of the Coursebook, such as *leads to, causes, means that, so,* etc.

- Cut up the photocopies in eight and divide the class into groups of six. To each group, hand out one of the two descriptions, Wotchester or Harley. Give the students time to read it.

Teaching notes for photocopiable activities

- Tell students that they have the opportunity to build something that will make the town more successful/popular. They must decide what it will be.
- To each student, give one of the six proposed improvements. Tell students that they should prepare an argument why their proposal is the best for the town. (If you've got more than one group doing the same town, one student from each of the groups can form pairs and work together.)
- In their groups, students now have a meeting where each student is given a minute to present their 'proposal' and explain why it should be chosen. Once all of the proposals have been presented, the group must decide on the one they will adopt.
- Have a class feedback session where representatives from each group will present their decision and explain why they took this decision.
- To finish, discuss what students think could be the best improvement for 'this town', the town where the classes take place.

Option: Students write a composition on what they would do to improve their home town.

8A Don't trust your future! (use after Lesson 8.2) **

Aim: to revise and practise future patterns (*going to, hoping, would like to, 'd like to*)

Grouping: whole work, then individual and group work

Procedure:

- Ask students if they had a dream last night. Ask them what they dreamt about. Elicit some answers and write them on the board.
- Tell students some people think that dreams tell you your future. Ask students if they think it's true (why/why not?). Elicit from the students what they think the dreams on the board might mean. Encourage students to use future patterns (*Katrina is going to …, this person is hoping to …, maybe he'd like to …*) to describe the meanings.
- Cut up and divide the Dream cards and Interpretation cards into two sets.
- Divide the class into two groups: one group will be dreamers, the other will be dream interpreters.
- Give the dreamers one dream card each. Tell them they have a few minutes to create their dream but must include the object or place on the card in their dream.
- Give the interpreters one interpretation card each and tell them that they have an interpretation for one object. Tell them this is the real one but if someone mentions an object that is not on their card then they must make a false interpretation. Students should spend a couple of minutes creating false interpretations (using *going to, hoping, 'd like to*).
- Dreamers should now go round the class telling the interpreters their dream. They must listen to the interpreters' meanings and decide which is the real interpretation (tell students that it doesn't matter if they get the wrong interpretation).
- When everyone has spoken to everyone else and noted the meaning of their dream, have class feedback. Ask each dreamer to tell their dream to the class and what

they think the meaning is. Then check with the correct interpreter if it is true.
- If you have time, now switch the students round (dreamers become interpreters and interpreters become dreamers) and hand out the cards you didn't use the first time round.

Option: Students write a composition discussing whether dreams carry meaning.

8B Preferences Bingo (use after Lesson 8.3) **

Aim: to revise language for expressing preferences

Grouping: whole class, then individual, pairwork and group work

Procedure:

- Write on the board *I love bananas!* Elicit from the students the verb in the sentence and then elicit the purpose of this verb (to express preference).
- Elicit from the students all the other structures that they have studied in Lesson 8.3 (*I prefer, I fancy, I'd rather, I'm keen on, I don't mind, I'm more interested in … than*)
- Elicit from students how to change the sentence on the board, using the other structures. Do this both in positive and negative forms (*I prefer bananas, I don't fancy bananas*).
- Cut up and hand out one bingo card to each student.
- Show students that three of the boxes have subjects. Tell the students that under the subject they should write an example sentence showing their personal preferences (positive or negative) in relation to that subject (e.g. if it says *chocolate*, they might write *I prefer chocolate to nuts*.)
- When they have completed this, they should then fill the remaining six boxes with subjects and personal preferences sentences e.g. *OLD MOVIES – I am keen on watching old movies*.
- When writing their sentences, students should use as many different structures as they can. They then work in pairs and check that their sentences are grammatically correct.
- Tell the students that they will now play 'Preferences Bingo'. Show students that you have a table with preference structures. Tell students that you will read out a structure. If the students have a box with that structure in, they can cross it out. Make sure, however, that they understand they can only cross out one box at a time.
- Tell the students that the first person to cross out all of their sentences is the winner. (Make sure you tick the structures you are reading out as you will need to check that the winner has not cheated.)

Option: Students may use these cards and their sentences to conduct a class survey of preferences.

9A The job for you? (use after Lesson 9.1) **

Aim: to practise vocabulary of job conditions

Grouping: whole class, then individual work followed by group work

Procedure:

- Ask students what jobs they would like to do. Ask them why they would like to do them. Write up some of the jobs they say on the board.

- Remind students of the job conditions they discussed in the first exercise of the unit, on page 74 of the Coursebook. Ask students to decide which conditions fit the jobs that you have written on the board.

- Tell students that they are now going to do a role-play. Cut up the photocopies into eight and divide the class in half. One half will be employers. The other half will be people looking for a job.

- Divide the halves into groups of four. Each member of a group is given either one job description card (the employers) or one job seekers' card.

- Tell students to read their cards. Tell job seekers that they have to prepare questions to find the answers they need. Tell employers that they really want the job seekers so they should make their answers as attractive as possible. (If you have a good class, you may like to tell them that they should never say no, rather, e.g., *Well, the pay is OK, but the training opportunities are fantastic.*)

- Students spend a few minutes preparing.

- Put one group of employers with one group of job seekers. Tell the job seekers that they must visit each employer to find out if it is the right job for them. Remind them that they must not show each other their cards.

- Get feedback from the class.

- Divide the students in half again. This time employers will be job seekers and vice-versa.

Option:

- Employers should create their own jobs, taking the conditions into account. Job seekers should write what they are looking for in a job.

- Now do the task again, this time with the students' self-created cards.

9B How to make … (use after Lesson 9.2) **

Aim: to practise the present passive

Grouping: whole class, then group work with groups of three; finally individual or pairwork

Procedure:

- Write *How to make …* on the board and then finish the sentence by writing *a cup of fresh coffee*. Elicit the ingredients: *coffee beans, grinder* (you may need to teach this), *coffee machine, water, milk* .

- Tell your students the first stage and write on the board *The coffee beans are put into a grinder*. Guide them to notice that the present passive is being used. Elicit why (the present passive is often used to describe a process, e.g. how to make something).

- Elicit the remaining stages (you may need to teach the verb *to grind*). You then have an example of how to make something on the board.

- Divide your students into groups of three and tell them that they are going to do a running dictation. Assign a recipe to each group, *Chocolate, Vegetable soup* or *Bread*.

- Having cut the photocopies in three, put the three different copies of the running dictation (headed *Chocolate, Vegetable soup* and *Bread*) in different places round the room (remember to place the copies furthest away from the group you have assigned the recipe to, otherwise you will have problems).

- Explain to the groups that they must nominate one runner, who has to go to the copy assigned to them, remember a sentence or words, come back and tell the two 'writers' who should both write down what the runner tells them.

- Make sure the runner knows that their recipe is in capital letters at the top of their copy, but that the sentences on that copy are not all relevant to their recipe.

- Tell students that when they have finished collecting everything from the copy, the three group members should compare the two documents prepared by the writers and create one document.

- When students have done this, explain that they need to trade sentences with the other groups to get their remaining sentences, the ones relevant to their recipe. Again, the runner is assigned to do this.

- Once students think they have got all the sentences appropriate for their recipe, they need to put them in the right order.

- The team that has their completed recipe in the right order first is the winner.

- To finish, divide students into pairs and let them create their own recipe. (This could be given as individual work for homework.)

> **Chocolate:** 1, IV, c), 4, VI, b)
> **Vegetable soup:** a), 5, III, e), II, 3
> **Bread:** I, f), 6, 2, V, d)

10A Firsts crossword (use after Lesson 10.2) **

Aim: to practise the past passive

Grouping: whole class, followed by individual and then pairwork

Procedure:

- Choose a famous event and date that all your students know (e.g. 1969 – First man on the moon). Make sure a past passive question can be made from your event (e.g. *When was a man first sent to the moon?*) Write the date on the board. Ask students what they think happened in that year.

- Tell them what happened. Ask them how they would ask the question to find out the date. Elicit answer from students. Draw their attention to the use of the past passive. Elicit the rule for past passives. You may now want to do a few more examples if you think your students are not strong on this structure.

- Tell the students that they are going to do a dates crossword on famous 'firsts' in history. Divide the class into Student As and Student Bs and hand out a half-sheet to each student. Tell them not to show their sheets to anyone else.

- Give students a few minutes to read all the clues. They may know some of the answers and be able to fill them in.

- Put students in pairs (A+B). It may be a good idea to pair students from different sides of the room in case they had already started talking while working alone.

- Tell students that their partner has the answers that have not been filled in their crossword. To get the missing answers they have to make the correct question in the past passive form. If the form is not correct their partner cannot tell them the answer.

Teaching notes for photocopiable activities

- When students finish they should let the teacher know.
- Now do feedback to check answers. Students should give the answers in full sentence form.

Option: Students can go on the Internet and find out more famous firsts and bring them to class for the following lesson. Such things can be found on Wikipedia and http://thelongestlistofthelongeststuffatthelongestdomainnameatlonglast.com/first.html

> **Across:**
> 3 1940; 5 1840; 7 1454; 8 1904; 9 1162; 10 1857; 11 1952; 12 1896; 13 1963; 14 1900 BC; 15 410
> **Down:**
> 1 400 BC; 2 1930; 4 1979; 5 1492; 6 1415; 7 1485; 10 1868; 11 1962; 12 1897; 13 1974

10B University opening (use after Lesson 10.3) **

Aim: to practise 'adding emphasis' phrases and 'Other useful phrases' from Lesson 10.3, as well as the present continuous for future arrangements

Grouping: whole class, followed by individual and then group work

Procedure:

- Do a quick review of Lesson 10.3. Remind students of the language they need to use for giving a talk to recommend something. Remind them too of phrases to add emphasis. Elicit some example sentences from the students.
- Tell students that today they are considering the opening of a new department at the university. Brainstorm with students the name of the possible different departments. Then tell them that it is a new Science Department that is being opened.
- Elicit from students what is needed for an opening – a ceremony, the media (e.g. journalists, TV, etc.), a famous person …
- Ask students what sort of person they would like to invite for such an opening. What characteristics should he/she have?
- Tell students that there is a shortlist of six famous people to invite to the opening ceremony. Divide the students into groups (four to eight groups depending on the size of the class).
- Hand out one candidate card to each group (if you have eight groups there will be two presentations on each person). Tell students they will prepare a speech supporting their candidate and saying why their famous person would be the best person to open the new Science Department.
- Give students at least ten minutes to prepare their presentations. Remind them to use the language from Lesson 10.3 that they revised at the beginning. Students should nominate a speaker.
- Before the talks are given, tell the groups that at the end they will have to vote for a candidate that is not their candidate. Tell them they will have to give reasons, based on the talk they have heard, why they chose that particular candidate.
- Students now give their talks.

- When the talks are completed, give the groups about five minutes to get their arguments together and present their decision with reasons.
- Students give their reasons (the person who gives this should not be the same as the original speaker).
- Announce the result.
- If you have time, you may get the students to plan the itinerary for the day for the special guest. This can be presented to the class and the best itinerary decided on.

11A Phrasal verb snap (use after Lesson 11.2) **

Aim: to revise and further practise phrasal verbs

Grouping: whole class, then group work

Procedure:

- Write the words *get up* on the board. Ask students what this is (verb; phrasal verb). Elicit what it is made up of (verb + particle, usually a preposition). Elicit example sentences to clarify the meaning.
- Tell the students they are going to play 'phrasal verb snap'. Ask if they know the game (there is usually an equivalent in every country). Tell them that snap is a game usually played with cards. Two players each have half a pack of cards that they lay face down on the table. Each player takes the top card on their pile and lays it face up on the table. If the two cards are the same, the first player to say 'snap' gets all the cards face up on the table. The person with the most cards at the end wins.
- Tell students this version of snap is a little different. Divide the students into groups of three. Give one student from each group the list of sentences 1–14. Give the second student the cut-up verb mini-cards, face down. Give the third student the cut-up particle mini-cards, face down. The student with the sentence list is nominated as the referee.
- Explain that the player with the verb cards will lay one of his/her cards face up on the table. The player with the particle cards will then lay his/her cards face up one by one. When one of the two players recognises a phrasal verb pairing from the two cards face up on the table, he/she should say 'snap'. The referee will then check his/her list of sentences and, if correct, fill the gap in the relevant sentence. If the referee fills in a sentence, the player who said 'snap' receives one point. The game carries on in this way till all the cards have been paired up.
- Tell students that some of the verbs need a different form to fit in the sentences – past simple or *-ing* form.
- Explain that when all the sentences are filled in, the game is over and the student with the most points wins.
- This game can be played as many times as you wish with students changing places. The more this is played, the more students are likely to remember the phrasal verbs.
- Finally, remember to do a feedback session to check that all the sentences are properly filled out.

> 1 throw away; 2 put on; 3 give up; 4 stop off; 5 take … back; 6 get up; 7 go out; 8 put … in; 9 pick up; 10 grew up; 11 going up; 12 cut down; 13 get into; 14 giving out

11B Missing persons (use after Lesson 11.3) **

Aim: to revise and further practise question tags

Grouping: whole class, then pairwork

Procedure:

- Write up *The weather's nice today* on the board.
- Ask students how they can ask what the weather is like today (*What's the weather like today?*).
- Ask students how they would ask the question if they thought they knew the answer and were just seeking confirmation. Elicit *The weather is nice today, isn't it?*
- Underline the question tag and ask students to identify it. Elicit from the students other types of question tag.
- Get students to practise on each other using a question tag. Tell them to look at their partner and to ask question tag questions referring to how their partner looks, what he/she is wearing or their mood, e.g.:

  You've got a new jumper, haven't you?

  You are a little tired, aren't you?

- Do some feedback to find out what questions were used.
- For the activity, divide students into pairs. Tell the pairs that they are police officers. Two people have gone missing. A missing person report was prepared and a few hours later a bad copy was made. The original report and the copy have now been mixed up. Tell the students they each have half of the original report and half of the copy. Tell students they must ask each other tag questions to correct the errors on the copy, e.g.:

  The man's name is Paul Smith, isn't it? – Yes, it is.

  He is 36, isn't he? – No, he isn't. He is 33.

- When they have completed this activity you can check the answers by using the copy and asking tag questions yourself.

12A Second conditional chains (use after Lesson 12.1) **

Aim: to revise and further practise the second conditional

Grouping: whole class, then group work and whole class again; individual work as an option

Procedure:

- Write up *If I had a million dollars …* on the board. Elicit from students endings to this question. Write an ending you particularly like.
- Using the example on the board, elicit the rule for the second conditional from the students.
- Cut the sheet up into eight slips of paper and divide the students into groups of no more than four people.
- Tell students that nowadays we are accustomed to things that make our life easier. Ask students what they would do if there were no cars, for example. Write *If there were no cars …* Elicit answers, getting students to discuss and finish the sentence.
- Hand out one slip of paper to each group.
- Tell students to look at the sentence start on their slip of paper. Tell them to complete the sentence by writing down two ideas that all the group agrees with, e.g.:

  If there were no computers … many people would lose their job.

- When all students have done this, tell the group to pass the slip round and then the next group adds its ideas.

- Continue doing this until the slips return to their original groups.
- In their groups, students should now look at all the sentences and put the sentences in order of importance.
- When they have done this, each group will present the three sentences they most agree with and explain why they believe these sentences to be the best. The class will then vote on the ideas.

Option: Students can write a paper discussing their group's topic for homework e.g. *What would life be like if there were no computers?*

12B Wordsearch (use after Lesson 12.4) **

Aim: to revise vocabulary from Unit 12

Grouping: whole class, then pairwork, individual, pairwork/ group work and whole class again

Procedure:

- Make sure students' Coursebooks are closed.
- Brainstorm with students the new vocabulary they learned in Unit 12. Ask them to say one or two words each. Write the words on the board. Do not add words students don't say or identify which are right or wrong.
- Get students to provide example sentences. (This can either be done as pairwork or whole-class work.)
- Hand out wordsearches to students.
- Tell students they should identify the words from the clues (1–15) and then find the words in the wordsearch.
- Allow students to do this individually.
- Put students into pairs to check. You can then put them in groups of four to double-check.
- Then check as whole class.

Option: As this is the end of the book, for final revision get students to create their own wordsearch puzzles like this one using important vocabulary items from all the units in the Coursebook. These can then be passed around the class as revision before the final class test.

A	G	G	R	E	S	S	I	V	E	Q	Q	S	O	Z	X
Z	F	B	O	P	Y	T	N	X	H	B	M	P	E	F	M
O	V	M	V	Q	Z	A	M	H	P	L	E	O	E	H	H
B	M	Q	J	T	P	D	W	K	B	S	M	N	P	V	Z
C	O	M	P	E	T	I	T	I	V	E	O	T	W	D	R
D	I	V	Y	Y	K	U	Z	Z	N	E	M	A	O	Z	Z
N	P	U	O	X	Q	M	X	J	S	U	U	N	R	V	P
Y	M	T	J	R	X	R	P	I	G	O	X	E	L	R	W
Z	H	B	R	D	M	L	B	B	P	B	S	O	D	O	P
T	T	G	T	E	N	D	T	O	O	O	N	U	W	W	F
S	O	C	I	A	B	L	E	A	L	X	O	S	I	I	D
M	A	J	O	R	I	T	Y	S	O	I	O	L	D	N	P
A	R	C	H	E	R	Y	Z	H	E	N	K	J	E	G	O
F	N	E	F	L	E	G	J	B	O	G	E	C	Z	W	L
M	O	T	O	R	R	A	C	I	N	G	R	K	W	R	O
F	E	N	C	I	N	G	C	O	N	Q	M	F	Y	T	O

1 snooker; **2** archery; **3** polo; **4** competitive;
5 spontaneous; **6** aggressive; **7** majority; **8** worldwide;
9 stadium; **10** sociable; **11** boxing; **12** fencing;
13 motor racing; **14** tend to; **15** rowing

WORLD WEATHER

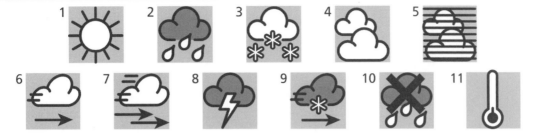

Student A

Student B

DICTIONARY CROSSWORD

Across:

1 /braɪt/ *adjective* something that is ... shines a lot or has a lot of light

2 /maɪld/ *adjective* ... weather is not too cold

5 /ˈræftɪŋ/ *noun* when people go down a river on a raft

7 /ˈhʌrɪkən/ *noun* a violent storm with very strong fast winds

9 /ˈθʌndəstɔːm/ *noun* a storm with lightning and loud noise

10 /tʃɪl/ *noun* a feeling of coldness

12 /ˈflaɪ-ɪŋ/ *noun* travelling by plane or controlling a plane

13 /ˈtʃeɪndʒəbəl/ *adjective* weather that changes quickly is ...

14 /fɒg/ *noun* cloudy air near the ground which is difficult to see through

15 /ˈsiːzən/ *noun* one of the periods of time into which a year is divided

16 /dɑːk/ *adjective* a ... place is one where there is little or no light

Down:

1 /ˈblɪzəd/ *noun* a storm with a lot of wind and snow

2 /ˈmeɪdʒə/ *adjective* large and important

3 /draʊt/ *noun* a long period of dry weather when there is not enough water

4 /ˈkʌntrisaɪd/ *noun* land that is not near towns or cities

6 /ˈtrekɪŋ/ *noun* walking a very long way, especially across rough ground

8 /kuːl/ *adjective* slightly cold, especially in a nice way

11 /ɪkˈstriːmli/ *adverb* very

14 /flʌd/ *noun* a very large amount of water that covers an area that is usually dry

Mr Grey

7 p.m. – in kitchen, making dinner

8 p.m. – in kitchen, making coffee

9 p.m. – in bathroom, having shower

10 p.m. – in bed, sleeping

Mr Red

7 p.m. – in library, reading

8 p.m. – in dining room, eating

9 p.m. – in games room, playing pool with Mr Green

10 p.m. – in bathroom, cleaning teeth

Mrs Yellow

YOU ARE THE CRIMINAL!
EVERYTHING YOU SAY IS A LIE!

7 p.m. – in dining room, eating

8 p.m. – in garden, smoking a cigarette

9 p.m. – in games room, playing pool with Mr Red

10 p.m. – in bed, reading

Miss Pink

7 p.m. – in lounge, watching TV

8 p.m. – in dining room, eating

9 p.m. – in kitchen, washing up

10 p.m. – in lounge, watching TV

Mr Green

7 p.m. – in bedroom, getting dressed

8 p.m. – in dining room, eating

9 p.m. – in games room, playing pool with Mr Red

10 p.m. – in kitchen, making a sandwich

Miss Orange

7 p.m. – in games room, playing cards with Mrs Yellow

8 p.m. – in dining room, eating

9 p.m. – in lounge, reading a magazine

10 p.m. – in bedroom, drinking hot chocolate

THE FAMILY COMPANY

Paul Smith

What he says:
'I don't like meeting people very much.'
'I'm good with numbers.'
'I work better on my own.'

What they say:
'He doesn't like meeting people.'
'He doesn't talk much.'
'He's very good at solving problems.'
'He works very hard.'

What was he doing this time last year?
Working in a bank.

Heather Smith

What she says:
'I love meeting people.'
'I'm always trying to win.'
'I always try to help people.'

What they say:
'She thinks she can do anything.'
'She never gets angry with people.'
'She never stops talking.'

What was she doing this time last year?
At university studying sports.

Graham Smith

What he says:
'I know I am the best.'
'I have lots of skills.'
'I work very hard.'

What they say:
'He is never polite.'
'He doesn't work very hard.'
'He doesn't have any friends.'

What was he doing this time last year?
Travelling around Europe.

Sarah Smith

What she says:
'I never stop working.'
'I love my job.'
'I'm always ready to help.'

What they say:
'People always want to work with her.'
'She has very good ideas.'

What was she doing this time last year?
Studying art at university.

Molly Smith

What she says:
'I love meeting people.'
'I love talking.'
'I don't like selling things.'

What they say:
'She always smiles.'
'People like to talk to her.'
'She is never rude.'

What was she doing this time last year?
Working in a computer shop.

Ali Smith

What she says:
'I know I can do any job.'
'I love meeting people.'

What they say:
'She knows a lot of things but doesn't like working.'
'People don't like working with her.'

What was she doing this time last year?
Living at home doing nothing.

NAME	Characteristics	Job?
Paul Smith		
Heather Smith		
Graham Smith		
Sarah Smith		
Molly Smith		
Ali Smith		

Student A

Tell your partner about what's on tonight, using relative clauses,
e.g. *At 8.00 there's a reality TV programme that shows people's problems.*

TIME	TV 1	TV 2	TV 3
8.00	**ASK PETE!** Reality TV programme about people's problems. (1 hour)	**ON TIME** News programme about the economy. (1 hour)	**SPRACH DEUTSCH** Education programme about learning German. (1 hour)
9.00	**SAME TIME TOMORROW** Comedy programme about milkmen.(30 mins)	**SPIDERMAN** Programme about finding things on the Internet. (1 hour)	**THE NEW ANIMAL** Documentary. Some animals have never been seen because they live, for example, deep in the sea. (1 hour)
9.30	**MAKE ME RICH!** Game show. People win millions of pounds by answering general knowledge questions. (30 mins)		

--- ✂

Student B

Tell your partner about what's on tonight using relative clauses, e.g. *At 8.00 there's an action movie that shows people on a mountain with no food or drink.*

TIME	FILM 1	FILM 2	SERIES 1
8.00	**A LONG WAY DOWN!** Action movie about people on a mountain with no food or drink. (90 mins)	**GEORGE CLOONEY – THE MAN** Documentary about the life of George Clooney. (30 mins)	**MY HOME** Soap opera about a typical street. (45 mins)
8.30		**LAST STOP HOTEL** Drama film about a hotel manager that helps people escape from a war. (90 mins)	
8.45			**THE BEAUTIFUL AND THE WEAK** Brazilian soap opera about film stars. (45 mins)
9.30	**COMING SOON** Preview programme on films for next week. (30 mins)		**CRIME SEATTLE** TV series about murders in Seattle. (1 hour)

Student A

You believe the newspaper should tell the news and only the news. It can be local or international but you believe people do not want to know what Robert De Niro's cat had for dinner.

Student B

You believe that gossip sells newspapers. This newspaper has not been selling well. Most of the customers are buying magazines. You believe that gossip, real-life stories and entertainment will sell more newspapers than news.

Student C

You believe news is important but not international news. People are only interested in local news about their own country. If there isn't enough local news then the newspaper can include some gossip and entertainment.

a **Prime Minister agrees new education plan**

b **Economic crisis expected next year**

c *Three people die in fire in the US*

d **New war starts in Africa**

e **President of Bogan goes to prison**

f *Our Queen loves the colour yellow*

g **Big Brother favourite leaves the House!**

h *What is Tom Cruise doing with Sarah Collier?*

i Local team get Brazilian World Cup player

j **Bogart – film of the year!**

k **What does the Prime Minister's wife do at the weekend?**

Student A

QUESTIONS	ANSWERS
1 England last won the World Cup in 1966.	1956
2 Madonna started living in England in 2000.	1936
3 Turkey became a republic in 1923.	1926
4 Man first traveled to space in 1961.	1952
5 Someone last saw a dodo in 1681.	1981
6 Hollywood made its first film in 1910.	1886
7 People first used the telephone in 1876.	1920
8 Poland had its first democratic government in 1989.	1954

- ✂

Student B

QUESTIONS	ANSWERS
9 We first knew about AIDS in 1981.	1923
10 People first watched TV in 1926.	1966
11 The Eurovision Song Contest first took place in 1954.	2000
12 People first used a credit card in the UK in 1956.	1961
13 People first drank Coca-Cola in 1886.	1876
14 The United Nations opened its office in New York in 1952.	1910
15 People listened to the radio for the first time in 1920.	1989
16 Pilots wore the first Ray-Bans in 1936.	1681

4B

THE ADVICE GAME

START

I always fail my tests.

I talk too much!

I work all day on a computer and my back always hurts.

I forgot Valentine's day and my partner is very angry.

I can't wake up in the mornings.

I can't stop eating chocolate.

My partner wants a dog but I hate them.

How can I learn English better?

My neighbours have a baby that always cries.

I can't stop smoking.

I can't sleep.

Someone stole my wallet.

I always get headaches when I watch TV.

How can I be more interesting?

I owe the bank a lot of money.

FINISH

SHIPPING REPRESENTATIVE
SOUTHAMPTON

You have: *apples* _____
cooking oil _____
sugar _____

You need: *bananas* _____
cabbages _____
tomatoes _____

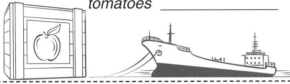

SHIPPING REPRESENTATIVE
DURBAN

You have: *bananas* _____
green peppers _____
ginger _____

You need: *apples* _____
tea _____
chilli peppers _____

SHIPPING REPRESENTATIVE
ADANA

You have: *chilli peppers* _____
coffee _____
chicken _____

You need: *sugar* _____
ginger _____
pineapples _____

SHIPPING REPRESENTATIVE
GDANSK

You have: *cabbages* _____
fruit juice _____
tea _____

You need: *green peppers* _____
chicken _____
beef _____

SHIPPING REPRESENTATIVE
BUENOS AIRES

You have: *beef* _____
pineapples _____
tomatoes _____

You need: *cooking oil* _____
coffee _____
fruit juice _____

A The World Animal Protection League

This is a very large organisation with offices in 42 countries. Its main job is to stop animals from becoming extinct. Over the last ten years it has saved more than six different animals from extinction. There are 750 volunteers working in the organisation and it receives money from 24 governments. At the moment it has only two projects running. The most important one is a sanctuary for ten different types of endangered birds in South Africa.

B The Peter Edwards Clothes for the Old Charity

This charity is based in your city and provides clothes for all the old people who live in old people's homes and have no money. Although it is more than 25 years old, the charity only has one office and ten volunteers. Recently it has been decided to close the charity because there isn't enough money to keep it running. Old people's homes in the city are very worried about this because many old people will suffer without the clothes the charity gives.

C The Helping Hands for Hearts Charity

This charity is five years old and now has 12 offices around the country. This charity provides money to build new clinics for heart transplants. These clinics are very expensive and very few towns have one. There are 550 people working full-time for this charity and it is now taking on a new project to train 2000 private nurses to work in the heart clinics. This charity is always in the media for doing charity events to make money.

D Think Environment!

This charity is only six months old but already has ten offices in eight countries, with about 250 volunteers. The charity's main role is to clean up as many polluted areas as they can find across the world. So far it has identified five major projects including the 'Green Fingers' campaign to rescue all the private parks in this country from rubbish and the 'Make your Lakes Transparent' campaign to clean up polluted lakes all over the world.

E Fight Obesity!

This charity is nine years old and has six offices in four countries, with 75 volunteers. For the first five years it only did research on how many people are fat and are suffering from illnesses or diseases caused by being overweight. Now they are preparing a campaign to train people about the dangers of eating too much or eating the wrong food. They are very unpopular with big governments and big food companies and their 'Junk your Junk Food' campaign was stopped by two large fast-food chains. The charity lost £500,000 in the court case and may now have to close.

Group A Student A

In 50 years' time …

1 People won't drive cars.

2 All banking will be on the Internet.

3 People won't smoke.

Group B Student B

In 50 years' time …

1 People will have holidays in space.

2 There will be more sea and less land in the world.

3 All countries will belong to organisations like the European Union.

Group C Student C

In 50 years' time …

1 All food will be organic.

2 There will be fewer types of animals.

3 Every country will give free education to children.

Group D Student D

In 50 years' time …

1 People will never retire.

2 There will be more divorces.

3 The birth rate will increase.

Student A

M	I	N	I	S	T	E	R	I	U	A
D	E	Y	R	E	T	I	R	E	D	D
O	A	G	R	A	D	U	A	T	E	I
I	C	F	I	A	N	C	E	E	F	V
S	L	P	I	E	F	A	N	I	I	O
P	E	R	M	I	S	S	I	O	N	R
O	A	D	M	W	R	N	F	R	I	C
C	N	I	I	N	L	A	W	O	T	E
K	I	F	A	S	H	I	O	N	E	D
E	N	E	U	F	I	H	K	E	L	F
T	G	R	U	N	L	U	C	K	Y	I

1 If I finish university I will be a _____.

2 Some people think I am old- _____ because I like records.

3 She used to be a teacher but now she is _____.

4 I lost the game again! I am so _____.

5 If I marry Susan, her brother Paul will be my brother _____.

6 Sarah only gets £2 _____ money a week.

7

8

9

10

11

12

✂ --

Student B

M	I	N	I	S	T	E	R	I	U	A
D	E	Y	R	E	T	I	R	E	D	D
O	A	G	R	A	D	U	A	T	E	I
I	C	F	I	A	N	C	E	E	F	V
S	L	P	I	E	F	A	N	I	I	O
P	E	R	M	I	S	S	I	O	N	R
O	A	D	M	W	R	N	F	R	A	C
C	N	I	I	N	L	A	W	O	T	E
K	I	F	A	S	H	I	O	N	E	D
E	N	E	U	F	I	H	K	E	L	F
T	G	R	U	N	L	U	C	K	Y	I

1

2

3

4

5

6

7 If you do the cooking, I will do the _____.

8 Before you leave the police station, you must get _____ from the policeman.

9 Sarah is my _____. We are getting married in June.

10 I'm sure! It _____ won't happen.

11 There is a new _____ for education in the government.

12 Paul and I _____ after five years of marriage.

QUESTIONS

... work in a laboratory?

... work with people?

... help people with experiments?

... work outside?

... work at night?

... work alone?

... always be clean?

... work at any time of day or night?

... use a scalpel?

... look at the sky?

... discover cures for diseases?

... work with students?

... meet people with personal problems?

... prepare exams?

... work with the police?

... help children?

Improvements

A new shopping centre

A new car factory

A new theme park

A new hospital

A new secondary school

A new metro

Descriptions

WOTCHESTER

HARLEY

Wotchester is situated in the centre of the country and is around 30 miles from the nearest town, Harley. Around 200,000 people live in the town, mostly outside the city centre. This is a problem because the bus system is not very good. It has only two hospitals and six secondary schools. Many of the schools are old and overcrowded. It has a lot of unemployment. A safari park is being built near Wotchester.

The council would like Wotchester to become a tourist centre.

Harley is a big town in the centre of the country. Around 500,000 people live in the town. It has only five secondary schools, which are very overcrowded and many students have to travel to Wotchester (around 30 miles away). It has six hospitals but they are very old. Unemployment is low but most people do their shopping in Wotchester.

The council wants Harley to be a tourist centre. They are already building an airport outside Harley.

PEARSON
Longman

DON'T TRUST YOUR FUTURE!

Dream cards

You had a dream last night. It was about … A bank	You had a dream last night. It was about … Eating bananas
You had a dream last night. It was about … A university	You had a dream last night. It was about … A candle
You had a dream last night. It was about … A bag	You had a dream last night. It was about … An actor
You had a dream last night. It was about … Cards	You had a dream last night. It was about … A beach
You had a dream last night. It was about … A carrot	You had a dream last night. It was about … A bath
You had a dream last night. It was about … A flying balloon	You had a dream last night. It was about … A new house
You had a dream last night. It was about … A balcony	You had a dream last night. It was about … A dentist

Interpretation cards

University – You are going to make a new friend.	Actor – You are hoping that someone will notice how hard you work. They will.
New house – You'd like to change your house or something about your life.	Bag – You are going to have a lot of responsibilities.
Balcony – You are hoping someone special will notice you soon.	Flying balloon – Life is going to get better for you.
Eating bananas – You are working hard but no one is going to notice.	Bank – You are going to get very tired and you will need a rest.
Bath – You'd like to forgive someone or say sorry to someone.	Beach – Life is very complex now and you are hoping it is going to get easier.
Candle – There is going to be a lot of luck in your life.	Cards – You are hoping for love or happiness in your life.
Carrot – Someone is going to offer you something. You'd like to have it.	Dentist – Things look bad now but they are going to be much better.

Teacher's card

PREFER	LOVE	KEEN
MORE INTERESTED ... THAN	RATHER ... THAN	PREFER
FANCY	KEEN	MIND
MIND	PREFER	KEEN
LOVE	FANCY	LOVE
RATHER ... THAN	MORE INTERESTED ... THAN	MIND
MORE INTERESTED ... THAN	FANCY	RATHER ... THAN

Bingo cards

Chocolate	Watching tv	Eating snails
Diving	Going to the theatre	Doing exams
Almonds	Swimming	Taking long walks
	Meeting new people	
	Watching football	
	Smoking	
Flying		
Eating fast food		
Science		

THE JOB FOR YOU?

Job descriptions

Serox Research

Serox, one of the most famous research companies in the world, is looking for a tele-research assistant. You will work in a friendly team with a very good manager. You will spend all day working on the telephone and the computer but there are opportunities to become a manager and we will give lots of training. Unfortunately, there is no training before the job begins, but the job is very well paid.

World Packages

This small, new company is looking for someone to travel around Europe and find new contracts and clients. There are lots of opportunities to travel and you will work with a friendly team on your visits around the world. The manager is very new and, like you, is learning the job. There is a training course before you start work. This is a very well-paid job. We also pay for more training every year.

Party Power

Our company is a small local company that prepares parties. Your job will be to find new clients. You will always be working on your own but you will meet lots of people. The job is lots of fun and is never boring. The pay is not good at the beginning but gets better if you find clients. We give training before you start work.

Market Marketing Inc.

We are the biggest marketing company in the country and we want a new marketing executive with new ideas. The job is a lot of fun. The pay is not great at the begining but can get much better. You will work alone and create your own marketing campaign. You will have to travel a lot to meet clients and we will give you lots of training. You also have the chance to be a manager in two years.

Job seekers' cards

What's important for you

Well-known company	Yes
Opportunities to travel	No
Good working conditions	No
Good manager	Yes
Friendly colleagues	Yes
Having fun	No
Opportunities to learn new skills	Yes ·
Training course before you start	No
Working as a team	Yes
Good pay	Yes

What's important for you

Well-known company	No
Opportunities to travel	Yes
Good working conditions	No
Good manager	No
Friendly colleagues	Yes
Having fun	No
Opportunities to learn new skills	Yes
Training course before you start	Yes
Working as a team	Yes
Good pay	Yes

What's important for you

Well-known company	No
Opportunities to travel	No
Good working conditions	Yes
Good manager	No
Friendly colleagues	No
Having fun	Yes
Opportunities to learn new skills	No
Training course before you start	Yes
Working as a team	No
Good pay	No

What's important for you

Well-known company	Yes
Opportunities to travel	Yes
Good working conditions	Yes
Good manager	No
Friendly colleagues	No
Having fun	Yes
Opportunities to learn new skills	Yes
Training course before you start	Yes
Working as a team	No
Good pay	No

CHOCOLATE

1 Cocoa beans are roasted at 400 °C for about 30 minutes.

2 Another three or four cups of flour are added until the mixture is thick and you can make a ball. The ball is then flattened and it is left for about 45 minutes to rise.

3 The mixture is cooked lightly until the potatoes are soft and then spices are included to finish the soup.

4 The liquid is heated in a pan for a few minutes and then put in a grinder again until it becomes a thick mixture.

5 Butter is heated with oil in a saucepan. Then the onion, carrots and green beans are heated lightly for 3–4 minutes.

6 Three cups of flour are added with one cup of milk, two spoons of sugar and three tablespoons of oil. This mixture is then stirred 100 times.

 -

VEGETABLE SOUP

a) Onion, carrots and mushrooms are cut into small pieces. Green beans are cut in half and potatoes are cut into quarters.

b) The mixture is finally put in the fridge to make it solid.

c) The little pieces are put in a grinder and are ground until they make a liquid.

d) Finally, it is divided into two loaves. The loaves are then baked at 425 °C for 25–30 minutes.

e) When the vegetables are softer, water is added with the potatoes and salt and pepper.

f) Two tablespoons of yeast are added to the bowl and the mixture is left for five minutes.

 -

BREAD

I One cup of warm water and one spoon of sugar are put into a bowl.

II The whole mixture is boiled. Then the heat is reduced.

III Mushrooms are added and then everything is cooked for 2–3 minutes.

IV They are then taken out of the oven and they are smashed into little pieces.

V The ball is now much bigger. It is now flattened and is left for about 45 minutes to rise.

VI Spices, sugar and vanilla are added to the mixture and the mixture is stirred.

Student A

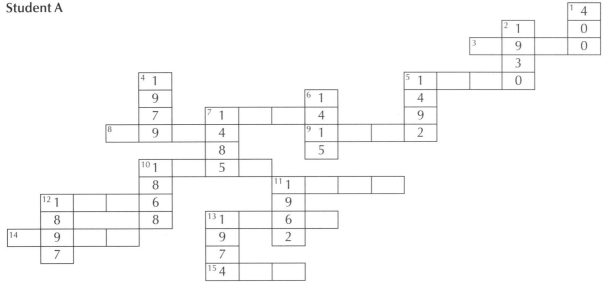

Across:
3 First Bugs Bunny cartoon shown.
5 First stamp sold.
7 First document printed.
8 First Olympic gold medal given.
9 First Mongol leader (Genghis Khan) born.
10 First toilet paper sold.
11 First computer game made.
12 First X-ray given.
13 First woman sent to space.
14 First known alphabet written (BC).
15 First trousers introduced.

Down:
1 First kite created (BC).
2 First World Cup played.
4 First modern bungee jump made
5 America discovered by Columbus.
6 First handgun fired.
7 Henry VIII's first wife born.
10 First traffic light used.
11 First James Bond movie made.
12 First motorised taxi driven.
13 First landing on Mars made.

Student B

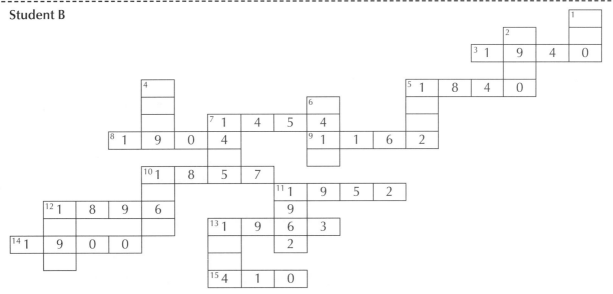

Across:
3 First Bugs Bunny cartoon shown.
5 First stamp sold.
7 First document printed.
8 First Olympic gold medal given.
9 First Mongol leader (Genghis Khan) born.
10 First toilet paper sold.
11 First computer game made.
12 First X-ray given.
13 First woman sent to space.
14 First known alphabet written (BC).
15 First trousers introduced.

Down:
1 First kite created (BC).
2 First World Cup played.
4 First modern bungee jump made
5 America discovered by Columbus.
6 First handgun fired.
7 Henry VIII's first wife born.
10 First traffic light used.
11 First James Bond movie made.
12 First motorised taxi driven.
13 First landing on Mars made.

Peter Arkwright

- ➡ famous writer
- ➡ written six best-selling novels
- ➡ writes crime novels and thrillers
- ➡ lives near the city
- ➡ very good-looking (in his thirties)
- ➡ good speaker
- ➡ can be rude
- ➡ staying with friends next weekend

Shanay Cross

- ◆ pop star
- ◆ in her early 20s
- ◆ born in the city
- ◆ didn't finish school
- ◆ very good-looking
- ◆ young people love her
- ◆ has never done this before
- ◆ coming to the city next week at 4 p.m.

Mohindar Khan

- ★ scientist
- ★ given the Nobel Prize for Science 30 years ago
- ★ studied at the University
- ★ written over 30 books
- ★ 89 years old
- ★ has been ill for some time
- ★ will be in the city next weekend
- ★ not well known any more

Sarah Patterson

- ⇨ Minister for Education
- ⇨ born in the city
- ⇨ worked at the University for ten years
- ⇨ good speaker
- ⇨ not popular
- ⇨ very political
- ⇨ happy to come next weekend if the TV channels come

Trevor Lloyd

- ➤ student in Science Department
- ➤ best student at the University
- ➤ 20 years old
- ➤ very good-looking
- ➤ shy
- ➤ lives at the university
- ➤ no one knows him

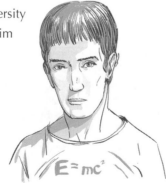

Harold Thompson

- ❱ mayor of the town
- ❱ has been mayor for ten years
- ❱ graduate of another university
- ❱ got sponsorship to build the department
- ❱ police suspect him of stealing money from the city
- ❱ media hate him

PEARSON
Longman

PHRASAL VERB SNAP

Verbs

go	put
give	take
stop	pick
cut	get
throw	give
go	grow
get	put

Particles

off	on
up	out
back	out
up	up
away	into
up	up
down	in

Sentences

1 Don't _____ my newspaper. I haven't read it.

2 Why don't you _____ your new jumper?

3 Don't _____ learning to play the guitar. You are good.

4 Please _____ and see us on your way home.

5 I don't like this book. Shall I _____ it _____ to the library?

6 On Sundays I _____ very late.

7 Would you like to _____ with me tonight?

8 Don't _____ your mobile phone _____ your pocket.

9 Always _____ your rubbish from the street.

10 I _____ in London but moved to Manchester when I was ten years old.

11 House prices have been _____ for some time.

12 You need to _____ on your smoking.

13 If I don't have my key, how will I _____ my house?

14 Some people are _____ free sunglasses on the street.

Student A

COPY	ORIGINAL
Name: Paul Smith	**Name:** Sarah Jones
Age: 36	**Age:** 26
Eyes: brown	**Eyes:** green
Height: 1.76m	**Height:** 1.62m
Face: beard and moustache	**Face:** big earrings
Hair: blonde	**Hair:** blonde
Clothes: white shirt, blue jeans, black jacket, black leather shoes	**Clothes:** striped red and white jumper, blue jeans, no coat, red and white sports shoes

OTHER INFORMATION FOR BOTH – COPY

Last seen: in a café at 7 p.m.

Doing: drinking coffee and talking on their mobile phones

With: a box containing an expensive painting stolen from Mr and Mrs Jones

✂ -

Student B

ORIGINAL	COPY
Name: Paul Smith	**Name:** Sarah Davies
Age: 33	**Age:** 26
Eyes: blue	**Eyes:** blue
Height: 1.78m	**Height:** 1.82m
Face: glasses	**Face:** glasses
Hair: blonde	**Hair:** brown
Clothes: white shirt, black trousers, black jacket, white sports shoes	**Clothes:** striped blue and white jumper, blue jeans, raincoat, white shoes

OTHER INFORMATION FOR BOTH – ORIGINAL

Last seen: at airport at 8.15 p.m.

Doing: getting on a plane for Spain

With: two shoulder bags containing sun cream, water, magazines

If there were no computers …

If there were no telephones …

If there was no electricity …

If there were no countries …

If there were no guns …

If there was no money …

If there were no hospitals …

If there were no fridges …

A	G	G	R	E	S	S	I	V	E	Q	Q	S	O	Z	X
Z	F	B	O	P	Y	T	N	X	H	B	M	P	E	F	M
O	V	M	V	Q	Z	A	M	H	P	L	E	O	E	H	H
B	M	Q	J	T	P	D	W	K	B	S	M	N	P	V	Z
C	O	M	P	E	T	I	T	I	V	E	O	T	W	D	R
D	I	V	Y	Y	K	U	Z	Z	N	E	M	A	O	Z	Z
N	P	U	O	X	Q	M	X	J	S	U	U	N	R	V	P
Y	M	T	J	R	X	R	P	I	G	O	X	E	L	R	W
Z	H	B	R	D	M	L	B	B	P	B	S	O	D	O	P
T	T	G	T	E	N	D	T	O	O	O	N	U	W	W	F
S	O	C	I	A	B	L	E	A	L	X	O	S	I	I	D
M	A	J	O	R	I	T	Y	S	O	I	O	L	D	N	P
A	R	C	H	E	R	Y	Z	H	E	N	K	J	E	G	O
F	N	E	F	L	E	G	J	B	O	G	E	C	Z	W	L
M	O	T	O	R	R	A	C	I	N	G	R	K	W	R	O
F	E	N	C	I	N	G	C	O	N	Q	M	F	Y	T	O

1 A game played with sticks, balls and a table. _____

2 In this sport you aim at a target. _____

3 You need a horse for this sport. _____

4 This means you like to win. _____

5 You do things without thinking. _____

6 You get angry easily. _____

7 Most people. _____

8 Everywhere in the world. _____

9 A place where sports are played. _____ .

10 You like meeting people. _____

11 Fighting with gloves on your hands. _____

12 Fighting with a sword. _____

13 A sport with cars. _____

14 Not always but sometimes do. _____

15 A sport on water. _____ .